THE SHAME OF IT

Global perspectives on
anti-poverty policies

Edited by Erika K. Gubrium, Sony Pellissery
and Ivar Lødemel

First published in Great Britain in 2014 by

Policy Press
University of Bristol
6th Floor
Howard House
Queen's Avenue
Clifton
Bristol BS8 1SD
UK
t: +44 (0)117 331 5020
f: +44 (0)117 331 5367
pp-info@bristol.ac.uk
www.policypress.co.uk

North America office:
Policy Press
c/o The University of Chicago Press
1427 East 60th Street
Chicago, IL 60637, USA
t: +1 773 702 7700
f: +1 773 702 9756
sales@press.uchicago.edu
www.press.uchicago.edu

© Policy Press 2014

British Library Cataloguing in Publication Data
A catalogue record for this book is available from the British Library

Library of Congress Cataloging-in-Publication Data
A catalog record for this book has been requested

ISBN 978 1 44730 870 6 paperback
ISBN 978 1 44730 871 3 hardcover

The right of Erika K. Gubrium, Sony Pellissery and Ivar Lødemel to be identified as editors
of this work has been asserted by them in accordance with the Copyright, Designs and Patents
Act 1988.

Cover design by Policy Press
Front cover image: Getty
Printed and bound in Great Britain by CPI Group (UK) Ltd,
Croydon, CR0 4YY
The Policy Press uses environmentally responsible print partners

To our families

Contents

Notes on contributors   vi
Acknowledgements   ix
Preface   x

one   Resetting the stage   1
Erika K. Gubrium

two   New urban poverty and new welfare provision: 17
China's *dibao* system
Ming Yan

three   Thick poverty, thicker society and thin state: policy spaces   37
for human dignity in India
Sony Pellissery and Leemamol Mathew

four   Self-sufficiency, social assistance and the shaming of poverty   61
in South Korea
Yongmie Nicola Jo and Robert Walker

five   'Not good enough': social assistance and shaming in Norway   85
Erika K. Gubrium and Ivar Lødemel

six   Pakistan: a journey of poverty-induced shame   111
Sohail Choudhry

seven   Separating the sheep from the goats: tackling poverty   133
in Britain for over four centuries
Robert Walker and Elaine Chase

eight   'Food that cannot be eaten': the shame of Uganda's   157
anti-poverty policies
Grace Bantebya Kyomuhendo and Amon Mwiine

nine   Shame and shaming in policy processes   179
Sony Pellissery, Ivar Lødemel and Erika K. Gubrium

ten   Towards global principles for dignity-based   199
anti-poverty policies
Erika K. Gubrium and Ivar Lødemel

Index   221

Notes on contributors

Grace Bantebya Kyomuhendo is professor of gender studies at the School of Women and Gender Studies, Makerere University, Kampala, Uganda. Her work focuses on vulnerable populations within Uganda, with a focus on women's work throughout Ugandan history. She is the author of numerous publications on women's work and reproductive health. She is co-author (with Marjorie K. McIntosh) of the award-winning book, *Women, work and domestic virtue in Uganda*, as well as co-editor of the upcoming *The shame of poverty: Global experiences*, to be published in 2014 by Oxford University Press.

Elaine Chase is research officer at the Department of Social Policy and Intervention, at University of Oxford, UK. Her research focuses on the sociological dimensions of wellbeing, health and the rights of individuals and communities, particularly those most likely to experience disadvantage and marginalisation. She is author of numerous publications in these focal areas, as well as co-editor of the upcoming *The shame of poverty: Global experiences*, to be published in 2014 by Oxford University Press.

Sohail Choudhry is a research assistant and DPhil student at the Department of Social Policy and Intervention, University of Oxford, UK. He has held public appointments in the Departments of Home, Education and Housing as well as the Minimum Wages Board and Community Development in Punjab, Pakistan. His dissertation work focuses on the dynamics of poverty-induced shame, social exclusion and public policy on vulnerable women, children and minorities in Pakistan.

Erika K. Gubrium is post-doctoral research fellow at the Institute for Social Sciences at the Oslo and Akershus University College, Norway. Her research applies qualitative approaches to investigate anti-poverty policies in Norway, with a particular focus on the discourses, norms and expectations surrounding both social assistance provision and the work activation approaches directed towards individuals receiving social assistance. She is author of several articles and chapters in these areas.

Yongmie Nicola Jo is research assistant and DPhil student at the Department of Social Policy and Intervention, University of Oxford, UK. Her dissertation work explores the social dynamics between poverty and shame, illustrating the social construction of shame through discourse analysis of popular films and analysing the role of government policy in ameliorating or accentuating poverty-shame in South Korea.

Ivar Lødemel is professor of social sciences at the Oslo and Akershus University College in Oslo, Norway. His research interests include social assistance policy and comparative social policy. He has served as a consultant for the World Bank, the Council of Europe, the European Union and the Organisation for Economic Co-operation and Development; he has authored numerous articles, chapters and reports on the issue of Norwegian social assistance policy and is co-author of the upcoming Oxford University Press volume, *Workfare revisited: The political economy of activation reforms*.

Leemamol Mathew is a consultant psychologist based in Bangalore, India. Her work focuses on the interpersonal relationships and mental health of children and disadvantaged populations. Her post-doctoral work focused on how positive mental health may be maintained among people living in poverty during unexpected economic crises. She has published several journal articles and has edited a special issue on 'Relationship research in India and South Asia' for *Interpersona: An International Journal on Personal Relationships*.

Amon Mwiine is assistant lecturer at the School of Women and Gender Studies, Makerere University, Kampala, Uganda. He has a Master of Arts in gender studies. His thesis (published with Lambert Publishing) focused on 'Space, gender and identity construction in students' hostels at Makerere University, Uganda'. He has professional experience as a gender auditor for the United Nations Development Programme Uganda, and is currently developing his PhD concept in 'Men, masculinities and poverty in Uganda'.

Sony Pellissery is associate professor at the Centre for the Study of Social Exclusion and Inclusive Policy at the National Law School of India University, Bangalore, India. He is a public policy specialist with key contributions on how social networks have shaped public policies through elite influence. His research has also examined how common resources are vital to the livelihoods of poor people, and how policies could make common resources replenishable. He has authored numerous articles and chapters investigating the impact and effect of social protection policies in India.

Robert Walker is professor at the Department of Social Policy and Intervention, University of Oxford, UK. He was the leader of the Economic and Social Research Council/Department for International Development project, 'Shame, social exclusion and the effectiveness of anti-poverty programmes: A study in seven countries'. He has personally undertaken over 60 research projects, many of them international and concerned with poverty and related issues, and is author of the upcoming volume, *The shame of poverty: Global perspectives*, to be published in 2014 by Oxford University Press.

Ming Yan is professor at the Institute of Sociology and Center for Social Policy Studies, Chinese Academy of Social Sciences, Beijing, China. Her research interests include the development and history of sociology in China, as well as the policy implications of Chinese urban development. She has written an award-winning book on the history of sociology in China and has also published numerous articles and chapters both in English and in Chinese.

Acknowledgements

Our express thanks go to the UK Economic and Social Research Council (ESRC) and the UK Department for International Development (DFID) for their financial support of the broader project, 'Shame, social exclusion and the effectiveness of anti-poverty programmes: A study in seven countries' (ESRC-DFID Joint Fund for Poverty Alleviation Research, grant number RES-167-25-0557), from which this volume is drawn. We also thank the Oslo and Akershus University College for full funding of a post-doctoral position during the duration of the project. Their support enabled the Norwegian team to conduct their research and supported the completion of this volume. We are grateful for the hard work put in by the project teams in each of the seven settings, which is reflected in the volume's empirical depth. We are grateful to our home institutions at the time of the writing of this volume for their support during its production: the Oslo and Akershus University College and the Institute of Rural Management Anand. We would also like to thank the anonymous reviewers to our earlier drafts and Arne Kristian Aas for sensible and helpful suggestions to improve the typescript. Our message is strengthened due to their feedback. During the two-and-a-half years of the project's span, a broad group of people helped to make this work possible. Most significant, however, were the families and individuals who participated in interviews and focus groups within each country setting, as well as those individuals who spent many hours helping us to establish contacts in the field. Our gratitude for their time and efforts cannot be overstated.

Preface

> The worst thing about living in extreme poverty is the contempt – that they treat you like you are worthless, that they look at you with disgust and fear and that they even treat you like an enemy. We and our children experience this every day, and it hurts us, humiliates us and makes us live in fear and shame.[1]

This is the first volume to take seriously the policy implications of the experience of this Peruvian mother. It is an experience shared by people living in poverty in countries as disparate as Norway and Uganda, the UK and Pakistan, South Korea, China and India. It is probably true of people in poverty everywhere.

Certainly, that is the view of Amartya Sen, Nobel Laureate, who has had a profound influence on recent global debates about poverty reduction. He argues that shame, specifically 'the ability to go about without shame', lies at the 'irreducible absolutist core in the idea of poverty.'[2] This link between poverty and shame is important for at least four reasons that are evidenced in this volume and in two companion volumes by the same research team.[3] First, shame hurts. Physiologically shame is recognised by increased pro-inflammatory cytokine activity and cortisol; psychologically it is associated with depression, anxiety and suicidal ideas. To live in shame every day adds to the pain of poverty.

Second, shame, while internally felt, is externally imposed by those of us who are not poor: the 'they' referred to by the Peruvian mother cited above. We impose shame whenever we speak of 'the poor' as an undifferentiated group; when we refer glibly to people in poverty as scroungers, lazy or good for nothing; when we justify our relative affluence in terms of our ability, hard work and motivation; or when we avert our gaze by not, for example, acknowledging a person begging in the street.

Third, social psychology reveals that shame is the most debilitating of the emotions, causing people to retreat socially, to lose faith in themselves and to find their sense of agency eroded. While we might naively wish to encourage people in poverty to help themselves by shaming them, we are, in fact, more likely to have the opposite effect. Shame undermines people's ability to help themselves.

Finally, and for similar reasons, policies that stigmatise and are shaming are likely to be ineffective. They demoralise and reduce individual agency. On the other hand, anti-poverty programmes that promote dignity have the potential to overcome the debilitating psychological and social effects of poverty as well as tackling material deprivation.

Drawing attention to the shame attaching to poverty risks people living in poverty being additionally blamed for feeling ashamed. However, the shame associated with poverty is structural; it is as much our responsibility as individuals and as non-governmental organisations (NGOs), companies and governments. It is for us collectively to change: to think before we speak; to ask before we act.

Treating people with respect is not only a matter of social justice; it is also likely to enhance policy effectiveness. This is the principal takeaway message of this volume. But this volume offers much more than a single policy lesson, important though this is. Through careful analysis of policies in seven countries spanning the global North and South, the authors demonstrate that shame can permeate and indeed define the framing, structure and delivery of policy. Sometimes this is deliberate, as when politicians seek the votes of taxpayers, playing them off against welfare recipients; or when governments try to tackle perceived abuse benefits through variants of naming and shaming. Sometimes it is inadvertent – when targeting creates groups that are categorised as eligible or ineligible for receipt of services, and people who come to be labelled 'deserving' and 'undeserving'. Moreover, the editors begin the process of thinking through the implications of this evidence for the design and implementation of policies in the global South and North. The challenge they pose to those in positions of power and decision-making is to find ways of shame-proofing policy.

The research on which this volume is based has already begun to shape global debates about the design of social protection policies worldwide. It led to the inclusion in the principle that every government should have 'respect for the rights and dignity of people covered by social security guarantees' in the vitally important 2012 International Labour Organization (ILO) Recommendation 202 concerning national floors of social protection. This provision is an invitation to all governments and analysts to review policies through the lens of shame, asking whether, in their design and implementation, they impose shame or promote dignity. The same research has been taken up by the international NGO, ATD Fourth World, in its endeavour to allow the voices of people in extreme poverty to be heard in global debates about the future of the Millennium Development Goals.[4] New research is being funded by the Norwegian Research Council, with the goal of developing shame-proofed policies. Public opinion has been engaged in East Africa with shame-related storylines appearing in a popular television soap opera, *Makutano Junction*, aired in Kenya, Uganda and Tanzania while in Britain, the Pegasus Theatre Company has produced an educational pack around a new play based on H.P. Albarelli Jr's novel *The heap*, which addresses some of these important themes.

No book is truly the work of a single person. The genesis of the original research can be traced to Lindsey Richardson, in 2007 a graduate Sociology student at the University of Oxford, who took trouble not only to read words that Sen had written, but also to think about them. Thereafter, a team of 11, the authors of this volume, together undertook a programme of research that was funded by the UK ESRC and DFID. The project advisory committee, comprising Jimi Adesina, Jo Boyden, Charlotte Heath, June Tangney and Timo Voipio, and chaired by Lutz Leisering, offered powerful critique and moral support while the initial findings were fruitfully discussed at meetings in Anand, Beijing, Kampala, Oslo and Oxford, and with representatives of DFID, the ILO, The World Bank, the Office of the UN High Commissioner for Human Rights, Oxfam and ATD Fourth World among other organisations. This volume, therefore, is not merely a collection of essays, but the product of a collective journey, from ideas to evidence and policy implications, which has been brought to a successful conclusion through the skill and energy of the editors. It has been my privilege, as principal grant holder, to participate in this journey of discovery and realisation. It is an equal privilege to commend the volume to you, the reader, in the hope that you will find it stimulating and valuable given your desire to use research evidence for the purpose of addressing poverty and for building a better world.

Robert Walker
University of Oxford
June 2013

Notes

[1] Quoted in ATD Fourth World (2013) *Towards sustainable development that leaves no one behind: The challenge of the post-2015 agenda*, New York: ATD Fourth World.

[2] Sen, A. (1983) 'Poor, relatively speaking', *Oxford Economic Papers*, vol 35, pp 153-69; Alkire, S. (2002) *Valuing freedom: Sen's capability approach and poverty reduction*, Oxford: Oxford University Press.

[3] Walker, R. (2014) *The shame of poverty: Global perspectives*, Oxford: Oxford University Press; Chase, E. and Bantebya, G. (eds) (2014) *The shame of poverty: Global experiences*, Oxford: Oxford University Press.

[4] ATD Fourth World, op cit.

ONE

Resetting the stage

Erika K. Gubrium

In 1971, sociologist Robert Pinker made a frank observation about the field of social policy: 'We know much more about the sentiments of philosophers and social scientists than those of ordinary people in everyday life' (1971, p 135). The statement is as relevant today as it was then. Whether focused in the global South on intensive development and reconstruction, or in the global North on moving the long-term unemployed into the labour market, public social policy approaches all too frequently 'take for granted the subjective perceptions of ordinary people' (1971, p 136) rather than subjecting them to empirical investigation. This is predicated on the understanding of poverty as a personal failure (Walker, 2014). This understanding has had a great bearing on the policy solutions that are posed.

The solutions typically derive from microeconomics and behavioural psychology (see Becker, 1976; Elster, 1989; Kahneman and Tversky, 2000). Both traditions habitually put into place experience-distant understandings of everyday life, distant from both the ordinary practices and the diverse contexts and relational meanings of socioeconomic differences. They rarely, if ever, attend to the everyday logics of conduct. The chapters in this volume feature the ordinary experiences and perceptions of those whose lives are directly affected, and subject them to empirical scrutiny.

New insights

If late in coming, the time is ripe for resetting the stage by placing the lives of the recipients of anti-poverty measures front and centre, bringing these life experiences into the world of policy research. This volume shares that mission with two concurrent texts – *Poverty and shame*, a monograph authored by Robert Walker (2014), and *The shame of poverty: Global experiences*, a volume edited by Elaine Chase and Grace Bantebya Kyomuhendo (2014). Different in emphases, these texts build on the same body of empirical research as do the chapters of this volume. The research was part of a broad, Economic and

Social Research Council (ESRC)-funded cross-national comparative qualitative study, titled 'Shame, social exclusion and the effectiveness of anti-poverty programmes: A study in seven countries'. With Walker at the helm, the study has had local teams of researchers across the seven settings engaged in intensely collaborative work for a two-and-a-half-year period. Across the seven settings in focus, the authors in this volume have explored in-depth the links that may exist between poverty and shame. They have analysed influential literature, film and theatre to identify dominant notions concerning poverty and individuals living in poverty. They have interviewed individuals living in poverty and receiving state-funded anti-poverty measures to gain a better understanding of what it means to be 'poor' within each setting. They have conducted focus group conversations with individuals of low to middle and middle to high status to explore perceptions and understandings concerning poverty and individuals living in poverty that are held by the general public. Finally, they have conducted in-depth analyses of both policy documents and newspaper coverage of poverty and individuals in poverty to explore how broader norms, values and expectations wend their way into public coverage of poverty and the policy-making that addresses it.

The volumes by Walker (2014) and Chase and Bantebya Kyomuhendo (2014) incorporate this rich data from extremely diverse settings in order to substantiate the global existence of a connection between poverty and shame, irrespective of socioeconomic, political, social and cultural context. Walker's volume applies psychological and sociological theory to the empirical evidence to consider the contention by Nobel Laureate Amartya Sen that there is a universal and immutable link between poverty and shame. In doing so, it offers a radical reappraisal of the concept of poverty and its social and personal meaning. The edited volume by Chase and Kyomuhendo Bantebya applies a sociological lens to poverty, and richly illustrates its psychological and social impacts across different contexts. It provides a narrative that carries the reader across diverse economic, cultural and political contexts and offers robust support for Sen's contention.

Together, this work substantiates the view that, not only is the experience of poverty among the cumulative causes of shame for individual respondents living in poverty, this shame also undermines their agency. These findings make the consideration of shame paramount when developing effective social policy. This volume builds on these findings and is the culmination of the group's work. It systematically considers the relationship between anti-poverty policy and the possibility for heightened shame in vastly different economic and cultural environments, linking substantive findings to policy relevance.

New global initiatives

This volume's publication comes shortly before the final year of the United Nations (UN) Millennium Development Goals (MDGs), whose 15-year strategy has focused on the development of the world's poorest countries through a broad focus on the improvement of social and economic conditions, with one aim being the reduction of absolute poverty (UN, 2000). The MDGs primarily set out aims for outcomes assessment according to a number of goalpost measures. Setting the stage for a new era, the UN family has recently passed an important measure in its post-2015 anti-poverty work: Recommendation 202 on national social protection floors (ILO, 2012). In contrast to the outcomes-focused broad aims of the MDGs (which asked *if* and *to what extent* goals had been met), the Recommendation explicitly includes a focus on process, asking also *how* goals are met. Most important is its focus on the social and material aspects of risk management. This broader focus is reflected in the commitment by its 185 signatory countries to offer a social protection floor that includes basic income security and healthcare access. Moreover, its guiding principles also bring a new global focus to the social psychological dimensions of anti-poverty policy. Of particular relevance to this volume is the Recommendation's 6th principle, 'Respect for the rights and dignity of people covered by the social security guarantees'. Informed by the broader ESRC study findings from which this volume is drawn, this principle acknowledges the importance of considering the dignity of anti-poverty measure recipients when crafting effective social policy (Walker, 2012).

Experiences of poverty are increasingly recognised as multidimensional, with more recent focus on its social aspects over the past decade (reviewed in Walker, 2014; see OECD, 2001). The focus by the Recommendation on the importance of recipient dignity reflects this turn towards both the interactive and the social in the arena of global policy development. Yet to our knowledge, there are no internationally comparable data on shame, much less on its impact within the context of social policy (see Zavaleta, 2007).

The empirical chapters fill this current knowledge gap between broader anti-poverty policy aims and the impact of implementation, across the span of the global South and North. The findings provide a useful framework for adhering to the consideration given by the

Recommendation to the importance of recipient dignity. They draw strength from a study design that merges a bird's-eye view of policy across vastly different settings with a grounded sensitivity to the very personal effects of policy discourses and practices. With the mission of bringing the lives and experiences of policy recipients to the foreground, each of the chapters explores the links between shame, social exclusion and the impact of anti-poverty measures in one of seven settings: China, India, Norway, Pakistan, South Korea, Uganda and the UK. The vastly different political, social and economic realities of the particular settings selected enabled a maximum difference design. Given this design, the empirical chapters are able to robustly demonstrate that shame and anti-poverty policymaking is intimately connected, albeit culturally nuanced, across highly varied settings. The concluding chapters bring this material together in a comparative manner, demonstrating how the policy process of each setting has the potential to heighten the shame experienced by recipients of anti-poverty measures. The relationship is robust: despite wide variation in the settings chosen, and indeed, in the policy processes themselves, there is nonetheless a strong and shared potential for generating shame through these processes. The considerations of minimising shame and building dignity must be a point of focus when evaluating the content and practice of anti-poverty measures.

The empirical chapters present a broad array of anti-poverty intervention types, including income-enhancement policies (for example, microfinance programmes) in Uganda, programmes to subsidise and support agriculture in Uganda and India, employment generation or public works programmes in India and South Korea, in-kind programmes (for example, the Public Distribution System of nutritional resources) in India, income maintenance schemes and workfare programmes in the UK, Norway and China, as well as human capital interventions in the UK, Norway and Uganda. Acknowledging these differences, the aim is not to compare policy interventions per se, but the discourses, assumptions and strategies that are tied to the cross-national interventions that have aimed to address poverty. Each empirical chapter thus identifies how ideas and language, structures and delivery practices relate to heightened shame on the receiving end. Conversely, each also aims to locate the discourses and practices that may build dignity among target groups. The poverty–shame nexus is a crucial consideration if we are to craft policy that is to prove effective in the longer term.

Poverty, shame and anti-poverty policy

Poverty is a concept attached to widely varying meanings and agendas. In the global North, it has been operationalised within a framework of varying policy aims and predicated on the use of differing indicators (Townsend, 1979; Murray, 1984; Walker, 1995; Wacquant, 1996; Room, 1999; O'Connor, 2002). In the global South, international development agencies had, before the mid-1990s, described poverty as an absolute phenomenon and measured it using a subsistence baseline. Since this time, the definition has included indicators reflecting social as well as material aspects, albeit often pre-defined by the agencies themselves (Walker, 2014).

Interactionism and policy

A focus on local context is warranted. The meaning of poverty extends to identity. We establish who and what we are – our selves – through social interaction (Mead, 1934/2003). Who we are draws from, and reflects in complex ways, where we are in social life – we reflexively construct our experiences and our selves in relation to available and prevalent social identities (Blumer, 1969; Rose, 1997). The concept of dignity pays recognition to the interaction between the social and the personal. The *Oxford English Dictionary* accords dignity both an externally imposed and internally felt status: it is simultaneously 'the state or quality of being worthy of honour or respect' and 'a sense of pride in oneself; self-respect'. In this respect, shame is arguably an opposing emotional force (Walker, 2014). Ruth Lister (2004, 2008) describes identity and social status as interactional, and uses this understanding to define poverty as more than just a lack of material wealth. Poverty is a 'shameful and corrosive social relation' characterised by a lack of voice, disrespect, humiliation, as well as reduced dignity and self-esteem (Lister, 2004, p 7). This volume continues the exploration begun in the two earlier volumes, asking if shame is, indeed, 'at the core of' poverty, but moreover, how shame has an impact on those who are living in poverty. This volume, however, aims its focus more particularly at the world of social policy.

Anti-poverty policy: social psychological impact

Anti-poverty measures may mediate the shaming and social exclusion process, as well as the promotion of dignity. At the same time, they may also at times exacerbate shame and social exclusion and consequently be

5

reduced in their effectiveness or even counter-productive to economic and relief-oriented aims, as well as to the goals of empowerment and self-help. Given the substantiation that shame heightens the negative experiences and impact associated with poverty (Walker et al, 2013; Chase and Bantebya Kyohumendo, 2014), the shame dimension is important to consider when developing and delivering effective anti-poverty measures. Yet to date, there has been a dearth of scientific literature systematically speaking to the issues of shame and anti-poverty policy delivery within a social policy context.[1] The field of social policy is currently dominated, on the one hand, by human psychology scholarship, which explores the connection between poverty and shame/shaming and, on the other, by social policy scholarship analysing specific anti-poverty policy interventions (Alkire, 2007). This volume works at the intersection of these two arenas of investigation.

Amartya Sen's (2004) concept of a policy-making approach that considers the 'capabilities' of its target groups provides a starting framework through which to analyse the connections between shame and social policies (Zavaleta, 2007). Like Lister, Sen (1983) contends that shame is basic to the experience of poverty in *all* societies, despite differences in the availability of material resources. Across highly varied settings, he argues, shame decreases one's capability to participate fully in society (Alkire, 2002). An evaluation of social policy using a capabilities approach focuses not only on the activities and statuses *achieved* (the outcomes), but also on the *process* by which outcomes are achieved and the agency and freedom that individuals have along the way to promote or choose the things and activities they value (Sen, 1992, 1999). Yet this volume moves beyond an aim to increase the capability level of the individual rational actor (Dean, 2009). It adds to this equation a consideration of the relational and social aspects of the policy process as these, too, shape the impact of policy measures (Taylor, 2011).

The strength of the focus on shame and reduced capabilities within a broader psychosocial context is that it is built on empirical data and a theoretical framework that speaks to experiences and impacts across seven highly varied settings (Walker et al, 2013; Chase and Kyomuhendo Bantebya, 2014; Walker, 2014). Each setting varies in terms of culture, the nature and scale of poverty and the policy approaches applied. The sociocultural variation of these settings offers the possibility for a wide-ranging analysis. Yet the unique character of each context could also be claimed to pose a formidable challenge to the broad conceptualisation of shame in the exploration of connections between a poverty–shame nexus and anti-poverty policy. We begin, therefore, with a rationale for how the concept of shame has been operationalised across highly varying cultural borders.

Cross-national conceptions of shame

Shame is said to be one of the self-conscious emotions, experienced with reference to images of 'the self' in the eyes of society (Tangney, 1991). Western-based models of shame uniformly characterise the emotion as a negative assessment of the core self. It is made with reference to one's own aspirations and the perceived expectations of others, and manifests itself in a sense of powerlessness and inadequacy (Tracy et al, 2007; reviewed in Walker, 2014). Within a Western context, shame's negative focus on the self is associated with negative behavioural consequences (Tangney and Dearing, 2002). Shame reportedly results in feelings of worthlessness and increases the tendency to escape or disappear. It is said to generate maladaptive responses such as aggression, self-directed hostility and negative long-term behaviours (Tangney et al, 1996, 2006; Jönsson and Starrin, 2000; Fontaine et al, 2004).

Moving beyond Western assumptions

In contrast, cross-cultural studies moving beyond a West-only focus are mixed in their views of the impact of culture on the experience of and responses to shame. Some report that shame is uniformly experienced as negative across cultures (see, for example, Tsai et al, 2006; Edelstein and Shaver, 2007). Those that distinguish between how shame is *experienced* and the *behavioural effects* that follow this experience suggest that shame may, in fact, have a positive effect – it may encourage behaviours that are considered adaptive within specific situations and according to particular personal dimensions (Fontaine et al, 2006; Tsai et al, 2006). It is perhaps not surprising that individual respondents associate the experience of shame with positive behaviour when it is applied in a regulative manner and directed towards *other* people (Edelstein and Shaver, 2007; Walker, 2014). Yet shame directed towards *oneself* has also been characterised as having a positive valence by individuals living in collectivistic or interdependent settings, where its experience parlays informational and motivational significance (Wong and Tsai, 2007). Other studies complicate the story further, suggesting that shame cannot be uniformly divided into a negative or positive entity according to an individualist/collectivistic dichotomy (Scherer, 1997).

All told, studies of the experience and effects of shame across cultures suggest that they are more complex, nuanced and situationally contingent than has been suggested by models limited to Western conceptions (Li et al, 2004; Fontaine et al, 2006; Goetz and Keltner, 2007; Wong and Tsai, 2007). The operationalisation of shame in this volume recognises that its particular experience is shaped according to 'local cultural emphases' (Edelstein and Shaver, 2007, p 194), norms and expectations (Furukawa et al, 2012).

Locating shame

While a cross-cultural lens may complicate the story, cultural psychologists Jennifer Goetz and Dacher Keltner (2007, p 167) make the important point that findings of 'positive' shame in non-Western settings are overwhelmingly connected to instances in which the feeling of shame matches the particular cultural norms and expectations at hand, and moreover, when shame is not highly 'moralised'. This situation is, however, in marked contrast to the experiences portrayed by the low-income respondents we spoke with across seven settings. The common experience of shame across the seven settings in focus is vividly depicted elsewhere (Walker et al, 2013; Chase and Bantebya Kyomuhendo, 2014). Individuals, by virtue of being 'poor', feel placed and/or place themselves outside of what is publicly accepted as the valued 'norm' (Walker, 2014). The empirical chapters comprising the core of this volume also demonstrate a common experience of shame in conjunction with their social and relational status as recipients of anti-poverty measures, a theme that resonates strongly. Individuals living in poverty are frequently marginalised, stigmatised and socially excluded. A heavy public moral judgement describes these individuals as 'undeserving'. When evaluating the positive or negative aspects of shame, it is thus crucial to keep in mind *who* it is that is experiencing shame. This caveat is supported by studies across highly varied cultures reporting shame as a negative experience with negative effects when elicited in response to a decrease in social status (Lynd, 1958/1999; Scheff, 2000; Goetz and Keltner, 2007). This shame 'feels bad everywhere in the world' (Edelstein and Shaver, 2007, p 201).

In addition to a negative experience of shame for those living in poverty, common to the empirical chapters that follow are the quite negative consequences that result. The individuals we spoke with described shame relating to the reduction of capabilities in many aspects of their lives. While we cannot generalise about experiences, each empirical chapter in this volume offers a more personal look at how social policy has affected the lives of these policy recipients. Looking across the settings, we may also begin to discern the policy mechanisms that may potentially heighten or lower the shame of individuals living in poverty.

Policy moments

This volume considers poverty and shame across local settings in seven nations. The seven empirical chapters offer an entrée to the local experiences of policy recipients in broadly differing milieus. Each describes how the experiences and consequences of shame play out for policy recipients at three moments in the policy-making cycle.

Each chapter begins with a focus on how shame and dignity are linked to the *framing* of anti-poverty policy. The focus is on the public discourse relating to the nature, manifestations and placement of accountability for poverty, as well as the broader political goals guiding the policy-making process. Next, each describes how shame and dignity are potentially generated through the *shaping and structuring* of policy, with a particular focus on how the relevant policies came into existence and what they look like. This discussion includes the specification of policy objectives; the balance between social control and the promotion of individual wellbeing; resource allocation; the balance between universalism and targeting; and the nature and adequacy of benefits. Finally, each links shame and dignity to the *delivery* of anti-poverty policy, considering how the policies have been implemented and prioritised during this phase. The focus is on mechanisms for delivery and access; administration and gatekeeping; the assessment of need; the implementation of conditionality; and the management of perceived abuse and corruption. While dividing the policy cycle into discrete moments, each chapter simultaneously demonstrates the ways in which impacts reach across the cycle. Each concludes with a discussion of key implications and recommendations emerging from the illustrative examples presented.

Seven national settings

These moments and emerging themes are presented across seven national settings. Taken together, the settings serve to foreground both similarity and difference, making it possible to both compare and contrast. Striking a balance between the two serves to democratise the analytic playing field, making it possible to understand and appreciate alternative pathways that poverty and shame are shaped through varying anti-poverty approaches.

Rapid economic reform and the subsequent expansion of the social safety net in China have contributed to reductions of absolute poverty in China. Yet, as Ming Yan shows in Chapter Two, China's past three decades have also witnessed heightened income inequality, as relative poverty has become a growing issue and the relationship between poverty and shame has changed markedly. The past 15 years of conditional social assistance have been aimed at the relief of absolute poverty, yet have had as its primary aim the goal of maintaining social stability. The discourses and practices surrounding this effort neglect to recognise the presence of intensified socioeconomic inequalities. Furthermore, locally discretionary assessment procedures that are shaming and intrusive are made worse by the fact that a large population of the very poor are not in the end covered by this measure. These elements have heightened the shame of China's most vulnerable.

Poverty in India is deeply tied to one's region, caste and gender. According to Sony Pellissery and Leemamol Mathew in Chapter Three, the country has a weak public space given strong identity-based politics, and those policy measures that are available are highly politicised. Within this setting, rampant corruption means the most vulnerable are the least likely to access support. While shame is, indeed, connected with the receipt of some services, it is more shameful to fail to access much needed help. A mismatch between lofty promises at the national level and the delivery of measures means that those that are accessible are of low quality and reinforce the low status that is attached to being poor.

National leaders in South Korea have also employed a productivist work approach in their welfare policies. As Yongmie Nicola Jo and Robert Walker report in Chapter Four, the work approach that has been tied to social assistance in the past 15 years has made work equivalent to welfare, all in the name of economic growth. National-level assumptions of deservingness tied to work capability do not, however, match the needs and challenges of the groups severely in need of economic support, nor has it acknowledged vast changes to family structure and social expectations in recent decades. The mismatched assumptions and conditions tied to social assistance have resulted in the immense shaming of measure recipients in South Korea.

In contrast to India, the story in Norway is not of the shame due to an inability to access anti-poverty measures, but rather one of intense shame felt by those on the receiving end of such measures. In Chapter Five, Erika Gubrium and Ivar Lødemel describe how the presence of a high standard of living, social equality and a generous welfare state means that those who have not fared as well feel palpable shame at their failure to live up to social norms. The country's strong work approach has worked well for most, yet it is a strategy that is mismatched to the realities of this small, disparate and often marginalised group. While it has provided increased opportunities for some (the work-able), it has resulted in heightened shame and new divisions for social assistance claimants.

Religion and social policy are tightly interwoven within the setting of Pakistan. As Sohail Choudhry shows in Chapter Six, this feature, along with a history of deep division between rich and poor, has shaped the development and design of anti-poverty policy. Whether or not offered under an overtly religious context, the two national policies described are greatly weakened by a failure to consider – and some might suggest, active avoidance of – how social divisions play out in terms of religion, gender and social class. These divisions are felt both in terms of how poverty is conceptualised as well as in the gap that exists between policy-making at the national level and (often corrupt) policy delivery at the local.

In Chapter Seven, Robert Walker and Elaine Chase describe how the development of social policy in the UK over the past 300 years has not only maintained the shaming aspects of the 17th-century Poor Law, but has, in fact, heightened them through increasingly indiscriminate categorisation of low-income people. The application of increased conditionality, guided by stark assumptions concerning the individual psychology of individuals as rational actors choosing to live in a state of dependent poverty, has served as a punitive device to reinforce their low status and limited options.

The broader economic picture of Uganda in recent decades has shown a move away from absolute to relative poverty. In Chapter Eight, Grace Bantebya Kyomuhendo and Amon Mwiine describe how older and more recent development approaches by national and international policy-makers have overwhelmingly focused on the income aspects of poverty, failing to acknowledge the deep divisions that exist within a strong social hierarchy. Nationally, a focus on accessibility over quality, a failure to provide the necessary infrastructure and resources to support broad welfare offerings, vast corruption at all levels and targeting criteria favouring those with some resources means that the new opportunities posed by national policies in the past decades have been felt instead as new systems for stratification and shaming by those who are most vulnerable.

Improving policy while respecting uniqueness

The seven settings explored in this volume represent vast differences in sociocultural setting and social policy tradition. Their macroeconomic health and infrastructural development vary widely. There is a broad continuum between the role of state and society within the arena of social policy-making and the level of social and economic inequality that exists. Settings are variably infused with strong religious beliefs or a strong sense of secularism. Work-related and gender-related norms also vary greatly. Finally, there is a vastly differing public sense across the settings concerning what poverty is and who is responsible for poverty.

Despite vast differences, however, the contexts for heightened shaming in each setting are empirically united by three broad themes that run strongly through the seven stories that are told. First, the social matters as much as the economic: the shame of poverty is not only about material deprivation, but also about weakened social resources. Second, a mismatch exists between national policy and local reality. This mismatch represents a failure to consider the myriad issues that pose a challenge to translating policy intent into delivery practices. Third, conditionality, when imposed within an anti-poverty policy setting, heightens the shame experienced by policy recipients.

The shared themes and unique elements shaping the connections between anti-poverty policy and shame are subsequently considered together in a final section, which describes policy-making principles for respecting the dignity of anti-poverty measure recipients in two concluding chapters. The principles stated in International Labour Organization (ILO) Recommendation 202 offer promising guidelines for considering and evaluating the social psychological aspects of social policy. In Chapter Nine, these principles are drawn on as a foundation for conducting a synthetic analysis of the volume's findings in terms of an understanding of poverty, shame and the promotion of dignity. Analysis of anti-poverty policy is sensitised by local social and user realities and is thus salient both for the introduction of new welfare policies in the developing world and in the reshaping of social institutions that may be under threat in post-recessionary times. At the same time, methodologies have been closely synchronised in order to gather data that has been functionally equivalent, thus allowing for a robust and meaningful comparison.

In Chapter Ten, the findings are presented as a set of policy lessons that are sensitive to the political, social and economic particulars of each setting. This chapter also offers a concrete strategy for moving the lessons forward at a future point to take the form of a concrete 'rubric'. Such a rubric would take seriously the task set forth by the ILO and would clarify the necessary standards for policy-making to respect the dignity of anti-poverty measure recipients. They would be used both to guide progress towards those standards and as a tool for evaluating, improving and crafting social policy.

Despite shared themes, each setting has very real and unique considerations. It is neither ethical nor appropriate to propose a static set of guidelines for best practices if our intention is to recognise the cross-cultural contexts for policy-making and delivery, much less the everyday realities for individuals living in poverty. Instead, our preliminary rubric offers a set of guidelines that are flexible and informed by national and local contexts and particularities – for improving and crafting anti-poverty measures with a focus on promoting human dignity. This set of broader guiding principles and recommendations can be used as a template for the evaluation and design of policy with a view to ensuring that anti-poverty policies succeed in enhancing social wellbeing by bolstering individual agency and promoting human dignity. The chapter thus offers an alternative framework that engages more specifically with the psychosocial dynamics of poverty and in particular with the social construction of shame – aspects of policy which have hitherto been largely ignored. In doing so this volume maps the possibilities for bringing the consideration of shame and dignity to the foreground in anti-poverty policy-making.

Note

[1] W.G. Runciman's 1966 report on the stigmatising effects of means tests on applicants, however, provides a relevant early example of a single country study theorising the relationship between social inequality and stigma. Ivar Lødemel's (1997) *Welfare paradox* continues this focus in his concluding comments to a comparative study of social assistance provision in the UK and Norway.

References

Alkire, S. (2002) *Valuing freedoms: Sen's capability approach and poverty reduction*, Oxford: Oxford University Press.

Alkire, S. (2007) 'The missing dimensions of poverty data', *Oxford Development Studies*, vol 35, no 4, pp 347-59.

Becker, G.S. (1976) *The economic approach to human behavior*, Chicago, IL: University of Chicago Press.

Blumer, H. (1969) *Symbolic interactionism: Perspective and method*, Englewood Cliffs, NJ: Prentice/Hall.

Chase, E. and Bantebya Kyomuhendo, G. (eds) (2014, forthcoming) *The shame of poverty: Global experiences*, Oxford: Oxford University Press.

Dean, H. (2009) 'Critiquing capabilities: the distractions of a beguiling concept', *Critical Social Policy*, vol 99, pp 261-78.

Edelstein, R.S. and Shaver, P.R. (2007) 'A cross-cultural examination of lexical studies of self-conscious emotions', in J.L. Tracy, R.W. Robins and J.P. Tangney (eds) *The self-conscious emotions: Theory and research*, New York: Guilford Press, Chapter 11.

Elster, J. (1989) *Nuts and bolts for the social sciences*, Cambridge: Cambridge University Press.

Fontaine, J.R.J., Luyten, P., Estas, C. and Corveleyn, J. (2004) 'Scenario-based and frequency-based approaches towards the measurement of guilt and shame: empirical evidence for unique contributions', in S.P. Shohov (ed) *Advances in psychology research*, Hauppage, NY: Nova Science Publishers, pp 141-54.

Fontaine, J.R.J., Luyten, P., de Boeck, P., Corveleyn, J., Fernandez, M., Herrera, D., Itzes, A. and Tomcsanyi, T. (2006) 'Untying the Gordian knot of guilt and shame: The structure of guilt and shame reactions based on situation and person variation in Belgium, Hungary, and Peru', *Journal of Cross-Cultural Psychology*, vol 37, no 3, pp 273-92.

Furukawa, E., Tangney, J. and Higashibara, F. (2012) 'Cross-cultural continuities and discontinuities in shame, guilt, and pride: A study of children residing in Japan, Korea and the USA', *Self and Identity*, vol 11, no 1, pp 90-113.

Goetz, J.L. and Keltner, D. (2007) 'Shifting meanings of self-conscious emotions across cultures: A social-functional approach', in J.L. Tracy, R.W. Robins and J.P. Tangney (eds) *The self-conscious emotions: Theory and research*, New York: Guilford Press, Chapter 9.

ILO (International Labour Organization) (2012) *Recommendation 202 concerning national floors of social protection adopted by the Conference at its one hundred and first session*, 14 June, Geneva, ILO.

Jönsson, L.R. and Starrin, B. (2000) 'Economi-skam modellen och reaktioner på arbetslöshet', *Socialvetenskaplig Tidskrift*, vol 3, pp 267-84.

Kahneman, D. and Tversky, A. (eds) (2000) *Choices, values and frames*, New York: Cambridge University Press.

Li, J., Wang, L. and Fischer, K. (2004) 'The organisation of Chinese shame concepts', *Cognition & Emotion*, vol 18, no 6, pp 767-97.

Lister, R. (2004) *Poverty*, Cambridge: Polity Press.

Lister, R. (2008) 'A human rights conceptualisation of poverty', Paris: International Conference on 'Exclusion, a challenge to democracy. How relevant is Joseph Wresinski's thinking?', Paris: Paris Institute of Political Studies, 19 December.

Lynd, H.M. (1958/1999) *On shame and the search for identity*, London: Routledge & Kegan Paul Ltd.

Mead, G.H. (1934/2003) *Mind, self, and society*, in J.A. Holstein and J.F. Gubrium (eds) (2003) *Inner lives and social worlds: Readings in social psychology*, New York: Oxford University Press, pp 52-3.

Murray, C. (1984) *Losing ground*, Chicago, IL: Basic Books.

OECD (Organisation for Economic Co-operation and Development) (2001) *DAC guidelines: Poverty reduction* (www.oecd.org/dac/povertyreduction/2672735.pdf).

O'Connor, A. (2002) *Poverty knowledge: Social science, social policy, and the poor in twentieth century US history*, Princeton, NJ: Princeton University Press.

Pinker, R. (1971) *Social theory and social policy*, London: Heinemann Educational Books.

Room, G.J. (1999) 'Social exclusion, solidarity and the challenge of globalization', *International Journal of Social Welfare*, vol 8, pp 166-74.

Rose, N. (1997) *Inventing ourselves: Psychology, power, and personhood*, Cambridge: Cambridge University Press.

Runciman, W.G. (1966) *Relative deprivation and social justice: A study of attitudes to social inequality in twentieth century England*, London: Pelican Books Ltd.

Scheff, T. (2000) 'Shame and the social bond: A sociological theory', *Sociological Theory*, vol 18, no 1, pp 84-99.

Scherer, K.R. (1997) 'The role of culture in emotion-antecedent appraisal', *Journal of Personality and Social Psychology*, vol 73, no 5, pp 902-22.

Sen, A. (1983) 'Poor, relatively speaking', *Oxford Economic Papers*, vol 35, pp 153-69.

Sen, A. (1992) *Inequalities re-examined*, Boston, MA: Harvard University Press.

Sen, A. (1999) *Development as freedom*, Oxford: Oxford University Press.

Sen, A. (2004) *Rationality and freedom*, Boston, MA: Harvard University Press.

Tangney, J.P. (1991) 'Moral affect: The good, the bad, and the ugly', *Journal of Personality and Social Psychology*, vol 61, pp 598-607.

Tangney, J.P. and Dearing, R.L. (2002) *Shame and guilt*, New York: Guilford Press.

Tangney, J.P., Steuwig, J. and Mashek, D.J. (2006) 'Moral emotions and moral behavior', *Annual Review of Psychology*, vol 58, pp 345-72.

Tangney, J.P., Wagner, P.E., Hill-Barlow, D., Marschall, D.E. and Gramzow, R. (1996) 'Relation of shame and guilt to constructive versus destructive responses to anger across the lifespan', *Journal of Personality and Social Psychology*, vol 70, no 4, pp 797-809.

Taylor, D. (2011) 'Wellbeing and welfare: A psychosocial analysis of being well and doing well enough', *Journal of Social Policy*, vol 40, no 4, pp 777-94.

Townsend, P. (1979) *Poverty in the United Kingdom*, London: Allen Lane.

Tracy, J.L., Robins, R.W. and Tangney, J.P. (2007) *The self-conscious emotions: Theory and research*, New York, Guilford Press.

Tsai, J.L., Levenson, R.W. and McCoy, K. (2006) 'Cultural and temperamental variation in emotional response', *Emotion*, vol 6, no 3, pp 484-97.

UN (United Nations) (2000) General Assembly Resolution 55/2: Millennium Declaration, 8 September.

Wacquant, L. (1996) 'The rise of advanced marginality: Notes on its nature and implications', *Acta Sociologica*, vol 39, no 2, pp 121-39.

Walker, R. (1995) 'The dynamics of poverty and social exclusion', in G. Room (ed) *Beyond the threshold: The measurement and analysis of social exclusion*, Bristol: Policy Press, pp 102-26.

Walker, R. (2012) 'Dignity and respect: A briefing note', Presented to the International Labour Conference, 101st Session.

Walker, R. (2014, forthcoming) *The shame of poverty: Global perspectives*, Oxford: Oxford University Press.

Walker, R., Bantebya Kyomuheno, G., Chase, E., Choudhry, S., Gubrium, E.K., Jo, N.-Y., Lødemel, I., Mathew, L., Mwiine, A., Pellissery, S. and Yan, M. (2013) 'Poverty in global perspective: Is shame a common denominator?', *Journal of Social Policy*, vol 42, no 2, pp 215-233.

Wong, Y. and Tsai, J. (2007) 'Cultural models of shame and guilt', in J.L. Tracy, R.W. Robins and J.P. Tangney (2007) *The self-conscious emotions: Theory and research*, New York: Guilford Press, Chapter 12.

Zavaleta, D. (2007) 'The ability to go without shame: A proposal for internationally comparable indicators for shame and humiliation', *Oxford Development Studies*, vol 35, no 4, pp 405-30.

TWO

New urban poverty and new welfare provision: China's *dibao* system

Ming Yan

Background

As the most populous country and carrying the oldest continuous civilisation, China has undergone drastic political and social changes in modern times. Its dynastic system that had lasted centuries was ended and replaced by the Republic in 1911, ending the Imperial rule of over 2,000 years. Following a series of civil wars, the Sino-Japanese War and revolution, the country regained peace and unity as the Communist Party established the People's Republic in 1949. For the past six decades, the development of the Chinese economy can broadly be divided into two phases: the planned economy or socialist period until 1979, and the market economy or post-reform period from 1979 to the present time.

Throughout Chinese history and until the late 1970s, subsistence poverty was a regular and severe problem for its vast population. However, China began to adopt reform and open-door policies in the late 1970s. With the end of the commune and new permission for private entrepreneurship, productivity increased and the poverty problem was quickly improved. China has long had a dual rural–urban system. This duality is not only marked in differing modes of production and degrees of modernity, but rural and urban areas are also separated by institutional mechanisms in such a way that urbanites have enjoyed and still enjoy more elaborate social benefits provided by the state in the areas of education, medical care and pension provision, among others. Rural residents, on the other hand, have been presumed self-supportive in all respects (Hussain, 1994).[1] Poverty alleviation programmes primarily targeted at the rural population and launched in the mid-1980s by the Chinese government, however, had the strong support of international organisations and resulted in impressive accomplishments. Measured according to The World Bank standard, China's poverty reduction performance has been even more striking. Between 1981 and 2004, the fraction of the population below this poverty line fell from 65 to 10 per cent, and the absolute number of poor fell from 652 million to 135 million, a decline of over half a billion people (The World Bank, 2009). Migration to urban areas has also helped to reduce poverty in rural areas (Ravallion and Chen, 2007).

Despite this forward movement, in recent decades several new concerns related to poverty in China have appeared. Nationally, the standard set for determining poverty has been inevitably low and the rate of poverty decrease has stagnated, with a more recent resurgence in the poverty population as the number of rural residents returning to poverty has increased. Furthermore, it has been difficult to combat environment-related poverty, as some of the poverty-concentrated areas are just not suitable for human habitation. While migration from these resource-scarce areas might be a solution, there are obstacles, including a lack of willingness to move, the level of resources required to relocate, and adaptation to the new environment in both material and cultural terms.

The overall poverty rate has also declined in China's urban areas, which now contain approximately 50 per cent of the country's population (Ravallion and Chen, 2007), yet urban China has in past decades been confronted with the so-called 'new urban poverty' problem. Urban poverty in China emerged and became increasingly severe after the beginning of the urban economic reform in 1984 and especially since the early 1990s when the marketisation process speeded up (Tang, 2003). During this period, thousands of employees in the state sector suffered both from unemployment and compromised social benefits as a result of the restructuring and privatisation of formerly state-owned enterprises (SOEs). This has translated into heightened absolute poverty, as well as increased relative poverty, felt most markedly in China's urban areas. A period witnessing high economic growth and the modernisation of the Chinese economy has been accompanied by the creation of vast income inequalities. This period of parallel growth and economic inequalities might represent an ideal case in which to explore Amartya Sen's (1983) notion of universal shame attached to poverty. It is against this background that this chapter unfolds.

The China case presented here focuses on the emergence of urban poverty and the main anti-poverty programme, which is aimed at *absolute* poverty – the Minimum Standard of Living Scheme (MSLS 1999) in urban China, popularly known as *dibao* ('subsistence allowance' or 'minimal needs'), a term used throughout the chapter. This chapter is divided into three sections: the first deals with the framing of

---

policy, with an emphasis on public discourses concerning the nature, manifestations and causes of urban poverty since the 1990s. It reveals the structural factors leading to the re-emergence of urban poverty: the national strategic shift of development, and restructuring and privatisation of SOEs and public understandings concerning the new poverty. The second section focuses on the shaping and structuring of *dibao*, discussing how the policy came into existence, as well as the policy specifications such as funding, criteria and benefits. The phases in policy-making and variation among regions/cities are discussed. The third section examines several features connected to policy implementation and delivery, including issues and problems in administration and procedures. The second and third sections attend to the possibility that shame has been heightened for individuals receiving *dibao*, due to particular specifications and procedures. The chapter ends with a discussion on implications and policy recommendations, with a particular focus on maximising the dignity of those living in poverty.

Policy framing: new welfare provision and the emergence of new urban poverty

The structural transition in China since 1979 bears witness to a shift from a planned economy to a market economy. It also marks the retreat of the state from welfare provision. It was under such a context that urban economic reform characterised by marketisation and privatisation took place. Urban poverty as an issue has since retained the attention of both scholars and policy-makers in China (Gustafsson and Wei, 2000; Khan and Riskin, 2001; Meng et al, 2005).

After the Communist revolution in China in 1949 and until the 1980s, the developmental strategies adopted included restoration and expansion of industrial production, especially of heavy industry. Full employment and comprehensive welfare provision were made available to urban industrial workers under state socialism and its planned economy. In brief, production and social protection were characterised as 'full employment, comprehensive welfare, low wages and high subsidy'. Production, employment and social provision were under state authority, and it was the so-called 'iron rice bowl'. This control was primarily embodied through the system of *danwei*. *Danwei* literally means 'unit' in Chinese, and its *de facto* meaning in the given context was closest to that of the English 'workplace'. *Danwei* as workplace referred to the institutional arrangements through which one sought employment and thus drew a source of livelihood. During this command economy period, it was through the affiliation with *danwei* that an individual was ensured permanent employment and labour-related benefits, among them: sick leave, maternity, disability and an old-age pension. Furthermore, as state employees, individuals were provided with a comprehensive social protection scheme that provided a subsidised food service, medical care, recreation and various allowances (utilities, transport, newspapers and books) via the *danwei*. Finally, it was a 'mini-society' that serviced workers and their families with childcare, school and housing. In exchange, individual work mobility was extremely limited. Thus, *danwei* was more than a productive and social protection unit; it played a core role in the centralised redistributive system and served as an essential and unique tool of totalitarian control in economic, social and political terms (Walder, 1986; Bray, 2005).

From the mid-1950s to the late 1980s, reference to poverty was primarily limited to 'households in difficulty' and there was no public discussion of 'urban poverty' (Guan, 1999, pp 137-8). These households were regarded as a minor affliction confined to a small minority: comprised of either working individuals who faced challenges due to family issues (having numerous children or older dependants) or those who fell into the '3 noes' category (no reliable source of income, no ability to work and no family support). In 1992, at an early stage of economic reform, approximately 190,000 people (0.06 per cent of the population) in China's urban areas received social assistance (Tang, 1998). These individuals were assisted by regular and irregular relief and, as the number of these households was fairly low, were thought to have little impact on social stability. It is possible that these households experienced the shame of marginalisation in an otherwise egalitarian society.

Towards the end of the 1970s, the Chinese government shifted its long-term ideological and political approach and refocused on economic development, with the reformist Communist leader, Deng Xiaoping, describing the new approach as 'allowing some to get rich first.' The urban economic reform that began around the mid-1980s and continued throughout the 1990s facilitated the transformation of SOEs toward marketisation. Policy reform was undertaken in the areas of labour contract provision, tax and wage regulations and the provision of old-age and unemployment insurance. The official goal was to shut down unprofitable enterprise, diversify ownership and move business enterprises to modern forms of corporate governance.

This modernisation was arguably achieved at the expense of displaced and marginalised workers (Solinger, 2008). Economic reform meant that responsibility for, and regulated provision of, social services was decoupled from individual enterprises, housing was privatised and responsibility for health insurance and pension provision was shifted to city or provincial governments. According to government statistics, from 1995 to 2001 the number of workers employed in the state-owned sector fell from 113 million to 67 million, a decline of approximately 40 per cent. During the same period, employment in the urban collective sector[2] fell by 18.6 million, or nearly 60 per cent. Reports concerning the total number of workers officially registered as 'laid off' varied widely, with estimates ranging from 28 to 43 million, including 34 million from the state sector (Liu, 2004, p 218; He and Hua, 2006, p 5).

With a rise in mass lay-offs in the 1990s, the issue of urban poverty began to attract more attention from policy-makers and researchers, who have tried to make sense of this phenomenon (Gustafsson and Wei, 2000; Khan and Riskin, 2001; Li and Knight, 2002). Indeed, urban poverty trends in China do not reflect the country's broader rate of economic development. Various studies show that throughout the economic reform of the 1990s, the poverty rate in urban areas was on the rise, mainly due to massive unemployment and inadequate social assistance (Li and Knight, 2002; Xue and Wei, 2004). In contrast, in terms of macroeconomic development, by the end of 2008 China's level of gross domestic product (GDP) per capita had grown enough to push the country up to The World Bank status of a low- to middle-income country. This contradiction is explained by the fact that although China has significantly reduced poverty, it has been less successful in narrowing income inequality, which has drastically increased since the start of the economic reform period (Li, 2011).[3]

In fact, however, the level of income inequality is starker than ever before in the history of the People's Republic of China. In addition to income inequality, the effects of economic reform in terms of the increased need to save money, the higher relative price of food, the need to spend more on medical services, education and housing, as well as growing income inequality, have offset the potentially positive effect of income growth on poverty reduction (Meng et al, 2005). In particular, a number of studies have noted that a rapidly rising consumer price index during the 1990s contributed to increased economic burdens on low-income families, and thus to the expansion of a poverty population in urban China (Zhu, 1997; Tang, 1998). As the modernisation of the Chinese economy has been accompanied by the creation of vast income inequalities, this has translated into heightened *relative* poverty, especially marked in urban areas.

In reality, the bulk of the new urban poor are made up of former state industrial employees. Thus, unlike the 'old urban poor', a large percentage of the 'new urban poor' are able and willing to work but have no jobs (Hussain, 2003). Unemployment-related poverty has been especially severe in cities suffering from a resource drain or de-industrialisation after having relied on a single source of production due to historical and geographic particularities. The level of poverty in urban areas thus varies widely, and it is estimated that the number of people living in poverty in urban China has ranged from 14 million to over 37 million (Hussain, 2003; Tang, 2003).[4] More specifically, unskilled or low-skilled and poorly educated female workers have been those most negatively affected by the economic reforms (Knight and Song, 2005), and laid-off and unemployed workers are very likely to fall into poverty as a result of low human capital, low skills and old age (Wang, 2007), thus the newer poverty trend has inordinately affected those groups considered most vulnerable.

The euphemistically articulated discourse and new policy approach of the Chinese government since economic liberalisation has reflected the increase in urban poverty, an exponential growth in income inequality and the changing composition of low-income urban dwellers. An analysis of public discourse concerning poverty shows that rhetorically, the government has emphasised the structural causes of poverty in its politically attuned mantra to providing basic welfare provisions in order to ward off the threat posed by the new urban poor, to 'social stability' and to maintain social 'harmony' (Yan, 2014a). In terms of policy, China's introduction of the *dibao* system provides a system of minimum relief via residual social assistance targeted towards unemployed people. The system has aimed to be, as Premier Li Peng has stated: 'an effective programme that costs little but is beneficial to social stability' (cited in Duoji, 2001, p 178). Thus officially, its objectives or functions have been described as a social safety net to ease labour risks, an adjustment mechanism of redistribution for lessening income disparity and as a shock absorber for social stability by providing a minimum living standard guarantee (Hu, 2009).

New urban poverty has emerged and had significant implications during fast economic growth and amidst widely improved standards of living. The new urban poor are a reflection of rapid socioeconomic transformation in China, and are more visible than 'older' urban poverty and the population living in rural poverty, as they are located in power centres – cities. Low-income urban dwellers are typically faced with two major issues: while those individuals who are securely employed possess elaborate employment-based pension and healthcare programmes, it is extremely difficult for the members of this group to find new employment and for those who have managed to do this, the jobs obtained are often insecure and poorly paid (Knight and Song, 2005).

Focus group conversations with individuals not experiencing economic challenges emphasise a rapidly growing economic disparity in the face of which urban poverty has become a crucial issue (Yan, 2014a). Furthermore, data gathered from interviews with people experiencing poverty in Beijing shows they have great difficulty adapting to the change in their status from advantaged to disadvantaged, from the 'glorified' master of the country to social assistance recipients. Longing for the 'good old days', their sense of deprivation, discontent and social injustice tends to be high (Yan, 2014b). This study shows that respondents in China, who as employees of SOEs had once been part of the vanguard of the working class enjoying high status as 'masters of the state', now largely had to be content with low-paying, insecure occupations because they lacked the entrepreneurial skills demanded by the reformed Chinese economy. They were angry at their lowered social status post-economic reform, and questioned the rapidly increasing economic disparity in China.

Despite a government focus on social responsibility for poverty and social harmony, the newer context of modernisation and advanced capitalism and the attendant growth of consumerism may, however, mean that those experiencing newer poverty may increasingly come to be publicly seen as personal failures, open to shaming because their situations are considered indicative of socially and economically dysfunctional behaviour in an arena that is increasingly status-oriented.

Combating urban poverty: policy-making and implementation

The social assistance programmes existing during China's period of planned economy reflected the marginalised status of the old urban poor. Social assistance coverage and funding before the period of economic reform were quite low and arguably insufficient. The number receiving support was modest and many struggling households were left out. The level of monetary support was also extremely low. In 1992, the total social assistance expenditure (including regular and temporary relief) totalled 120 million yuan, or 0.005 per cent of GDP and less than 0.03 per cent of the national revenue. On average, a level of 38 yuan/month was provided to recipients, equivalent to about 25 per cent of the cost of living and less than one third of the per capita food expenditure for urban residents in China (Tang, 1998).

The old social assistance programme was inadequate to deal with new forms of poverty. Discontent and protests from former workers was profuse, imposing pressure on the Chinese government (Lee, 2007). To deal with the looming problem of massive 'redundant labourers' and to ensure the basic livelihoods of the unemployed in urban areas, new policy or institutional arrangements were developed.

Initially, a policy of 'three security lines' took form, which provided sequential cash transfers: basic living security aid for three years, unemployment insurance for two years, and then *dibao*. These programmes drew on the combined financial sources of the former SOEs and on central and local governments. The approach of enterprise-focused provision, however, was eventually phased out. During the early days of *dibao*, the Chinese government placed rhetorical emphasis on the need for welfare reform in order to minimise the financial 'burden' of providing for former employees on former state and now private enterprises, easing the way for the further retrenchment of state workers in later years (Solinger, 2008). By 2000 the *dibao* scheme was officially recognised as an integral part of the social security system independent of the earlier enterprise-based one (Tang, 2003, p 23). By 2002 financial support from enterprises had dwindled to a trickle as the government assumed greater responsibility for the social welfare of former workers, as they were forced to relinquish contractual links with their former work units. *Dibao* became the primary social assistance programme in urban China.

The development and implementation of *dibao* was a gradual and cautious process that took eight years (1993-2001), from initial experimentation on the local level to national adoption. In 1993, Shanghai, China's largest city, took the initiative with a pilot *dibao* programme issued jointly by the Shanghai Bureaus of Civil Affairs, Finance, Human Resources, Social Insurance and the Trade Unions. Together, these entities stipulated a 'Notice to establish the urban residents' Minimum Scheme of Living Standard in Shanghai'. In this early stipulation of the terms and conditions of *dibao*, it was noted that the municipal government and *danwei* would share financial responsibilities. This emphasis on the role of *danwei* in the funding mechanism, popularly known as 'taking one's own child', reflected remnants of the earlier *danwei*-based approach to welfare provision (Shen, 2009).

Shanghai's pilot programme soon won the support of the national Ministry of Civil Affairs, which urged China's cities on the east coast – more financially resourceful and yet experiencing the stark pressures of growing poverty – to introduce their own pilot programmes. Policy explorations of *dibao* by local governments continued their expansion into China's urban areas. These efforts were rhetorically supported by the central government's Ministry of the Civil Affairs through organising a series of policy discussion meetings at which various policy practices were assessed.

The formal establishment of *dibao* in China with the central government's 'Regulations on the *dibao* for urban residents' took place in 1999 after the scheme had been implemented in all urban areas, representing 668 cities and 1,638 towns. The 1999 Regulation states that *dibao* is 'the right of those whose family income is lower than the MSLS criteria and should seek basic material support from the local government', which signifies universal coverage. Indeed, by 1999 *dibao* had been extended to approximately 2.82 million urban residents, of whom 79 per cent were new recipients, a tenfold increase compared with the population covered by the old social assistance scheme in 1992 (Tang, 2003).

In reality, however, coverage would prove to be far from universal. The lack of social assistance coverage for migrants is a case in point. China's unique registration system (*hukou*) divides the Chinese population into rural and urban localities according to birthplace. Those born in urban areas are registered as such, and, as suggested above, are granted access to the various urban-only social services provided by the government. Those born in rural areas, on the other hand, are not entitled to the more extensive publicly provided social provisions in the realms of health and education, but do possess the right to land. An individual moving away from his or her birthplace faces the loss of either the right to these services or to his or her land. Those with high levels of resources may convert their registration files into an urban identity, yet this is not the case for most rural people (Chan and Zhang, 1999, cited in Chen, 2012).

While urban and rural *dibao* systems have been established, this has been done separately (the rural variant since 2007), and the urban system provides a transfer only to *locally registered* urban households with incomes below a municipally designated line. This practice denies eligibility to the thousands of migrants whose official registration remains in their hometown. Despite concerns over migrant poverty, official discussions within the realm of Chinese policy-making and implementation have yet to effectively address this issue.

From 1999 to 2008, receipt of *dibao* by registered urban households grew eightfold, yet coverage even of this population remains low, a widely acknowledged problem. By 2008, 3.8 per cent of the urban population received the benefit (22.73 million people) (MCA, 2008).

Despite the scheme's broad aims this represented, however, only approximately one quarter of households with an income level below the *dibao* line (Solinger, 2008). Thus, despite its expansion, coverage is still extraordinarily limited. It has reduced poverty according to the absolute poverty definition, but has had little impact on inequality or poverty more broadly defined (Chen, et al, 2006; Appleton et al, 2010). The result is that there is a large urban population that continues to languish while being surrounded by increasing levels of urban wealth.

Delivery of dibao: problem or promise?

The lack of universalism associated with social assistance provision in China is not entirely surprising as China's decentralised fiscal system cannot support a nationwide universal welfare system. The decentralised nature of this system is reflected in the fact that local – not central – governments have become the main players in welfare administration and provision. For instance, local governments have received the authority to set their own poverty line standards in determining eligibility, and there is no detailed national framework to guide this process. In principle, cities set the poverty line using the direct method of costing 20 items of goods and services considered necessary for basic subsistence (the so-called 'basic needs' approach), yet methods vary across cities and some cities rely on no more than an informed guess in standard setting. As for the *dibao* line, according to the 1999 Regulation, local governments decide on appropriate criteria, based on the local consumer price, consumption pattern and income levels, as well as the economic development and financial capabilities of the given local government. Therefore the poverty line is usually equivalent to the *dibao* line, which might well be determined by the local government based on its fiscal constraints at its own discretion (Duoji, 2001; Hong, 2004; Li and Yang, 2009).[5] The implication is that the current *dibao* in some cities or regions, especially those economically less developed areas, could be far from adequate in meeting the basic needs of those in poverty.

While the benefit is to be available to those whose family income is lower than a locally determined *dibao* line, there is a public concern with minimising 'dependency' and 'cheating' (Yan, 2014a). The process for applying for and obtaining *dibao* is also arduous. Provisions for all urban households are registered in a specified locality. Because local authorities lack the personnel to deal with the tedious paperwork involved, the vetting process has been delegated to the neighbourhood committee, a self-organised group handling public affairs in the local area. The committee's familiarity with the particular situations of neighbourhood residents is also thought to effectively separate the deserving from the undeserving, but this structure may also be both invasive and stigmatising (Solinger, 2010).

As it is a huge challenge to verify the income or assets of the applicant, many committees apply a variety of strategies to help make the decision, much of these based on an assessment of consumption (Ding, 2008). The review process can include household visits and interviews with those familiar with the applicant (Duoji, 2001). Cases must be reviewed and reapproved at a minimum of every six months. The reliance on familiarity as a strategy for decision-making in the *dibao* system has meant that obtaining registration in a new location has been difficult (not least for those living in poverty and socially disconnected), so in practice programme eligibility has been confined to well-established local residents. Furthermore, in order to limit fraud, there is a community inspection process whereby the names of proposed claimants are displayed on notice boards and community members are encouraged to identify non-eligible applicants. This practice has, in particular, raised concerns about stigma effects, and has had the potential of producing a sense of shame among those awaiting their peers' evaluation concerning their deservingness.

A review of pertinent policy documents shows that the challenge of verifying the income and assets of applicants also relates to the debate on deservingness, and consumption level is variably taken into account when local committees determine eligibility. The expectation of minimum subsistence is also prevalent in this setting. Among the criteria for receiving the benefit is that claimants cannot have a consumption level that is deemed as markedly higher than the local minimum standard of living. It is, however, up to local committees to determine what this standard should include. Thus, the committee might reject claimants for owning a car and highly priced appliances, such as air conditioning units. Additionally, those applicants of working age and physically able are required to make three attempts to find employment prior to seeking the benefit, and a claimant cannot have refused a job offer without legitimate reasons. Furthermore, in exchange for receiving *dibao*, claimants are expected to engage in community service, such as street patrolling. A study among Beijing residents who had experienced poverty suggests that these criteria are potentially shaming for some claimants. One respondent, for instance, described the humiliation she experienced when forced to provide documentary evidence as to why a potential employer had not considered her fit for a position in her previous job searches (Yan, 2014b).

Another challenge concerns the level of benefit provided and the process in determining it. As income, consumption, fiscal resources and priorities vary widely, so do benefit standards from city to city and from region to region. A significant issue is whether the *dibao* income is sufficient for the recipient, especially in light of the relative disparity of growing income inequality within urban areas. As a whole, the income is only a small proportion of the income per capita according to local standards, reportedly ranging from only 16 to 26 per cent (Gu and Gao, 2007). Thus, the *dibao* focus on absolute poverty precludes a policy focus on the very real issue of relative poverty experienced by many of China's new urban poor.

The aforementioned processes and emphasis on determining deservingness have drawn scholarly concern about the stigma and shaming effects that might be attached to *dibao* application and, more specifically, to the community vetting process. Indeed, a sense of stigma or shame felt by *dibao* recipients may mirror the classical debate concerning the deserving and undeserving poor that is now deeply engrained in Chinese discourse concerning benefit provision. Public opinion in China is clear and strong that the category of deserving poor includes older people, children and those with disabilities, and that these groups are entitled to receive social assistance. The undeserving poor include those within working age who are physically fit to work but do not, and those possessing a criminal record. The mass media focus on welfare dependency (Zhang, 2006) has been especially focused on the former group (Guangwei, 2003; Lai and Wang, 2006), and one report suggests that 85 per cent of *dibao* recipients are physically able to work (Huang, 2007). As to the latter group, people acknowledge the fact that due to discrimination, the chance of finding employment for someone with a criminal record is slim, yet the public is especially unhappy about those who feel entitled to *dibao* as soon as they come out of prison (Yan, 2014a).

Studies examining recipient perceptions of the stigma and shame that they experience via benefit receipt, however, vary in their findings. One study has reported a common public perception that an unemployed person of working age and physically able to work is incompetent and the disdain cast towards these individuals when applying for benefits (Ma, 2010). However, studies, including our own interviews with benefit recipients in Beijing, have generated rather inconsistent findings. Respondents in our study consistently emphasised that they had sought *dibao* out of dire financial necessity and that their situations had finally enabled them to overcome their reluctance to apply for the benefit (Yan, 2014b). A survey on *dibao* receipt, however, shows that the majority of the respondents described themselves as 'very happy' (59.4 per cent) or 'at ease' (9.5 per cent), and only 15.9 per cent described feeling embarrassed (Zhu and Lin, 2010). Another survey-based study also indicates that while some *dibao* recipients perceived that receiving the benefit was a matter of 'losing face' (21 per cent), more did not think so (38.6 per cent) (Ma and Zhao, 2006). Two factors may be at work to explain this contradiction. First, *dibao*, if considered along with the associated wide range of supplementary assistance provided, is rather comprehensive and badly needed by those living in poverty, which may compensate for the reluctance of application due to the attached stigma and social shaming.[6] Further, as *dibao* has been increasingly described as a basic right, the stigma attached to it may have decreased when contrasted with the earlier charity approach to social assistance (Zhu and Lin, 2010). Yet many urban *dibao* recipients were also former SOE workers. They perceived the scheme as a minimal means of compensation, given the loss of job security they had experienced (Yan, 2014b).

With regard to concerns about the community vetting process, our own discussions with respondents who had experienced poverty showed that many were accepting of the procedure as legitimate. Some noted that their neighbours and community members had already been familiar with their financial struggles, and one respondent emphasised that he had explained to his daughter that it was their "right" to receive the benefit (Yan, 2014b). Similarly, a 2007 report by The World Bank describing the results of a survey of benefit recipients in Liaoning Province found that only 10 per cent were ashamed or uncomfortable with disclosure of their household information in the application process (Ravallion, 2009).[7] There is, however, evidence that the vetting process is shaming for some. Some low-income respondents described feeling reluctant to submit the application for benefits, referring to the tedious nature of the application process. Several also expressed feeling uneasy or embarrassed during and after this process, some especially concerned about their school-aged children "losing face" by belonging to a family on *dibao* benefits (Yan, 2014b).

Implications and recommendations

Overall and in practical terms, the establishment of the *dibao* system as the institutional framework of poverty relief was a policy response to the restructuring of the SOEs and retreat of the enterprise social provision and resultant political pressure to maintain 'social stability'. For such a rapidly established and growing programme, the implementation and delivery of the system has not been without question or even challenges. Its implications and policy recommendations are further discussed here.

While the *dibao* system has rhetorically been described as a basic right for urban residents to have their basic necessities met (Hu, 2009), and as a necessary scheme for poverty alleviation (Li and Luo, 2009), this quickly expanded programme has generated controversy. Some argue that despite its effect on poverty alleviation, the system has a very limited impact on narrowing income inequality in urban China. Several scholars have argued that policy cannot be an effective means of broader poverty prevention until the basic benefit level is raised and coverage expanded (Li and Luo, 2009; Zhang and Tang, 2009).

Additionally, policy-makers and scholars have provided confusing messages concerning what should be the target of social protection policy in China. Much of this work has been aimed at providing quantitative estimates of poverty lines within varying settings, estimates of the levels of absolute versus relative poverty and on the poverty–growth–inequality nexus. The findings from these sorts of analyses have been quite inconsistent. While new region-specific strategies for determining absolute poverty lines appear to better reflect current conditions (Ravallion, 2009), it could well be that while these scientifically determined poverty lines are valid for absolute poverty consideration, as the general standard of living continues to rise, it is a matter of drawing a poverty line in *relative* terms in which political, economic and social factors play an increasingly significant role. While reports suggest that the aggregate poverty rate has tended to fall over time, it has been generally agreed that *relative* urban poverty is an issue in the context of increased income disparity, and a high representation of this has been reflected in the struggles of the laid-off workers of former SOEs, the focus of this study. Given the issue of relative poverty, the policy strategies implemented must grapple with the rapidly increasing income inequality in order to effectively address the rapidly changing socioeconomic reality in urban China (Zhang and Tang, 2009; Li and Yang, 2009).

Another challenge concerns the public stigmatisation of benefit receipt. Concerns over welfare dependency expressed are strong in scholarly writings as well as the mass media. The scholarship focused on minimising dependence via system design has attempted to determine a level of income at which recipients presumably maintain an incentive to work. The implication here is that the scheme may create a poverty trap, whereby participants do not face an incentive to raise their own incomes (see, for instance, Ravallion 2009). This emphasis mirrors a public focus on benefit receipt that is more concerned with 'cheating' and 'dependency' and less with a consideration of the larger issues at play in shaping economically challenging conditions. Scholarship focused on measuring fraud has not cited broad evidence that this is, in fact, a real problem in practice, with few reports citing instances of fraud (see, for instance, Ge and Yang, 2004). On the other hand, researchers engaged in fieldwork observations have indicated that the notion of 'imputed income' has been frequently applied in practice. This level of income that reflects a presumed *potential* for income given the household labour force has apparently been applied with the aim of reducing work disincentives. Scholars focused on balancing incentives and disincentives hold this practice up as confirmation that, in fact, the process of community vetting for *dibao* eligibility has attenuated the disincentive effects implied by its design (Chen et al, 2006).

Rather than focusing on the presence of generous benefits as a disincentive to work, in reality, work disincentives instead often take the form of strenuous and demanding labour conditions, employment instability and the extra expenses related to work such as transportation, meals, clothing and childcare. The fact that *dibao* receipt serves as a link to the receipt of a series of additional benefits such as medical expenses reimbursement, school tuition reduction or remission and housing subsidies have proven to be quite attractive to low-income families, some of which have focused on add-on benefits, as opposed to the income benefit, as motivation to seek *dibao* (Huang, 2007; Li and Xiao, 2007). In this respect, policy should focus on the enhancement of social provision in general, not only for people living in poverty in urban areas but for the whole population as well.

Our respondents frequently described a feeling of marginalisation in relation to their fall in status after economic liberalisation. These individuals had not reaped the rewards of broader economic prosperity: respondents described the vast economic inequities as a troubling and rather new experience. Despite the seemingly draconian eligibility process associated with the granting of *dibao*, however, in our discussions with Beijing respondents who lived in poverty they less frequently described a sense of shame or shaming connected with this process than similarly situated respondents in other countries (see, for example, Chapters Five, Six and Seven, on Norway, the UK and Pakistan, this volume). Our respondents were drawn mostly, however, from a population of individuals who *had* managed to access benefits within the context of general low coverage. The involvement of local community members in decisions concerning the award of benefits may have enabled these individuals who had – after a gruelling effort – been deemed eligible for benefits to internalise a sense of deservingness.

Thus, the potential for shame may have been displaced through the very arduous nature of the process. Yet, the process is tedious and difficult; the potential for shaming and heightened marginalisation by the large number of people who have *not* been deemed eligible for benefits is still a matter of concern. Thus, the issue of coverage is a crucial issue in China.

Another concern is that *dibao* recipients are becoming a special group who bear a stigmatised label. In the long run, both the regulations that shape this programme and the regimens used in enforcing it – whether by design or by subterfuge – marginalise the most vulnerable among the urbanites (Hong, 2005; Solinger, 2010). A policy remedy could be to stress the 'right' to *dibao*, not only rhetorically, but also through the methods used in evaluating applicants and by following through on rhetorical promises to offer universal coverage.

In conclusion, China's rapid and drastic transformation has brought about many changes and problems, among which urban poverty and the resultant *dibao* system is but one. This particular social assistance programme has been effective in that it has met the goal of poverty alleviation to some extent, as well as, from an official perspective, served to maintain political stability. At the same time, while issues with the benefit level, coverage, dependency and a concern with delineating the deserving from the undeserving might seem minor given the enormity of the task at hand, in order to build a system that effectively grapples with the economic and social psychological effects of income inequality and relative poverty, their significance must not be overlooked.

Notes

[1] In recent years, social security has been rapidly expanded to rural residents through the offer of social assistance (*dibao*), medical care and an old-age pension scheme.

[2] During the planned economy period, the urban collective sector, compared with the SEOs, offered lower wages and fewer comprehensive benefits (Walder, 1984).

[3] The Gini coefficient for the entire country was estimated at approximately 0.47 in 2007 compared to 0.30 in the early 1980s. In urban China, the coefficient surged from 0.16 in 1978 to 0.36 in 2007 (Li, 2011).

[4] Some studies, however, refute the massive growth in poverty during this period. In particular, one suggests that while the withdrawal of subsidies during 1988-95 lowered the real income of the poorest in urban areas, this

policy change was subsequently outweighed by growth in other sources of income. Thus, this study suggests, despite the rise of mass unemployment after 1995, absolute poverty continued to fall, irrespective of where the poverty line was set. This implies that the concern that *absolute* poverty has risen during urban reform is misplaced (Appleton, et al, 2010).

[5] Local variation is also reflected in the level of benefit offered. The average benefit level is 208 yuan per person/month (US$31), while the range has been between 150 and 400 yuan (MCA, 2008).

[6] In 2001, China's central government stipulated in its 'Notice to strengthen urban MSLS work' its intention to provide aid to urban *dibao* recipients in the areas of housing, medical care, education, taxes and utilities, among others. This was followed by a series of official notices, stipulating provisions in each area.

[7] These results may, however, reflect a biased sample if those deterred by public disclosure chose not to participate.

References

Appleton, S., Song, L. and Xia, Q. (2010) 'Growing out of poverty: Trends and patterns of urban poverty in China 1988-2002', *World Development*, vol 38, no 5, pp 665-78.

Bray, D. (2005) *Social space and governance in urban China: The danwei system from origins to urban reform*, Stanford, CA: Stanford University Press.

Chan, K.W. and Zhang, L. (1999) 'The Hukou system and rural–urban migration in China: Processes and changes', *China Quarterly*, vol 160, December, pp 818-55.

Chen, J. (2012) 'Beyond the invisible wall: Urbanization paradox in China caused by the Household Registration System', Unpublished paper.

Chen, S., Ravallion, M. and Wang, Y. (2006) *Di Bao: A guaranteed minimum income in China's cities?*, World Bank Policy Research Working Paper, No 3805, January, Washington, DC: The World Bank.

Ding, J. (2008) 'Problems and strategies in urban MSLS management – a case study of Wuchang, Wuhan City', *Study and Practice*, vol 9, pp 140-7.

Duoji, C. (2001) *Research and practice of the Minimum Standard of Living Scheme in China*, Beijing: People's Press.

Ge, D. and Yang, T. (2004) 'Minimum income schemes for the unemployed: A case study from Dalian, China,' *International Social Science Journal*, vol 56, no 179, pp 47-56.

Gu, X. and Gao, M. (2007) 'Coverage and fairness issues in the social safety net of urban and rural China', *He Bei Journal*, vol 2, pp 74-9.

Guan, X. (1999) *Urban poverty*, Changsha: Hunan People's Publishing House.

Guangwei, (2003) 'Why do those *dibao* recipients with the ability to work not do so?', *Beijing Evening*, 27 October.

Gustafsson, B. and Wei, Z. (2000) 'How and why has poverty in China changed? A study based on microdata for 1988 and 1995', *China Quarterly*, vol 164, pp 983-1006.

He, P. and Hua, Y.F. (2006) *Study on the social security policy and implementation measures of the urban poor groups*, Beijing: Chinese Labor and Social Security Press [in Chinese].

Hong, D. (2004) *Social assistance in China's transition*, Shenyang: Liaoning Education Press.

Hong, D. (2005) 'When responsibility becomes institution – on the effect and trend of the urban MSLS', *Comparative Social and Economic Institutions*, vol 3, no 119, pp 16-25.

Hu, X.Y. (2009) 'Social security', in *Social security system in contemporary China*, Beijing: Chinese Labor and Social Security Press [in Chinese].

Huang, C. (2007) 'On the factors affecting job seeking behavior of the urban MSLS recipients and the relevant institutional arrangements', *Sociological Studies*, vol 1, pp 137-60.

Hussain, A. (1994) 'Social security in present-day China and its reform', *American Economic Review*, vol 84, no 2, pp 276-80.

Hussain, A. (2003) *Urban poverty in China: Measurement, patterns and policies*, Geneva: International Labour Office.

Khan, A.R. and Riskin, C. (2001) *Inequality and poverty in China in the age of globalisation*, New York: Oxford University Press.

Knight, J. and Song, L. (2005) *Towards a labour market in China*, Oxford: Oxford University Press.

Lai, Z. and Wang, F. (2006) 'Claiming MSLS rather than seeking jobs, many lazy men among young MSLS recipients', *Beijing Evening*, 31 March.

Lee, C. (2007) *Against the law: Labor protests in China's rustbelt and sunbelt*, Berkeley, CA: University of California Press.

Li, S. (2011) 'Issues and options for social security reform in China', *China: An International Journal*, vol 9, no 1, pp 1-29.

Li, S. and Knight, J. (2002) 'Three types of poverty in urban China', *Economic Studies*, vol 10, pp 47-58.

Li, S. and Luo, C.L. (2009) 'Impact of public policy on income distribution in our country', *Chinese Social Sciences*, vol 12, November.

Li, S. and Yang, S. (2009) 'Impact of the urban MSLS in China on income distribution and poverty', *Chinese Population Science*, vol 5, pp 19-27.

Li, Y. and Xiao, Y. (2007) 'Three serious problems in the urban MSLS', *People's Forum*, vol 4, pp 38-9.

Liu, G.X. (2004) *A brief history of labor security in the new China 1949-2003*, Beijing: Chinese Labor and Social Security Press.

Ma, F. (2010) *Involution of social welfare during the transitional period and its institutional implications – An analysis on the experience of the urban laid-off or unemployed women seeking and receiving assistance*, Beijing: Beijing University Press.

Ma, J. and Zhao, S. (2006) 'Exploratory study on the disincentive effects of MSLS', *Journal of Chongqing University of Science and Technology* (Social Science edn), vol 4, pp 43-6.

MCA (Ministry of Civil Affairs) (2008) 'Construction of the social policy support system for urban and rural poor families in China', Unpublished report.

Meng, X., Gregory, R. and Wang, Y. (2005) 'Poverty, inequality, and growth in urban China, 1986-2000', *Journal of Comparative Economics*, vol 33, pp 710-29.

Ravallion, M. (2009) 'Decentralizing eligibility for a federal antipoverty program: a case study for China', *The World Bank Economic Review*, vol 23, no 1, pp 1-30.

Ravallion, M. and Chen, S. (2007) 'China's (uneven) progress against poverty', *Journal of Development Economics*, vol 82, pp 1-42.

Sen, A. (1983) 'Poor, relatively speaking', *Oxford Economic Papers*, vol 35, pp 153-69.

Shen, Z. (2009) *Weaving the last safety net for combating poverty*, Shanghai: Shanghai People's Press.

Solinger, D. (2008) 'The *dibao* recipients: mollified anti-Emblem of urban modernisation', *China Perspective*, vol 4, pp 36-46.

Solinger, D. (2010) 'The urban *dibao*: Guarantee for minimum livelihood or for minimal turmoil?', in F. Wu and C. Webster (eds) *Marginalization in urban China: Comparative perspectives*, Basingstoke: Palgrave Macmillan, pp 254-77.

Tang, J. (1998) 'The last safety net – the framework of the MSLS for urban Chinese residents', *Chinese Social Sciences*, vol 1, pp 117-28.

Tang, J. (2003) *Report on poverty and anti-poverty in urban China*, Beijing: Huaxia Publishing House.

Walder, A. (1984) 'The remaking of the Chinese working class, 1949-1981', *Modern China*, vol 10, no 1, pp 3-48.

Walder, A. (1986) *Communist neo-traditionalism: Work and authority in Chinese industry*, Berkeley, CA: University of California Press.

Wang, M. (2007) 'Emerging urban poverty and effects of the *dibao* program on alleviating poverty in China', *China & World Economy*, vol 15, no 2, pp 74-88.

World Bank (2009) *From poor areas to poor people: China's evolving poverty reduction agenda – An assessment of poverty and inequality in China*, Washington, DC: World Bank.

Xue, J. and Wei, Z. (2004) 'Unemployment, poverty and income gap in urban China', in S. Li and Sato Hiroshi (eds) *The cost of economic transformation – An empirical analysis on unemployment, poverty and income inequality in urban China*, Beijing: China Financial and Economic Publishing House.

Yan, M. (2014a, forthcoming) 'Society and shaming: Views of the non-poor on those in poverty in Urban China', in E. Chase and G. Bantebya Kyomuhendo (eds) *The shame of poverty: Global experiences*, Oxford: Oxford University Press.

Yan, M. (2014b, forthcoming) 'Experiences of poverty and shame in urban China', in E. Chase and G. Bantebya Kyomuhendo (eds) *The shame of poverty: Global experiences*, Oxford: Oxford University Press.

Zhang, H. (2006) 'Investigation and reflections on MSLS in the City of Zhengzhou', *Macroeconomic Studies*, vol 6, pp 37-40.

Zhang, S. and Tang, J. (2009) 'New stage of the urban and rural minimum standard of living scheme', in X. Ru, X. Lu and P. Li (eds) *2009 China's society: Analysis and forecast*, Beijing: Social Science Documentary Press.

Zhu, J. and Lin, M. (2010) 'Social construction of welfare stigma – a case study of the urban MSLS families in Zhejiang Province', *Zhejiang Journal*, vol 3, pp 201-6.

Zhu, Q. (1997) '1996-1997 people's living conditions', in L. Jiang et al (eds) *1996-1997 China's society: Analysis and forecast*, Beijing: China Social Science Press, pp 126-136.

THREE

Thick poverty, thicker society and thin state: policy spaces for human dignity in India

Sony Pellissery and Leemamol Mathew

Introduction

India is home to the largest number of poor people in the world. Of 1.13 billion people, 27.8 per cent live below the conservative income-based poverty line set by the Indian government and can thus be said to live in absolute poverty (Planning Commission, 2012). The face of this deep and persistent poverty is observable in minimal health expenditure, in the fact that more than 50 per cent of the population lives without sanitation facilities, in the presence of undignified ageing, as well as in poor educational standards, malnourished bodies, inferior housing, poor infrastructure resulting in deterioration in the quality of life, widespread child labour and poor service delivery. All of these attributes have severe implications for interpersonal relationships within the Indian household, village, workplace and broader community.

As a polity, India is a democratic country with huge diversity (28 federal states[1] and 7 union territories, over 1,500 languages, 16 climatic regions and various orientations of faith). While this cultural richness of diversity has been celebrated, it has also been a primary challenge to the country's economic progress.[2] This complexity is reflected in the web of social relationships that we allude to in the title for this chapter. This 'thicker society' creates poverty and undermines the policy efforts to eliminate poverty. Although India has made tremendous economic strides in recent years, this has primarily been the case in the country's urban centres, yet over 68 per cent of the population still resides in rural areas.[3] While close to 60 per cent of the workforce is involved in the less mechanised agricultural sector, the contribution of agriculture to gross domestic product (GDP) is as low as 15 per cent. Inability to move people from agriculture to industrial or service sectors has been largely due to the limited spread of education, and this is reflected in low literacy rates and a limited supply of skilled manpower. Poor agricultural productivity and limited mobility to other sectors has, in fact, reportedly led to multiple waves of farmer suicides in the past two decades (Reddy and Mishra, 2009). Moreover, while daily casual wage labour in rural and urban areas is considered to be the last resort to make ends meet, this currently represents the situation for approximately 40 per cent of the total workforce. The overwhelming dominance of the informal sector is reflected in the fact that only 10 per cent of India's total population receives the full social security coverage that is connected with employment in the formal job sector (Pellissery and Walker, 2007).

The presence and effect of widespread poverty and lack of social security coverage are heightened by India's strong sociocultural traditions of social stratification. Three associations of poverty-induced shaming in India are widely recognised and are related to the variables of geography, caste and gender. Geographically, rural poverty is pervasive although urban poverty is deeper. Traditionally, five states in India – Bihar, Madhya Pradesh, Rajasthan and Uttar Pradesh[4] – have been described as *bimaru* ('sick'), with reference to their persistently high poverty levels. People hailing from these states and travelling to the metropolitan areas of Delhi, Mumbai, Kolkata, Bangalore and Chennai seeking work, experience stigmatisation associated with their place of origin, and this has led to the denial of work, the boycott of their business or even collective violence against them (CSP, 2001). There is, however, less resistance to highly skilled, upper middle–class workers hailing from these states.

In addition to geographical stratification, the more general social stratification of the caste system is still strongly prevalent in India. Although the traditional purity-based practice of 'untouchability' aimed towards *dalits* (lower caste members, literally meaning 'oppressed') and indigenous tribal communities has been reduced,[5] other forms of discrimination continue. Poverty adds to the dimension of shame that is already culturally shaped through humiliating practices towards group members. Poverty is much more pervasive in these groups: while the overall rural rate of poverty is 38 per cent, among scheduled tribes it is 47 per cent and among scheduled castes it is 42 per cent. These two historically oppressed groups, which together make up 24 per cent of the total population, are 'scheduled' in the constitution of India for special protective welfare measures such as affirmative action. These measures provide 'reservation' (quota positions) in hiring processes and political elections. The past two decades have, however, shown the reservation system to be divisive in practice, as it has been resisted by a broader society that tends to attach shame to people who benefit from the policy.

The feminisation of poverty in India is associated with the humiliation to which girls and women are subjected. The primary issue is not about the number of women who live in poverty; it is about unequal intra-household allocation, the vast wage differences between women and men and about female-headed households broadly experiencing poverty. Furthermore, India's traditional patriarchal cultural traditions are reflected in social control mechanisms that overwhelmingly place shame on women living in poverty. The most important of these mechanisms is symbolised by the idea of *izzat* ('honour'). *Izzat* is said to be a woman's greatest possession, but can be taken away from her when she deviates social norms: for instance, if she is raped or engages in prostitution, even if for the purpose of feeding her children. In this way *izzat* acts as a principle that forces women to live according to the principles of society. This issue has variable bearing on the participation of women in the broader labour market, as one's honour is more likely to be kept intact if one stays safely at home. Seemingly with more honour at stake, the labour market participation of women also decreases as one goes up the social strata. While women from lower caste groups may engage in farm labour or small businesses, higher caste women tend not to. The emphasis on 'keeping *izzat*' means that higher class as well as higher caste women, although educated, tend not to participate in the labour market. The strong preference for male children also results in social stigma for parent couples bearing only female children, as that couple is then shamed and ostracised by the community, and also frequently leads to the break-up of marriages. This strong preference for boys has led to the neglect of female children (represented most strongly as female infanticide), the abandonment of widows and a minimal decision-making role for women inside the family.[6]

Hence, India's high poverty levels reflect strong social stratification and shaming practices. One important question that rises is in a context such as India's, where culturally determinant social norms act as root causes of poverty (as in the case of poverty associated with lower castes): how can one separate out shame as a result of poverty from the shame resulting from one's sociocultural position? There is evidence to indicate that a high economic status achieved by a lower caste household does not end the discrimination experienced (Guru, 2011). In a similar way, a high caste household experiencing poverty does not necessarily experience a reduced social status. Such distancing between caste and economic (if not social) status is now recognised as 'difference' rather than hierarchy (Gupta, 2000). Yet this does not mean that India is no longer a hierarchical society. Hierarchical norms have merely been transferred to other realms such as the increased acceptance of class or political authority. Whether from poverty or from one's particular sociocultural location, it is arguably the role of policy to minimise the inequities and sense of shame that have been created by these sorts of norms.

This chapter examines the ways in which the dignity of people living in poverty has been considered in national interventions designed to tackle poverty. The focus is on two flagship national anti-poverty policies: a food security policy, the Public Distribution System (PDS) and an income-maintenance policy, the National Rural Employment Guarantee Act (NREGA). The chapter is structured in three sections. The first provides a historical overview of anti-poverty policies in India, the second details how shaming occurs in the formulation, structuring and delivery of two national-level anti-poverty policies, and the final section summarises the implications of these shaming components.

Anti-poverty policies: a brief historical overview

To understand how India's anti-poverty policies have been instrumental to poverty reduction, four broader phases can be identified. After India's 1947 Independence,[7] national policy attention focused on macroeconomic development, particularly on the need to build energy sources and state-owned public enterprises (SOEs). 'Community development programmes' were established through which local village communities and national government agencies were to collaborate to implement a variety of anti-poverty programmes. The State, however, quickly found the close-knit nature of village communities and strong social rules to be impenetrable, and the 'growth' approach failed to reduce economic inequalities (Vaidyanathan, 2001). The first phase ended with a realisation that centralised policy-making was a faulty strategy.

The second phase of poverty reduction history in India began with the general election of 1971, when Indira Gandhi's election slogan, *Garibi Hatao* ('Abolish poverty') for the first time in Indian history attached 'political worth' to the masses living in poverty (Nayyar, 1998). Following an astounding election victory, a broad array of anti-poverty programmes was introduced and non-governmental organisations (NGOs) began to enter the mainstream development intervention sector.

The third phase involved the cynical political practice throughout the 1980s of announcing anti-poverty programmes primarily as 'freebies' just before an election in order to gain the 'feedback' benefit of votes. Constitutionally, poverty reduction was primarily the responsibility of federal state government rather than central government. While this practice led to the constitutionally backed institutionalisation of varying levels of welfare systems in each federal state, political compulsions forced a system of patronage-based welfare regimes rather than fully institutionalised service delivery. This practice continues today.

The final phase arguably began with economic liberalisation in 1991, wherein India formally adopted open market measures. A short period of hope that the market would solve India's poverty issues was followed by the rapid increase of economic inequality. At the same time, social security programmes were introduced by central government in 1995 and 2005, serving as a complement to the federal state-level social security programmes of the 1970s and 1980s. To counter-balance the exclusion of certain groups by market forces, the politicisation of ethnic identities according to caste and religion intensified, with a public increasingly focused on political inclusion (Nayyar, 1998). Policy emphasis was also placed on entrepreneurial strategies for poverty reduction, including micro-finance, women's self-help groups and corporate social responsibility activities.

Despite the many discontinuities marking India's long history, its culture has maintained a common thread that is widely similar across the South Asian continent, albeit with subtle variations. Its long existence has been marked by the creation of and reliance on numerous symbolic forms or 'codes of honour and dishonour' (Casimir, 2009, p 307) to regulate social processes. Together, these codes have functioned as a hierarchical society, a system for social control and legitimation. In each stage of policy process described below, these codes are deployed in the relationship between the State and its citizens.

Framing policy

The 17th-century idea of a social contract has long informed the Western social welfare setting. A contract between the state and the individual legitimates the authority of the state and the limits posed on individual freedom. This is in exchange for the protection of individual rights. The Indian policy context – including the ideas, actors and institutions involved – has undergone tremendous change, yet a weak social contract ideology still permeates. This weakness simultaneously limits the legitimacy of public policy spaces and their potential to either shame or to facilitate the dignity of the Indian people. This difficulty plays out at three levels.

First, each federal state possesses a unique history dating back to the presence of multiple kingdoms in pre-colonial India. Thus, the formation of a single Indian State is an ideal that is still a work in progress (Khilnani, 1999). Any unified sense of national policy-making is further limited by the fact that primary responsibility for anti-poverty policy has been constitutionally placed with federal state governments. Since economic liberalisation, each federal state has also been left to manage its own economy and programme planning, while the role of central government is limited to the provision of overall guidelines (Chelliah, 1998).

Second, in post-colonial India the 'State' – and its related arms of parliament, bureaucracy and judiciary – is popularly perceived to have objectives that are antagonistic to popular interests. This antagonism emerges from the fact that each 'independent' state is governed by elites who have stronger connections with colonial/global powers than with the local population. A strong distinction has resulted between political society and civil society (Chatterjee, 2004). This further underscores the distance between people and the State (Mathew and Pellissery, 2010) and reduces the legitimacy of the State, as well as the potential for social contract formation via the State.

Finally, the sense of social identity is extremely forceful in a setting where the mix of caste, religion and birth region creates its own obligations and rights. In recent times, these identities have also been variably used for political gain across the party spectrum. This 'differentiated citizenship' (Jayal, 2011) presents a strong challenge to the emergence of a more general 'public space' to enable the successful development and implementation of redistribution policies. It is the very absence of this space that, in fact, defines the sort of policy approach typically offered. Kuldeep Mathur and James Bjorkman (2009, p 159) summarise this approach succinctly: 'Policy strategy has come to represent a political strategy that serves a particular vote bank rather than working for the public interest.'

Indian policy processes are also characterised by a strong disconnect between centralised decision-making by 'experts' and rampant interference by politicians (Mooij, 2007; Mathur and Bjorkman, 2009). The disconnect is reflected in a tendency for policies introduced in an idealistic, rights-based and technically correct manner to fail to live up to their emancipatory and dignity-building objectives in practice. As a result, centrally introduced policy becomes unrecognisable in its delivery after myriad interpretations by politicians and lower level bureaucrats (Harriss-White and Janakarajan, 2004). Politicians frequently invoke social institutions rather than policy instruments to achieve desired social goals (since implementation capacity is limited). For example, in 2012, Jairam Ramesh, India's Rural Development Minister, made a public plea to the parents of young brides not to marry their daughters off to homes where there was no toilet. The Minister expressed the hope that the public stigmatisation attached to this remark would prompt households to construct toilets (a sanitation mission that the government has attempted many times and failed). Such an exhortation reflects the perception that societal forces and norms are more instrumental for development efforts than public policies.

Furthermore, in the context of anti-poverty policy-making, experts and elites engage in strong 'othering' through a combination of cognition, values and norms (Reis and Moore, 2005), in which a double standard for appropriate behaviour is applied depending on one's socioeconomic status. The double standard is also reflected in general popular opinion concerning poverty and people experiencing poverty (Pellissery and Mathew, 2014a). In the midst of this generally negative attitude, however, the newspaper media is a notable exception in its pro-poor stance. In addition to accusing the state, newspapers also accuse businesses and the corporate sector for accelerating poverty through exploitative processes such as land acquisition or the use of child labour (Pellissery and Mathew, 2014a). These conflicting attitudes towards poverty and people living in poverty represent the colliding value frames within which anti-poverty policy has been formulated.

The differing value orientations that collide in the process of policy-making become more intense in a multi-party democratic institutional arrangement. This makes it difficult to reach consensus in order to move ahead, and frequently leads to policy paralysis. An early example of this conflict was the ideological competition between Mahatma Gandhi (who wanted self-reliant villages at the centre of development) and Jawaharlal Nehru (who wanted an industrialised India). A solution to these ideological battles was to move policy into a technocratic frame. As early as 1948 this was achieved by constituting a group of experts (often economists) as India's Planning Commission. This group was central to formulating all of the country's anti-poverty programmes, yet as it applied a technical approach to solving policy dilemmas, it was often insensitive to the everyday realities of those living in poverty.

A case in point has been the question of determining 'who is and who is not poor'. This matter has been left to the Planning Commission to deal with 'objectively'. Since 1977 three expert groups have applied differing criteria in developing a benchmark definition of what it means

Shaping and structuring anti-poverty policy

India's vast array of poverty alleviation policies are mostly designed by central government and are financed jointly with federal states and delivered by local self-governments. They generally fall within five main types: income enhancement policies, basic minimum service policies (education, housing, sanitation and health), natural resource management policies, food and nutritional security policies and income maintenance policies. The PDS and NREGA, analysed in this chapter, fall into the last two categories, respectively.

Apart from the policies falling into these major categories, there are approximately 100 additional programmes spread over 12 different national ministries (World Bank, 2011). With the inclusion of federal state-developed anti-poverty programmes, the number rises exponentially. As mentioned earlier, the plethora of programmes (and absence of unified policy) is primarily due to their short-term introduction by parties vying for votes (Guha, 2009; Barrientos and Pellissery, 2012). Politicians often affix their names to such programmes as a signal to the voter. This sort of clientelist rationale belittles the 'rights' of groups living in poverty, treating them as worthy only in their connection to 'purchasable' vote commodities.

At the same time, the multiplicity of piecemeal programmes without a unified approach to poverty reduction also creates a huge challenge for convergence. Ironically, this systemic weakness mitigates the shame experienced by those partaking in programmes and receiving benefits. While the application of stringent criteria for programme eligibility may shame an individual applicant, the presence of numerous, overlapping programmes provides the 'opportunity' to similar benefits or services elsewhere. In turn, community members perceive those who are able to receive the benefit of more than one programme as 'smart' people making the most of the system, a response frequently cited by respondents in our fieldwork (Pellissery and Mathew, 2014b).

For the purpose of tracing avenues of shame that may exist within the context of anti-poverty policy-making and provision, we selected two national-level policies for the focus of our analysis, the PDS and NREGA. Both are flagship anti-poverty programmes receiving substantial resources and affecting a large number of people.

Public Distribution System

Approximately 1 per cent of India's GDP is spent on the PDS of food grain, introduced in 1965. PDS has twin aims related to food security:

it distributes food grain and essential items (wheat, sugar, rice and kerosene) to needy households at subsidised rates and offers security to the agricultural sector through government provision of a minimum support price for products. The system represents a network of approximately 500,000 fair price shops, and it reflects the rent-seeking strategies often tied to such programmes. At the federal state level it is frequently promoted with the chief minister's photograph to emphasise that its associated benefits are 'big brother's gift' (Olson, 1989).

PDS was designed to address the insufficient availability of food in the country, a challenge that gained international visibility after a series of famines. While programme participation was originally a universal right, it was turned into a targeted programme in 1997 following India's 1991 economic liberalisation. With targeting, the programme was made available only to those people designated as falling into the BPL category.[9] For the rest of the population, grain was to be available only at the market rate. Targeting may well have reduced the market for grain, in turn affecting the livelihood of farmers; however, the lobby of five major grain-producing states (Punjab, Haryana, Uttar Pradesh, Chhattisgarh and Andhra Pradesh) resisted the proposal to reduce procurement so strongly that the central government was forced to continue buying grain (Mooij, 1999). The continuous procurement of grain benefited rich farmers on the one hand, and reduced food demand on the other, resulting in an ensuing situation of 'hunger with surplus food' as reserve stocks of grain rapidly grew. This immense system failure disturbed civil society and the media deeply. Cases filed before the Supreme Court in 2001 resulted in the release of stocks of food grain for the hungry masses. The special Supreme Court Commission appointed to review the case has since cast the situation as a shameful paradox:

> The experience of chronic hunger in distant villages as much as on city streets is one of intense avoidable suffering; of self-denial; of learning to live with far less than the body needs; of mind and bodies stymied in their growth; of the agony of helplessly watching one's loved ones – most heartbreakingly, children – in hopeless torment; of unpaid, arduous devalued work; of shame, humiliation and bondage; of the defeat and the triumph of the human spirit. Such high levels of hunger and malnutrition are a paradox, because they stubbornly survive surging economic growth and agricultural production. (CSC, 2008, p 4)

This paradox can be said to be a policy creation since India's 'soft state' (Myrdal, 1968) was unable to contain the social forces of the rich agrarian political lobby, leaving little space for the State's independent action. In other words, the effectiveness of government to shame-proof the economically vulnerable from richer grain-owning famers has been absent. A similar phenomenon has taken place with respect to India's employment guarantee approach, as described below.

National Rural Employment Guarantee Act

India's NREGA is a relatively new programme that began in 2005 to provide 100 days of guaranteed employment to any person seeking work. The programme was introduced to address the limited job opportunities available in rural areas during lean agricultural seasons.[10] Participants receive manual labour work, often engaging in public works projects that will improve local conditions. Such projects are primarily coordinated efforts between the local village government and district government. It is stipulated that 60 per cent of project expenditures should be paid out to workers as wages. The programme is self-targeting in that programme participants receive lower wages than the standard market rates, yet, as there are no eligibility criteria, officials are not to deny work to any person seeking it (Dreze and Khera, 2009).

Does NREGA provide an opportunity for participants to engage in dignified work? This question has not been considered. Rather, the primary policy focus has been on estimating the number of people that have benefited from receiving wages through the programme and on total asset creation. The programme's founders (Dreze and Khera, 2009) have sought to answer this question by comparing NREGA results with the situation in India's hugely exploitative private agricultural labour sector and, unsurprisingly, have easily reached the conclusion that NREGA provides a more dignified option for workers. Indeed, there is evidence that the programme has provided an important escape route from the humiliating working conditions on private farms or in forced labour where workers must be at the beck and call of the farm owner. In these situations, women are especially vulnerable to wage discrimination and exploitation. Notably, women are also more frequent participants in NREGA (Khera and Nayak, 2009, p 5, as cited in Singh, 2012a). Auxiliary offerings for workers, such as the provision of a supply of drinking water, childcare facilities, shades for rest periods and first aid kits have been touted as dignity-building features of the programme. Yet survey after survey has shown that these offerings are merely available on paper and not actually in practice (Shah, 2012).

While the NREGA may have offered some of its participants a way to escape highly exploitative or forced working conditions, there is much to be desired about the programme itself. The promise attached to NREGA was that it would provide the means to ensure a national 'minimum wage' for programme participants. The government has, however, refused to provide this. The system of paying lower than average wages to programme workers has been an adaptation of the British Poor Law 'workhouse test'. By engaging in programme-related work, participants implicitly declare that they are in such a position of vulnerability that they are willing to receive substandard remuneration. Public pressure mounted in response to this situation forced central government in 2011 to concede to providing inflation-indexed wages for NREGA workers.

Furthermore, NREGA is structured in such a way that participants' autonomy and agency are constrained. According to the definitions specified in the Universal Declaration of Human Rights (Article 23.1) and the International Covenant on Social, Economic and Cultural Rights (Article 6.1), one's labour may be characterised as 'dignified' only if one can choose how to creatively engage in activities leading to moral worth and self-satisfaction. Guy Standing (2002, p 273) argues that this norm is an essential feature of the full realisation of the employment guarantee, noting: 'the right to a job that is chosen for you by somebody else against your wishes ... is no right at all.' In contrast to this ideal, NREGA participants are matched with jobs in a top-down manner. In response, a recent government proposal for programme revisions recommends the participatory identification of jobs in order to generate longer-term benefits (Shah, 2012). Fitting a 'workfare' rather than human capital approach (Lødemel and Trickey, 2000), the programme is not concerned with the skill improvement of its participants. Designed primarily to achieve basic material security, it fails to consider the social aspects that may be key to longer-lasting income security. Instead, the routinised manual activity of 'digging earth and shifting earth' represents a new means for engaging in 'soulless labour' (Marx, 1844). Norms concerning what constitutes 'valuable' work pervade user and public perceptions of the stigma that is associated with NREGA participation. This blunt method of job creation under a 'workfare' approach has also been found to heighten system user shame in advanced Western welfare states (Dean, 2007), as described in Chapters Five and Seven, this volume (Norway and the UK).

Finally, the NREGA is yet another instance of the huge gap that exists in India between policy promises and outcomes. While we earlier blamed this gap on the fact that national policy is filtered through the interpretive practices of local bureaucrats and practitioners, the design of anti-poverty policies are also clearly to blame and reflect a foundational bias. The very intention of 'relief' and social reproduction that is reflected in the design of much of India's anti-poverty policy is humiliating to its recipients, and has been noted by one leading policy-making adviser:

> The policy maker treats the rural poor in exactly the same way as we as individuals treat the beggar. We do not ask the beggar how he was reduced to his present state or what he will do tomorrow. We indulge in a bit of charity in giving alms to the beggar without any intention to help him acquire a better status. This is how the employment programmes and PDS work. The policy maker proudly announces the amounts spent and the poor who benefited, but there are no arrangements at all to ensure food security and employment security to the poor. (Rao, 2009)

Delivery of anti-poverty policy

Our analysis of Indian newspapers shows that the sympathy expressed in the quotation above has also been widely prevalent in the media, where criticism has been directed at the political and bureaucratic apathy shown towards the economically vulnerable (Pellissery and Mathew, 2014a). The low-income individuals we spoke with described being constantly confronted with demeaning treatment from bureaucrats. Yet they also highlighted how important it was for their survival to reject the shaming they received. They mitigated the internalised effects of shaming by describing how these bureaucrats did not belong to their particular moral community (village). This strategy is arguably plausible in highly segmented societies, where inter-group trust is low (Gupta, 1995; Widmalm, 2005).

Gaining eligibility as 'poor'

While the NREGA is self-selecting, recipients of PDS and many other anti-poverty benefits face a high level of discretion at the local level. The local process of eligibility determination frequently involves mediation between applicants and local politicians. What typically results is the use of prevailing community moral norms to judge 'need' rather than a reliance on pre-stipulated norms and guidelines (Pellissery, 2007). Such applications of normative evaluations reinforce the social control that already exists within India's hierarchical society.

The national effort to craft an objective technical method for eligibility determination has ironically resulted in the inclusion of many economically secure groups and has excluded many economically vulnerable groups. A national survey in 2004 revealed that 16.8 per cent of India's richest quintile and 30.5 per cent of the next richest quintile possessed BPL cards, whereas 61 per cent of households belonging to the poorest quintile were excluded from being identified as poor (Expert Group, 2009). This reflects the reality of deep levels of corruption in India. In order to be identified as a poor household, one must possess the social and financial resources to place pressure on the local politicians making this evaluation. This includes paying bribes to local politicians, who make a tidy profit out of the high level competition that exists to get onto the BPL list. Within this context, attaining the designation of 'poor' becomes a matter of savvy rather than shame. Our female respondents, for example, frequently bemoaned their husbands' lack of ability to obtain a BPL card. One respondent emphasised the positive associations with making it to the BPL list, noting: "if a household feels shame and doesn't want to appear ... the loss is theirs. Households with hundreds of acres of land are on the BPL list. So, why be ashamed?" Another argued that "everyone knows each other's economic status" and that, moreover, "Getting onto BPL also shows how capable you are" (Pellissery and Mathew, 2014b).

Federal state governments do not argue for the need to fix the systemic corruption that is tied to the process for determining eligibility for BPL-related benefits. Rather, they place public focus on the need to distinguish the 'genuine poor' from 'well-off fakers'. In 2009 the government of Madhya Pradesh resorted to the branding of poor households. In an attempt to distinguish the 'genuine' from the 'fake', the district authorities of Khandwa and Seoni painted the walls of households on the BPL list in bold letters, reading 'I am poor'. The district collector explained that this was a strategy to discourage ineligible people from availing benefits meant for people living below the poverty line. Our analysis of newspaper media coverage during this period suggests that those individuals living in economically vulnerable situations did not, however, find this a good solution. As one noted: "Yes, we are poor but should the government try to address our poverty or mock us by branding us poor in this humiliating manner?" (Singh, 2012b). An interesting backlash to this explicit shaming occurred during a 2011 grassroots movement led by the middle and upper middle class against corruption. Adopting a similar strategy of shaming by labelling, movement followers painted the houses and offices of politicians with the words, 'I am corrupt'.

Public Distribution System: low access and low quality

While the PDS encountered new challenges after the introduction of targeting in 1997, it remains an important source of food for many households. In 2010 approximately 30 per cent of households purchased food grain from PDS shops. Here too, however, corruption is a huge challenge. Three related elements serve to heighten the shame of grain recipients.

Corruption and shaming are felt first and foremost at the point of access. Approximately 44 per cent of food grain procured for the purpose of distribution is instead diverted for primary use by private markets (grain dealers and shop owners) to fetch market rates and thereby reap huge profits (Khera, 2011).[11] Households experiencing poverty who are officially entitled to receive the subsidised grain are humiliated through two mechanisms. First, the same shopkeepers who distribute PDS grain are also those who typically run private market food grain shops, as this arrangement enables them to easily divert the grains. When a poor household seeks grain, the shopkeeper may report that the PDS stock has not yet arrived (or that a limited stock has sold out), yet market-priced grain is always available. The poorest households are thus forced to make many rounds to the shops to catch the PDS grain at subsidised rates. Repeated exposure to shops where they cannot afford market-priced products first results in uneasiness and then a sense of disgust. This sentiment is aimed towards the corrupt shopkeeper. Yet it is also directed at themselves for being in a situation where they are unable to effectively protest against the shopkeeper, often a powerful person in the locality, in order to obtain their necessary entitlements (Pellissery and Mathew, 2014b).

A second mechanism through which humiliation occurs is through the adulteration of PDS grain by the shopkeeper, a common phenomenon according to one study (PEO, 2005). In a deliberate action, the shopkeeper carefully separates the grain received according to quality. Higher quality grain is placed for sale at market prices and poor quality grain is displayed for PDS sale. One of our respondents noted the remarkably poor quality of PDS grain, describing it as "worth giving only to cattle and hens" (Pellissery and Mathew, 2014b). Public awareness concerning the low quality of the grain means that only those who have no other choice frequent PDS shops. Data from states with targeted PDS have shown that this phenomenon started with the movement from universal to targeted provision. Before the 1997 shift, people from all income levels availed food grain from PDS shops, and the quality of grain was better (Himanshu and Sen, 2011).

The third element heightening the shame of those partaking in the PDS has a gender dimension. Long PDS queues have resulted from the artificial 'shortages' that are often generated by shopkeepers, causing a subsequent panic among system users. Many female respondents during our fieldwork study reported feeling ashamed of being forced to stand in long queues to obtain PDS food grain, sometimes even without the necessary money to buy it. Their sense of shame and powerlessness was compounded by the fact that they found themselves in their current situations not due to their own choices, but to what they described as their husbands' irresponsible actions (Pellissery and Mathew, 2014b).

The relationship between PDS and the level of user shaming reported varied according to geographic location. We observed that in a tribal hamlet where everyone was poor, the inauguration of a new PDS shop in the community was a matter of broad celebration. No one experienced stigma because everyone bought grain from fair price shops. On the other hand, in a big village where economic inequality was visible, the PDS shop was perceived as being the 'poor person's' shop (Pellissery and Mathew, 2014b). This indicates the consideration that should be given to the effect of 'relative' poverty within anti-poverty provision settings, and provides an insight into the dynamics of anti-poverty provision and shame.

National Rural Employment Guarantee Act: 'undignified' labour

Compared to the experience of engaging in hugely exploitative daily wage work on private farms, for the many women (approximately 55 per cent of workers) and lower caste members (approximately 37 per cent) in the NREGA, the programme represents an escape and the opportunity to gain some dignity (Dreze, 2010). The provision of 'dignified labour' is not, however, part of the programme's design. Poorly paid and mostly manual labour jobs are assigned to low-income workers with no focus on building long-term skills. Furthermore, programme participation is stigmatised in the eyes of their higher income peers. The higher income people we spoke with interpreted engagement in the programme itself as a shameful act. As one said: "Those who are lazy and do not want to do any work go and stand at the NREGA work site all day and collect wages. On private farms they are closely monitored and they can't be so lazy." This interpretation has some bearing on a superficial level as many of the NREGA workers we spoke with did, in fact, report heading to NREGA worksites to earn wages rather than to participate in the productive engagement of labour. This practice is, however, unsurprising given the highly unappealing nature of the work entailed (Pellissery and Mathew, 2014b).

Much of the rhetoric used to publicly describe NREGA is connected with images of corruption and the moral unworthiness of those engaged in this sort of labour, whereby the potential of both NREGA workers and work is dismissed completely. In the state of Kerala, NREGA is translated in the local language to *Thozilurappu Paddhathi* (Work Guarantee Scheme). Locally, however, people have changed the name slightly, and emphasise its stigmatised nature, calling it *Thozhiluzhappu Paddhathi* (Lazy Work Scheme). In most states the 'job card' provided when a worker registers his or her name for NREGA is popularly referred to as a 'joker card', playing on the understanding that workers are non-serious and act like jokers, and that the card may not provide real work.

Unsurprisingly, there is no national-level data available that pertains to the level of corruption within NREGA.[12] Localised surveys have, however, shown corruption to be higher in NREGA than other government programmes, and this is reflected in the numerous newspaper reports of official suspensions within this context (CUTS, 2011). While many types of corruption are possible in the delivery of NREGA (see Pellissery, 2007; Shankar and Gaiha, 2012), it is the practice of underpaying programme workers that arguably provides the most significant means. Sixty per cent of the total cost of the programme is to be set aside for worker wages, and so officials and politicians associated with the programme take advantage of this formula to make windfall profits. Worksite inspectors, in collusion with local politicians and workers at many NREGA worksites, engage in the manipulation of lists to represent lower worker numbers. While this practice results in only a portion of the budget for wages actually being used to this end, it also saves inspectors and workers from exposure concerning inferior work outcomes. The truly pervasive corruption in NREGA can be traced, however, back to the State's inability to provide a labour opportunity that workers find meaningful and morally worthy of participation.

Implications and recommendations: possibilities for improved policy spaces in a weak state setting

India has been termed a 'prismatic society': it reflects the co-existence of a fused traditionalism, along with a more diverse and specialised modernism (Riggs, 1964). In this setting of traditional influences juxtaposed with the modern, shame is often experienced and perceived in diametrically opposing directions. This multiplicity of perception is succinctly illustrated in the short story, *Poisoned Bread*, from India's *dalit* literature, wherein out of shame the educated *dalit* grandson refuses to eat food thrown to cattle by the high caste farm owner, yet his grandfather considers the same food as his right and proudly eats it (Mathew and Pellissery, 2014). The perception of shame from the receipt of aid is a matter of one's personal history and current social position.

Our analysis of food security and employment guarantee policies has shown the drastic differences in shaming that depend on one's social location. This comparison informs us that when need-based policies are designed, it is important to provide complimentary services for capacity building to reduce dependency, which in turn brings more dignity for clients.

Shaming discourses also have multiple dimensions in a prismatic society. The proverb from the South Indian language of Malayalam aptly demonstrates this, and is roughly translated as 'the wealth that one acquires shamelessly can rescue one from shame'. Within an Indian context, this proverb indicates the great paradox of forbearance: a person who refrains from engaging in certain activities (such as taking up an undignified job) because this would be perceived as 'shameful' is likely to make little progress beyond his or her original status or situation. This proverb is frequently cited by elders to encourage young people to enter into traditional jobs, such as cattle rearing or agriculture, which are publicly viewed as 'shameful' in their characterisation as a last resort option.

As pointed out in the introduction to this chapter , shaming plays a legitimised role in a hierarchical society such as India. As the policy examples have shown, the State has not effectively overcome societal forces, and thus these forces enter strongly into delivery of public policy-making. The condescending perception by most policy-making elites concerning individuals living in poverty finds no fault with shaming them. On the contrary, their participation in anti-poverty programmes because of lack of other avenues to keep them going, or, in the words of Geoff Wood (2004, p 50), the 'no-exist' option, is construed as a reason to assert denial of shame.

Whereas India's public policy arena has thus far proved a limited means for facilitating honourable living, the Indian political arena has played a crucial role in achieving this. Mass resistance against the explicit labelling of individuals as 'poor', as well as political pressure resulting in standardised wages for NREGA workers and for PDS grain to be released to the broader populace, are examples of the key role that political pressure can play in ensuring that empowerment-based policies are more than just talk. Acting as a model for the sort of dignity-building role that politics can play, in the north Indian state of Uttar Pradesh, where caste politicisation has been intense, *dalit* political parties have gained immense power, encouraging *dalits* to demand respect on an everyday level (Jaffrelot, 2003). Thus, while corruption has seeped into the politics that are played within the context of anti-poverty policy structuring and delivery, a corresponding public pressure on politicians and a watchdog media may help to correct injustices done and further, to encourage the development of policies with dignity-based objectives in mind. Thus, grassroots initiatives for dignity-based policy may begin a shift towards policy improvement.

Any initiative must, however, take serious issue with the objectives that continue to inform India's anti-poverty policy-making. Despite emancipatory language, Indian policy-making follows a tendency common within the context of developing countries towards strategic design for the purpose of managing outcomes that have been created by the inefficiencies of the State (for example, as a result of having facilitated profit-making at the expense of the economically vulnerable), rather than the proactive promotion of welfare. True citizen empowerment would involve the avoidance of such inefficiencies to begin with. As we have shown, this requires changes at two levels: a more informed polity that challenges clientelist policy introductions and changes at societal level to inculcate citizenship values. The second will require a long process.

Notes
[1] The term 'state' refers to one of the 28 federal states, whereas 'State' refers to the Indian State in its entirety.

[2] After Independence in 1947 and until 1991 India maintained a low economic growth rate of 3.5 per cent, termed the 'Hindu growth rate'.

[3] 'Rural' is not homogeneous in India. The 2011 census estimated that there were 640,867 villages in India with uneven levels of habitation, and this diversity is a huge problem for governance.

[4] Orissa was later added to this list.

[5] Although space does not allow us to elaborate on various types of stigma with indigenous communities, one gross practice of discrimination cannot

go unstated. The poorest of the indigenous tribal communities were classified as 'criminal tribes' since they lived by stealing from others. Such groups were considered dangerous to the general public and were kept physically segregated during British colonial time. Although the law to treat these groups as criminal was repealed after Independence, such groups are still socially segregated and continue to be treated as 'criminal tribes'.

[6] In 2001, the sex ratio of children aged 0-6 stood at 927 girls to 1,000 boys, and in 2011 it has come down to 914. The ratio for all age groups in 2011 is 940 female to 1,000 male.

[7] The nature of poverty before colonisation is under serious debate. A group of economic historians attribute the creation of poverty in India to British colonial administration, which extracted wealth and rearranged the land-owning pattern tied to resource extraction, leaving the country to economically perish (Naoroji, 1901; Maddison, 2004). On the other hand, some scholars argue that high levels of poverty date back to India's feudal structure prior to British arrival (Mukherjee and Frykenberg, 1969).

[8] In 1989 the Indian government released the Prevention of Atrocities Act, which enabled the legal registration of cases against higher caste people who verbally or physically abused lower caste individuals. Implementation of the Act has, however, varied across states, and often is predicated on whether or not the political class counts members of the *dalit* caste among its necessary vote bank.

[9] While some state governments (Tamil Nadu, Chhattisgarh) still offer a universal programme using additional subsidies from their treasuries, the economically well-off population in these states tend to opt out from buying PDS food grain. This practice has been used as evidence to support the claim that targeting leads to both stigma as well as to leakage (Himanshu and Sen, 2011).

[10] The introduction of the programme was opposed by right-wing lobbies arguing that such a programme would result in the mere doling out of resources, which would then be inefficiently used (Dreze and Khera, 2009).

[11] Representing figures from 2007.

[12] The central government website currently, however, reports 62 cases of action taken against putatively corrupt officials/politicians in various federal states.

References

Barrientos, A. and Pellissery, S. (2012) *Delivering effective social assistance: Does politics matter?*, ESID Working Paper No 9, Manchester: Effective States and Inclusive Development.

Casimir, M.R. (2009) 'Honor and dishonor and the quest for emotional equivalents', in B. Rottger-Rossler and H.J. Markowitsch (eds) *Emotions as bio-cultural processes*, New York: Springer, pp 281-316.

Chatterjee, P. (2004) *Politics of the governed*, New York: Columbia University Press.

Chelliah, R. (1998) 'Liberalization, economic reforms and centre–state relations', in I.J. Ahluwalia and I.M.D. Little (eds) *India's economic reforms and development*, New Delhi: Oxford University Press, pp 344-74.

CSC (Commissioners of Supreme Court) (2008) *'A special report on the most vulnerable social groups and their access to food'*, in the case PUCL vs UOI & Ors Writ Petition (Civil) No 196 of 2001.

CSP (Crisis State Programme) (2001) *Collaborative research states of crisis in South Asia*, Crisis State Programme Working Paper No 3, London: London School of Economics and Political Science.

CUTS (Consumer Unity and Trust Society International) (2011) 'Pre and post RTI ground realities and corruption vulnerability analysis in NREGA, SGSY and IAY'. (www.cuts-international.org/CART/pdf/Pre_and_Post_RTI_Ground_Realities_Survey_Report.pdf).

Dean, H. (2007) 'The ethics of welfare to work', *Policy & Politics*, vol 35, no 4, pp 573-80.

Dreze, J. and Khera, R. (2009) 'The battle for employment guarantee', *Frontline*, vol 26, no 1, pp 36-41.

Dreze, J. (2010) 'NREGA is not artificial employment', *Civil Society*, May issue, pp 7-8.

Expert Group (2009) *Report of the Expert Group to advise the Ministry of Rural Development on the methodology for conducting the below poverty line (BPL) census for 11th five-year plan*, New Delhi: Ministry of Rural Development.

Gupta, A. (1995) 'Blurred boundaries: The discourse of corruption, the culture of politics and the imagined state', *American Ethnologist*, vol 22, no 2, pp 375-402.

Gupta, D. (2000) *Interrogating caste: Understanding hierarchy and difference in Indian society*, New Delhi: Penguin Books.

Guha, R. (2009) 'The dance of India democracy', BBC News, 4 March.

Guru, G. (2011) *Humiliation*, New Delhi: Oxford University Press.

Harriss-White, B. and Janakarajan, S. (2004) *Rural India facing the 21st century: Essays on long-term village change and recent development policy*, London: Anthem Press.

Himanshu and Sen, A. (2011) 'Why not a universal food security legislation?', *Economic and Political Weekly*, March 19, pp 38-47.

Hirway, I. (2003) 'Identification of BPL households for poverty alleviation programmes', *Economic and Political Weekly*, vol 38, no 45, pp 4803-8.

Jaffrelot (2003) *India's silent revolution: The rise of the lower castes in North India*, Columbia, NY: Columbia University Press.

Jayal, N.G. (2011) 'A false dichotomy? The unresolved tension between universal and differentiated citizenship in India', *Oxford Development Studies*, vol 39, no 2, pp 185-204.

Karat, B. (2011) 'An exercise in undercounting the poor', *The Hindu*, June 9.

Khera, R. (2011) *Trends in diversion of PDS grain*, Working Paper no 198, Delhi: Centre for Development Economics.

Khera, R. and Nayak, N. (2009) *Women workers and perceptions of the National Rural Employment Guarantee Act in India*, Rome: Food and Agriculture Organization (FAO)-International Fund for Agricultural Development (IFAD)-International Labour Organization (ILO).

Khilnani, S. (1999) *The idea of India*, London: Farrar, Straus and Giroux.

Lødemel, I. and Trickey, H. (eds) (2000) *'An offer you can't refuse': Workfare in international perspective*, Bristol: Policy Press.

Maddison, A. (2004) *The world economy: Historical statistics*, Paris: OECD Development Centre.

Marx, K. (1844) 'Economic and philosophic manuscripts', in *Early Writings* (1975), Harmondsworth: Penguin.

Mathew, L. and Pellissery, S. (2010) 'Enduring local justice in India: An anomaly or response to diversity?', *Psychology & Developing Societies*, vol 21, no 1, pp 13-31.

Mathew, L. and Pellissery, S. (2014) 'Film and literature as social commentary in India', in E. Chase and G. Bantebeya Kyomuhendo (eds) *The shame of poverty: Global perspectives*, Oxford: Oxford University Press.

Mathur, K. and Bjorkman, J.W. (2009) *Policy making in India: Who speaks? Who listens?*, New Delhi: Har-Anand Publications Pvt Ltd.

Mooij, J. (1999) 'Food policy in India: The importance of electoral politics in policy implementation', *Journal of International Development*, vol 11, no 4, pp 625-36.

Mooij, J. (2007) 'Is there an Indian policy process? An investigation into two social policy processes', *Social Policy & Administration*, vol 41, no 4, pp 323-38.

Mukherjee, N. and Frykenberg, R. (1969) 'The Ryotwari system and social organization in the Madras Presidency', in R.E. Frykenberg (ed) *Land control and social structure in Indian history*, Delhi: Manohar, pp 237-46.

Myrdal, G. (1968) *Asian drama*, New York: Pantheon.

Naoroji, D. (1901) *Poverty and un-British rule in India*, New Delhi: Publications Division, Ministry of Information and Broadcasting, Government of India.

Nayyar, D. (1998) 'Economic development and political democracy: Interaction of economic and politics in Independent India', *Economic and Political Weekly*, 5 December, pp 3121-31.

Olson, W. (1989) 'Eat now, pay later: Impact of rice subsidy scheme', *Economic and Political Weekly*, vol 24, no 28, pp 1597-611.

Pellissery, S. (2007) 'Local processes of national corruption: Elite linkages and their effects on poor people in India', *Global Crime*, vol 8, no 2, pp 131-51.

Pellissery, S. and Mathew, L. (2014a) 'Shaming in India', in E. Chase and G. Bantebeya Kyomuhendo (eds) *The shame of poverty: Global perspectives*, Oxford: Oxford University Press.

Pellissery, S. and Mathew, L. (2014) 'Experiences of poverty and shame in India', in E. Chase and G. Bantebeya Kyomuhendo (eds) *The shame of poverty: Global perspectives*, Oxford: Oxford University Press.

Pellissery, S. and Walker, R. (2007) 'Social security options for informal sector workers in emergent economies and the Asia and Pacific region', *Social Policy & Administration*, vol 41, no 4, pp 401-9.

PEO (2005) *Performance evaluation of targeted public distribution system*, New Delhi: Planning Commission.

Planning Commission (2012) *Approach paper for 12th five-year plan*, New Delhi: Planning Commission.

Rao, V.M. (2009) 'Policy making in India for rural development', Paper presented during the fourth annual international conference on 'Public policy and management', Indian Institute of Management, Bangalore.

Reddy, N. and Mishra, S. (2009) *Agrarian crisis in India*, New Delhi: Oxford University Press.

Reis, E.P. and Moore, M. (2005) *Elite perceptions of poverty and inequality*, London: Zed Books.

Riggs, F.W. (1964) *Administration in developing countries*, Boston, MA: Houghton Mifflin Company.

Shah, M. (2012) *Report of the Committee for revision of MGNREGA operational guidelines*, New Delhi: Ministry of Rural Development.

Shankar, S. and Gaiha, R. (2012) *Battling corruption: Has NREGA reached India's poor?*, New Delhi: Oxford University Press.

Singh, A.K. (2012a) 'Caste – The actual cost of empowerment? Dalit women and NREGA: A study of the poverty, social exclusion and shame nexus', Master's thesis, Oslo: Oslo and Akershus University College.

Singh, M.P. (2012b) 'The problem of identifying BPL households? Brand them poor', *The Hindu*, 15 July, Bhopal Edition.

Standing, G. (2002) *Beyond the new paternalism*, London: Verso.

Vaidyanathan, A. (2001) 'Poverty and development policy', *Economic and Political Weekly*, vol 36, no 21, pp 1807-1822.

Widmalm. S. (2005) 'Explaining corruption at the village and individual level in India', *Asian Survey*, vol 45, no 5, pp 756-76.

Wood, G. (2004) 'Informal security regimes: The strength of relationships', in I. Gough, G. Wood and A. Barrientos (eds) *Insecurity and welfare regimes in Asia, Africa and Latin America: Social policy in development contexts*, Cambridge: Cambridge University Press, pp 49-87.

World Bank (2011) *Social protection for a changing India*, Washington, DC: World Bank.

FOUR

Self-sufficiency, social assistance and the shaming of poverty in South Korea

Yongmie Nicola Jo and Robert Walker

South Korea was re-established in 1948 as an independent democratic nation after being annexed by Japan in 1910 for 35 years and experiencing three years of militaristic rule by the US between 1945 and 1948. However, the Korean War (1950-53) subsequently led to its partition into the Republic of Korea, better known as South Korea, and North Korea, the Democratic People's Republic. Since the end of the war, South Korea has experienced a dramatic transformation in virtually every aspect of its social and economic life. From a country characterised by abject poverty, it has become the world's 15th largest economy, with 50 million people, acquiring the status of being a long-term member of the OECD (Organisation for Economic Co-operation and Development).

National economic success is demonstrated in the lives of three generations, each generation being much better off financially than the previous one, with many individuals themselves experiencing a life that has literally taken them from rags to riches. Many have succeeded economically in an environment that has been uniquely conducive to economic success, and they are now celebrating their success through ostentatious consumption. This has fuelled a belief that economic failure and poverty equate with a person's own social failure and must be the result of personal failings. Policy continues to reflect this reasoning and often serves to reinforce the shame that people feel when they are characterised as being social failures, misfits and miscreants. This chapter first documents the economic and social transformation that has taken place in South Korea from 1953 onwards and which has shaped this conception of poverty. It then examines how such transformation has influenced the framing, structuring and implementation of social assistance provision.

Poverty in South Korea

In 1953, South Korea was ranked as one of the poorest countries in the world, with an absolute poverty rate exceeding 60-70 per cent according to some figures (PSPD/UNDP, 2000), comparable at the time to many African countries, including Uganda (see this volume, Chapter Nine). Its economy and social infrastructure was mostly destroyed during the war, creating mass unemployment, large numbers of displaced war orphans and widespread hunger. The situation was aggravated by refugees from the war returning home in large numbers, but with no means of livelihood (Ku, 2006, p 10; Kim et al, 2007, p 44).

The country was also politically unstable. The government, with no experience of democracy or economic capitalism, seemingly adopted the US practice. A semi-presidential representative democratic republic was established with the president as the head of state supported by a multi-party political system. However, the first president, Lee Seung-Man, elected in 1948, abused his power and ruled as a dictator through corruption and the manipulation of elections for 12 years until being ousted by a major popular uprising, the April 19 Revolution (Seo, 2007, p 44). Park Jung-Hee, who assumed power in 1961 with a military coup, headed a military dictatorship himself for 19 years and was followed by two more militaristic leaders, Jun Doo-Hwan (1980-87) and Noh Tae-Woo (1987-92). Democracy was instigated in a formative sense with the 1987 election (Kim et al, 2007, p 64), although it was only established in practice towards the late 1990s, following a long period of civil unrest and at times brutal oppression.

South Korea's economic transformation coincided with military rule, and by the late 1960s, during the period referred to as 'the Miracle of the Han River',[1] the country experienced annual growth rates exceeding 10 per cent in consecutive years (Kim et al, 2007, p 52). The government pursued a policy of state-led export-oriented industrialisation, which, with high growth, resulted in low levels of unemployment. Somewhat unusually, growth was not accompanied by greatly increased income inequality, a feature that has been attributed to land reform (Ku, 2006, p 9). The Land Reform Act in 1949 led to the dismantling of the pre-modern pattern of land ownership, undermining the power and wealth of the land-owning ruling class. In this scenario of high and comparatively egalitarian growth, poverty and deprivation fell rapidly, with the absolute poverty rate falling down to 8.6 per cent by 1972 (see Figure 4.1), and continuing to decrease until the mid-1990s down to 3.4 per cent (Park, 2001) or even much lower, depending on the statistics.

Figure 4.1: GDP growth and absolute poverty rate change, 1966-92

Sources: GDP per capita (US$): Statistics Korea, Absolute poverty rate (%): Kim et al (2007, p 251)

During this period of industrialisation and high employment, poverty came to be conceived as a residual phenomenon, and as affecting only those who could not or for whatever reason did not participate in the job market. Those who were able-bodied and therefore capable of work were assumed to be able to work their way out of poverty, had they only the sufficient willpower and diligence. The only people countenanced to be in poverty were pregnant women, children, old-aged people and those who were sick or physically disabled, all with an acceptable or pardonable reason for not working (Kim et al, 2007). Poverty during this period was seen as a consequence of personal failing or due to the lottery of ill health. Economic and political developments were accompanied by enormous social change, affecting people's cultural values, behaviours and lifestyle. The neoliberalistic capitalism that has since shaped the economy has created an era of 'limitless competition', with full-blown consumerism in which displays of wealth, consumption and economic status higher than others have become the main measures of social respect. If not obliterating traditional values, individualistic perspectives on life, influenced by Western and US culture, are now often found alongside Confucian values requiring families to behave in accord with moral obligations for parental piety and kinship.

These changes have all contributed to the development of a social environment in which the sense of shame that is attached to poverty is greatly heightened (Jo, 2014). Not only has consumption become the principal marker of social success, but the family ties that once functioned as the main provider of basic welfare have withered as a result of individualisation, the increasing predominance of nuclear family forms and divorce (rates of divorce in South Korea are among the highest in the world; see Yeo, 2004; Yeo, 2005; Lee and Ku, 2010). With the demise of the traditional social safety net provided by the extended family and community, individuals are now left to negotiate the highly risky labour market on their own. The social assistance system reportedly covers less than half of the population living in poverty, and provides only a bare minimum level of support (Moon, 1999a; Yeo, 2004; Lee, 2009).

For much of the post-war period until 1997, family continued to be the main social safety net for people of working age and, indeed, for elderly people. The first anti-poverty policy, the Livelihood Protection Law, was introduced in 1961 (Kim et al, 2007, p 54). It was first and foremost a political gesture designed to legitimate dictatorial rule, and was largely residual with very strict and non-universal eligibility criteria (Nam, 2004, p 43). Indeed, it reflected the charitable provisions that had previously been available as a result of foreign aid, first under US military rule and subsequently under President Lee Seung-Man (Kim et al, 2007, p 45). Economic growth, low unemployment and the dominance of Confucian family values, especially in the early period, meant that the residual welfare system appeared viable, and indeed, accorded a degree of political legitimacy to successive authoritarian governments until the Asian financial crisis of 1997. The crisis and the subsequent economic structural reform implemented according to the International Monetary Fund's (IMF) principles resulted in the bankruptcy of numerous medium to small size businesses, and the substantial lay-offs of workers from the country's large industrial conglomerates (*Chaebol*) over a very short period of time. The unemployment rate rose rapidly from 2.6 to 8.7 per cent in 1999 (Moon, 1999a, p 101), and the absolute poverty rate rose from 3.8 per cent in 1996 to 7.9 per cent in 2000 (Ku, 2004, p 68), and up to 21 per cent in urban areas (Lee, 1999). The popular news media were replete with stories of both laid-off workers and the former owners of now bankrupt businesses committing suicide, leaving dependants with nothing but insurmountable debt (Lødemel and Dahl, 2000; N. Park, 2002; Huh, 2009). With no real social safety net in place and with the reduced capacity of the extended family to provide support, the victims of the financial crisis and the structural reform plans were exposed to immense suffering with nowhere to turn.

The 1997 national crisis demonstrated to the body politic that poverty could not be solely attributable to individual failings, but was instead a product of structural failure. The focus shifted to poverty as a social problem beyond an individual's capacity to resolve (Lee, 1999; Huh, 2002; Yeo, 2005). The crisis also highlighted the absence of any effective social safety net, and precipitated demand for the introduction of the first universal social assistance programme for poverty relief, the National Basic Living Security Scheme (NBLSS), which was enacted in 2000 and which remains the main social assistance programme with minimum subsequent change.

Having experienced abject poverty in the post-war period, a rapid decrease in poverty associated with the industrialisation period, and mass unemployment and increased poverty following the Asian financial crisis, South Korea is currently confronting the emergence of a multiplicity of new forms of poverty affecting different groups of the population. Often referred to as the 'new poverty', it is the product of disparate causes including growing inequality, in-work poverty that fails to lift incomes above the minimum living expense threshold, growth in non-standard employment characterised by insecurity and low wages, a high level of unemployment among young people in their twenties, a rapidly ageing population, and increasing numbers of single parents and single-headed households without familial support (Kim et al, 2007, 2009).

The emergence of new forms of poverty has yet to be adequately addressed in the current policy design, not least because the conception of poverty forged during the era of industrialisation remains dominant in political and policy discourse despite the legacy of the Asian financial crisis. People are deemed to be poor for reasons of their own making. With policies designed according to this premise, low-income people are trapped in systems of provision that exacerbate the shame that they are often already experiencing due to being unable to acquire social status through conspicuous consumption.

Framing of anti-poverty policy

It is a major irony that the abject poverty that was endemic at the time of the formation of South Korea and that triggered the drive for economic growth was thereafter dropped from the political lexicon (until it returned with the Asian financial crisis of 1997). The focus instead was placed on the development and economic growth that was to achieve welfare or a welfare society (Kim et al, 2007, p 53). The presumption was that poverty would automatically be eliminated through the trickle-down effect of growth, and that its eradication did not therefore need to be accorded the status of an objective in its own right (Kim et al, 2007). Poverty became invisible in policy discourse as, for the most part, did those people who continued to be poor (Ku, 2006, p 16). Correspondingly, while enhancing welfare has been a central tenet of every national South Korean government in the modern era, it has not been until recent elections that *welfare policy* has been directly promoted as a means of achieving a welfare society.

The era of industrialisation: 'growth first, redistribution later'

Progress in the decade following the Korean War was insufficient to significantly reduce the poverty rate which, measured in absolute terms, still stood at 49 per cent at the time of the military coup that brought Park Jung-Hee to power in 1961. Park, in his presidential inauguration speech in 1963, clearly articulated the economic developmental approach to welfare that South Korea had adopted under his leadership and that was to frame subsequent policy debates:

> What this generation of Korea in the 1960s must experience as an unavoidable historical fate is the *modernisation* of the country in every aspect: that of politics, economy, society, and culture.... The people as individuals should strengthen the notion of improving their lot through building an independent and autonomous *self-supporting mentality*. In order to establish *democracy, prosperity, and welfare society* in this land, the people of our nation must bear a *nationalistic identity,* the mentality of *spontaneous participation* and a strong *hard-working mindset.* (emphases added)

Four years later, in the 1967 inauguration speech marking his second term as president, Park Jung-Hee further elaborated similar themes:

> In order to achieve our goal to build a *welfare society without poverty* and corruption, with trustworthy, hard-working, simple, and diligent citizens, I desire for us all to be more faithful to our *jobs* and the execution of *work* ... I am convinced that such a welfare society of justice can be achieved through our current path towards national *industrialisation.... Without building the economy, there is no*

> *poverty elimination*, without building the economy there is
> no way to abolish the unemployment that breeds *corruption*,
> and without it we cannot accomplish a beautiful vision in
> comparison to that of *communism*, nor reunify the country
> and liberate our brothers through the power of freedom
> flowing into the North. (emphases added)

Taken together, these inaugural speeches capture the thrust of policy thinking in South Korea over 30 years. The language is important although not transparent. In the first speech, democracy precedes prosperity and the creation of a welfare society as a policy goal, and yet was not to be achieved for over a quarter of a century, long after considerable strides towards prosperity had been accomplished. The reality was that Park Jung-Hee's regime pursued economic growth above all else, while sustaining a highly centralised and oppressive political dictatorship (Kim et al, 2007, p 50; Seo, 2007). In the second speech, welfare society is more or less defined as a society without poverty, which, he reiterated, could only be achieved through economic growth based on the then current path towards industrialisation: 'without building the economy there is no poverty elimination.' The political framing of poverty provided the justification for his government to concentrate on economic development policies without reference to any specific poverty alleviation programme, under the rationale that everyone would eventually benefit, and the 'trickle-down' effect of economic growth would subsequently relieve the mass poverty that existed.

Further reading of the excerpts from the presidential speeches during this period demonstrates that economic growth was not just perceived as the panacea to domestic problems but was geopolitical in its motivation. North Korea was presented as a threat to national security, and the economic success of South Korea was viewed as an essential demonstration of the ideological superiority of democratic capitalism over North Korean communism. Leaving to one side the fact that South Korea was neither democratic nor free at the time – the education system was infused with anti-communist ideology while the National Security Law was used as a mechanism of political repression (Seo, 2007, p 96) – nationalism was promoted as a spur to concentrate on economic growth. Given the legacy of recent occupation by Japan and the US, it was not lost on the population that economic success would also allow South Korea to win back the North: 'to liberate our brothers through the power of freedom'. Instilling the work ethic was not just about personal gain; it was about national security, identity and pride. Work and personal economic success were, in effect, civic duties that were used politically to justify the exploitative working hours and conditions that were widespread during this period (Kim et al, 2007).

Also evident from Park Jung-Hee's speeches is the focus on individualism: 'hard-working individuals' with an 'independent self-supporting mentality' were deemed necessary for economic success and for the broader populace to escape poverty. Such individualism was a marked departure from the Confucian thinking that had for centuries shaped Korean culture. This thinking had prioritised the interests of the family above individual success and promoted parental piety and support within extended families (Yeo, 2004, p 8). Ironically, in the absence of state social protection, individualism and economic self-sufficiency would be sustained by an informal safety net based on the moral obligation and collective reciprocity within families and neighbourhoods. Nonetheless, the government's emphasis on independent self-sufficiency continued, reinforced by the growing influence of Western cultural ideas and the rules of the capitalistic market economy. Whether or not they were the result of government rhetoric or a consequence of industrialisation, urbanisation or modernity itself, the individualistic values of self-sufficiency took hold. This was reflected in the sustained growth of the nuclear family in tandem with the weakening of broader family ties and sociocultural norms around familial obligations of mutual support (Yeo, 2004; Lee and Ku, 2010). As a result, individuals were exposed to greater economic risk as government rhetoric underlined personal responsibility over one's own fate. Yet as economic growth was strong, the loss of the collective insurance that had once been provided by strong familial networks would only become fully apparent in the aftermath of the 1997 financial crisis.

The policy trajectory initiated by Park Jung-Hee has proven resilient (no doubt in part due to the economic success enjoyed by South Korea), and the attachment to an economic growth-oriented and minimal welfare model remains strong in policy discourse to this day. What has changed, however, is the arrival of truly democratic politics. Along with this has come public pressure to realise the aspiration inherent in the development idea that growth first is subsequently to be followed by redistribution. Newly politicised industrial workers who had been sustaining the export-oriented economy, along with intellectuals and college students, led the civil movement in opposition to the dictatorships in the 1980s (Kim et al, 2007; Seo, 2007). This opposition precipitated several welfare policy reforms during the 1980s, including the enactment of the National Pension Law and the expansion of medical insurance, both in 1986 under the Jun Doo-Hwan military government and more fundamentally under the last military ruler, Noh Tae-Woo. In his 1988 inaugural speech, Noh Tae-Woo acknowledged the need for 'redistributing justly and honestly the fruit of rapid growth that has been achieved so far' and that 'the unfair sacrifice of the individual's share that has been undistributed for the sake of focusing on the national development should no longer be'. Notable reforms in the Livelihood Protection Law were undertaken in 1982 and the policy became more inclusive in terms of eligibility. The term of Noh Tae-Woo also saw the implementation of a national pension scheme and universal health insurance. Corporation-based welfare was also introduced as an alternative to state welfare policies.

While the welfare structures implemented in Korea during the 1980s and early 1990s sound reminiscent of a corporatist welfare state such as Germany, overall spending remained low as a proportion of GDP, and benefits were minimal by international standards, while familial support necessarily remained high. Despite eased eligibility standards, social assistance provision via the Livelihood Protection Law remained largely unchanged and provided only for recipients who were demonstrably poor, unable to work or who had no responsible family members to support them. Limiting social assistance provision to the 'worthy' poor reinforced the notion that anyone falling outside the narrow scope for eligibility was morally deficient. Thus, coverage remained low, never more than half of the poverty population due to strictness of eligibility criteria and to the stigma associated with claiming (OECD, 2000; Lee, 2009). While larger numbers were incorporated into the social insurance system, the distinction increased between this mainstream society with access to insurance protection and those dependent on social assistance.

The expansion of social insurance within a 'Growth first and redistribution later' approach to welfare continued well into the democratic period. During Kim Young-Sam's presidency (1993-97), the idea of a 'Korean welfare model' was first promulgated based on the pursuit of harmony between growth and welfare. This entailed provision by multiple providers, yet at a minimal level so as not to hinder economic growth. This approach has subsequently been categorised as 'neo-liberalistic welfare pluralism' (Huh, 2002, p 52; Kim et al, 2007, p 71). It prioritised economic growth over welfare provision and redistribution, portrayed welfare spending as a great potential burden on the economy and delimited the notion of welfare to that of a minimal charitable provision reserved for the poorest minority.

Progressive, yet still anachronistic, reform

The 1997 Asian financial crisis proved to be a critical juncture for South Korean welfare policy. The crisis was followed by the election of a democratic government under Kim Dae-Joong (1998-2003) that was necessarily more sensitive than ever before to political pressure from below, as well as to the importance of civil and social rights. The crisis saw unemployment soaring from 2.6 per cent to 8.4 per cent between 1997 and 1999 (Y. Park, 2002, p 272). An increasing number of people could neither find work nor depend on financial support from their extended families, because family members were similarly affected and because relationships had been fractured due to social change. As a result, a great number of people fell into poverty overnight and were burdened with debt, yet had no access to a public means of support (Y. Park, 2002). The impact of the crisis became a major social problem, and the government came under pressure from pan-national joint civil society movements that lobbied for a universal social assistance programme that would, for the first time, embrace those people capable of work (Lee, 1999, p 12; Y. Park, 2002, p 276; Nam, 2004, p 44). The national response was the enactment of the NBLSS as the first universal social assistance programme available to everyone on the basis of need.

NBLSS adheres to an incongruous hybrid of ideals. It is, on the one hand, based on a progressive notion of civil rights. On the other, it represents path dependency as it maintains an economic developmental welfare model prioritising self-support through work (Y. Park, 2002, p 279). This disconnect reflects the fact that the aspiration to universality was met with strong resistance from certain economists and government officials, most notably, the Ministry of Planning and Budgets (Huh, 2002, 2009). The primary objections were that the establishment of universal assistance would increase costs, generate abuse and waste finance. Most predominant was the argument that universal assistance would generate moral hazard and a decline in work motivation (Huh, 2002; Ku, 2006, p 94), resulting in 'welfare disease' (Moon, 1999a, p 112; Y. Park, 2002). Thus, while the resultant policy aimed to alleviate poverty that had been induced by mass unemployment among the work-capable population, it nevertheless still discriminated against them. Not only did the work-capable receive a lower benefit, but they were also required to enrol in workfare-like projects, thus creating a two-tier system in which even individual recipients evaluate each other as more or less deserving than themselves based on their presumed work capability (Jo, 2014).

A division based on work capability is, however, inappropriate in a post-1997 scenario. 'New poverty' is mostly due to widespread unemployment and, moreover, to growing levels of casual and non-standard employment. While the labour market is no longer capable of providing sufficient work for work-capable people, the policy discourse effectively holds individuals, if not responsible for the market's failure, responsible for their failure to find adequate work. This focus on the individual blame serves to shame people in poverty as a whole, since in reality many have no alternative but to claim NBLSS.

In short, consecutive governments since the very beginning of South Korea's modern history have prioritised economic development above all else, frequently promoting the concept of 'growth first and redistribution later'. In the aftermath of near total devastation poverty reduction was a dominant objective. Yet poverty, individual welfare and social policies were subsequently framed as secondary to a more prominent growth discourse. Poverty was constructed as an individual and household issue to be resolved through participation in the newly strong economy or through support by the extended family with minimal state intervention. Rapid economic growth, combined with low inequality, helped create a future-oriented optimism concerning improvements in general welfare. This diverted attention away from the hardships taking place. Indeed, as the term 'welfare' was equated with aggregate national prosperity, there was little political space in which to consider social policy as a viable means to improve the welfare of individuals. Furthermore, minimal social assistance provisions were justified by locating the blame for poverty with those individuals who did not take up employment opportunities or with families who did not provide an appropriate level of support. Despite the fact that the 1997 financial crisis illuminated the structural causes of poverty, this propensity to blame the victim is still inherent in the structure of NBLSS, the current social assistance scheme.

Shaping and structuring public assistance policy

The structure of NBLSS reflects the contradictions that shaped its format: the aspirations for reform based on a framework of rights in contrast to the lasting legacy of an economic developmental welfare model that had served South Korea well economically until the crisis of 1997. These contradictions create divisions among recipients and impose conditions that stigmatise and shame, hindering the effectiveness of policy implementation.

The social assistance scheme that was in place in 1997, the Livelihood Protection Policy, was a direct descendent of the charitable aid that had been provided during the post-war period. Aid had been made available through the international donor community, which offered minimal support, with no capacity to earn and with no access to financial support through the extended family. Aid was restricted to only the most vulnerable, on grounds of age, physical health or disability (Nam, 2004, p 43). The 1997 crisis demonstrated both the vulnerability of the people to structural change, and the weakness of the social safety net then in place. Civil society-driven reform (Kim et al, 2007, p 99) resulted in the establishment of NBLSS by the Kim Dae-Joong government in 2000. Its policy objectives closely reflected Article 34 of the National Constitution, which stated that 'Every Korean national has the right to a humane living, and those who are not capable of making a living due to physical disability, health, old age, or other reasons are to be protected by the country according to the legislation' (Moon, 1999b, p 19). The reform effectively redefined welfare. It was no longer a zero-sum burden on the economy, but instead became a positive-sum tool supporting economic growth (Kim et al, 2007, p 35). Nevertheless, the actual reform fell short of the original plan requested by the civil society movement: to redefine 'welfare' as a social human right that needed to be fully and universally protected.

Conceptually, NBLSS was a notable advance. It enhanced the legal status of people who successfully claimed assistance: 'beneficiaries' became 'qualified recipients', with a legally enforceable right to an adequate livelihood secured through the national government (Lee, 1999, p 13). This change represented a paradigm shift in the policy framework regarding poverty. Rather than individuals being solely responsible for providing for their own welfare, the national government was to ensure that everyone enjoyed at least the national official minimum standard of living (Nam, 2004; Huh, 2009). For the first time a scheme was put in place that was to be available to everyone in material deprivation, irrespective of age, health status and ability to work, criteria that had limited the effectiveness of the Livelihood Protection Law at the time of the 1997 financial crisis (Lee, 1999; Huh, 2005).

While NBLSS marked a radical change, shifting from the realm of political gestures and government charity to proactive and worthwhile policy, the structure of the scheme still reflects an overriding concern about the possibility of moral hazard, abuse and the creation of welfare dependency. As a consequence, stigma remains in the structure of the scheme and undermines the goal of dignity inherent in a human rights approach to social assistance provision (N. Park, 2002, p 14). The most important of these structural limitations are work orientation, the obligation of financial support from kin and the process of benefit renewal.

Work orientation and self-sufficiency

While people capable of work are not debarred from NBLSS, as they were under the Livelihood Protection Law, the structure of the benefit replicates the earlier distinction based on work capability and thus creates several sites of potential shaming. The work capability clause places the condition that recipients capable of work must participate in public service in order to receive benefit, a form of workfare. The requirement reinforces the notion of deserving and undeserving in its implication that those capable of work should, in fact, support themselves (Kim, 2010; Lee, 2010). The imposition of this condition was up for debate before the reform was enacted, yet in the end it was retained because of the developmental legacy and expectation that people would support themselves through employment (N. Park, 2002). Due to its inclusion, the work-capable who are receiving benefit are open to suspicion and claims of abuse, potentially adding to the shame of financial failure and the stigma of benefit receipt.

The work to which work-able NBLSS claimants are assigned is, for the most part, menial and of low status. As there is a general public distinction attached to those who must be engaged in the work programme as a condition of NBLSS receipt, such employment is a public sign of failure rather than success. Furthermore, evidence suggests that the work or 'self-sufficiency' programmes, as they are called, do not, in fact, help people to move out of NBLSS receipt. Rather, those engaged in the programme tend to become trapped in an intermediate labour market that is publicly not recognised as 'proper' employment and which thus offers few long-term career prospects (Ku, 2006, p 96).

The supplementary nature of the benefit system operates according to a monthly means test, such that monthly income is not permitted to exceed the eligibility threshold, the minimum living expense line. This provides no financial reward or incentive for finding a job that would pay less than the benefit itself. There is also no incentive for finding a job that would take recipients just above the threshold for entitlement to additional NBLSS-related support packages, including healthcare, education and housing benefits (N. Park, 2002, p 10). However, when people are, for whatever reason, unable to participate in work programmes, their livelihood benefit may be denied altogether, thus throwing them into abject poverty (Huh, 2009). This all-or-nothing scenario presents recipients with a moral and emotional dilemma: to risk their only source of support for the sake of finding a better paying job. Therefore, in effect, the policy structure intended to encourage self-sufficiency through work (Lee, 1999, p 16) serves instead to exclude benefit recipients from proper employment. This has the potential to undermine their sense of agency and self-respect, while denying them the security of an unconditional cash benefit. Recipients capable of work not only find themselves in a poverty trap that makes it difficult for them to move on to decent work situations, they also experience a shaming trap, since they have to continuously demonstrate that they are incapable of finding better paying work.

A further site of shaming is imposed by the fact that the employment criterion operates at the household level (Huh, 2009, p 281). People incapable of work are denied access to NBLSS if they happen to live in households that include people capable of working. For example, elderly parents living with or having near-poor adult children are likely to be ineligible for the programme. This almost inevitably leads to resentment by the applicant and exposes work-capable family members to the shame of, first, not being able to adequately support their own kin, and second, to the fact that their own inadequacy has resulted in the denial of rightful state support to these kin. Moreover, even when families receive NBLSS, there is no guarantee that economic hardship will be substantially reduced as benefit levels are set at the low level of less than 35 per cent of median household income (Jung, 2011).

The retention of the work capability clause echoes the long-lasting political emphasis on self-sufficiency, a preoccupation with the risks of moral hazard and welfare dependence and the media's portrayal of recipients as abusing the benefit system (Ahn and Song, 2006; Kang et al, 2008). However, as in the other settings represented in this volume, interviews with NBLSS recipients indicated their overwhelming desire to work, not merely for financial returns, but as a source of emotional and mental stimulus that they longed for, especially given their impoverished situations (Jo, 2014). These respondents daily confronted the indignity of being physically 'able-bodied', yet unemployed and finding it difficult to secure the sort of work that would accommodate their household situation or take them off benefits altogether. Proving the necessary documentation concerning their incapacity to be self-supporting was shaming, disheartening, and discouraged their future claims for public support (Park, 2008; Lee, 2010).

Family obligations

Social assistance programmes in South Korea have always obliged applicants to make efforts to secure support from their extended family prior to the receipt of state support. This requirement, however, has the potential to bring shame on the entire family, not just the person claiming benefits. Prior to partial reform of NBLSS in 2004, the obligation included grandparents, grandchildren and their spouses, even if they were not living with the person claiming NBLSS. Table 4.1 shows the current situation.

Table 4.1: Family obligation support clause: scope of application

	Post-2004 reform
Scope of application	Regardless of cohabitation: applicant's spouse, direct family kin and their spouses In case of cohabitation: applicant's siblings, grandparents and grandchildren
For example	Wife, husband Parent, grown-up children, etc Son/daughter in-law, etc Further included, if living in the same household: siblings, grandparent, grandchildren, grandson/daughter in-law, etc

Source: Yeo (2004)

The family obligation clause requires applicants to personally solicit the agreement of all relevant family members to means-testing, even if the quality of the actual relationship is such that the applicant would otherwise consider it inappropriate to ask for financial help. This process has the potential to be triply shaming. First, potential applicants are obliged to divulge their precarious financial state to their wider family. Second, they have, as a result of their own failings, committed their relatives to a detailed investigation of their financial circumstances by the NBLSS authorities. Third, applicants are placed in a situation in which their relatives may be made financially worse off as a result of their own financial dependence. The official calculation for determining the supportability of family kin requires only that one eligible family member earn 130 per cent or more of the combined minimum living expense lines for the applicant and relevant family member. If the applicant is denied recipient status should this threshold level be surpassed, it becomes a substantial emotional burden for the applicant to depend on the family member in question, who may need to set aside nearly half of their income or more towards support, depending on the extent of asset that is taken into calculation. In practice, the family member who is expected to provide support tends to provide either insufficient or no financial support at all, leaving the failed applicant to live in the throes of poverty (Yeo, 2004; Yeo, 2005; Huh, 2009, p 286).

Not surprisingly, research findings indicate that the family obligation clause is a crucial barrier to the take-up of NBLSS (Huh, 2002, p 60; 2005, p 24; Nam, 2004, p 46). In some cases, relatives ignore the request to cooperate in the application procedure, a deeply shaming experience, possibly for both parties. For elderly people claiming benefit, the issue is often one of losing face and, certainly prior to 2004, the potential for imposition even on distant children. Divorced lone families, who are likely to be exposed to more severe poverty, are particularly affected since ex-partners are often uncooperative and applicants themselves may prefer to avoid contact for fear of reopening old personal wounds, renewing dependence or for other personal reasons (Jo, 2014). If the process of seeking financial assistance from relatives is shaming, their failure to help can be even more so. Given the legacy of filial piety and familial support inherent in a Confucian culture, it means that family members may risk being stigmatised for being incapable of providing support to family members in need or being accused of amoral behaviour for refusing to fulfil the family obligation clause. For some applicants, it can manifest as shame of being rejected by family members for their impoverished circumstances (Jo, 2014).

The clause is a legacy of the times when extended family forms were the dominant social structure before urbanisation and individualisation changed the fabric of South Korean society (Yeo, 2004). The mismatch between the administrative logic of NBLSS and social reality helps to explain the notoriously low take-up of the scheme (Jung, 2011). In 2004, before the clause was modified, nearly half of those refused benefit (a number exceeding the total active caseload) had been rejected for failing to fulfil the family obligation clause. Of these cases, many of the relatives of refused applicants had been proven unable or unwilling to provide support (Nam, 2004; Yeo, 2004; Park, 2008; Lee and Ku, 2010). Even today, a major impediment to claiming assistance is the presence of family members who are too poor to contribute support or too distant to reasonably approach (Lee and Ku, 2010). Our low-income respondents saw the clause not only as a substantial barrier to accessing the social assistance system, but also as a factor that had further contributed to the disintegration of the extended family (Jo, 2014).

Sustaining low recipient status

NLBSS benefit regulations mean that the shaming processes described above have to be repeated regularly through the period of receipt. Once or twice a year, depending on the type of benefit, recipients are required to submit documentary proof that substantiates their continuing inability to independently support themselves, along with the unwillingness or inability of kin to assist them. The amount of documentation is considerable and the task stressful since the outcome merely reinforces a sense of personal failure and social rejection.

Furthermore, the need to repeat the process regularly means the continual reinforcement of a sense of risk and uncertainty for the claimant, as for reasons beyond their control claimants stand to lose benefit during the renewal process. For example, an offspring may have turned 18 and therefore no longer fit the category of dependent child, instead being defined as an adult who is required to contribute financial support irrespective of employment status. Claimants report high levels of stress attached to this process, which reinforces their sense of dependency on others when policy and culture demands that they should be financially independent (Lee, 2010). The unpredictable nature of the process has the potential to undermine claimants' sense of agency and control by underlining their powerlessness (Jo, 2014).

The original civil rights-based approach towards poverty and welfare provision envisioned by civil society activists has been severely compromised within the policy's design. Family-based means-testing and work requirements restrict the rights of claimants and expose claimants and recipients alike to stigma and shaming, not to mention extreme poverty (Park, 2008). Whether by accident or design, the imposed conditions reflect the earlier assumption that individuals and families are primarily responsible for their own welfare, and that they alone are to be blamed and shamed for falling into poverty.

The point of delivery: shaming practised face-to-face

Under the authority of the central state Ministry of Health and Social Welfare, NBLSS is run and delivered by local governments through the mechanism of community administrative (*dong*) offices in cities and counties. The workfare component – comprised of work ability maintenance work, internships, socially useful work and market-based work – is delivered directly by local government or by local self-reliance centres. It is possibly at the point of delivery that the most salient shaming and experiences of feeling shame occur, as it involves direct and personal interaction between officials and those reliant, or potentially reliant on, NBLSS. Evidence suggests that recipients repeatedly find themselves in situations where they are exposed to shaming practices that include being treated with a lack of respect, interrogated under the presumption of guilt, subjected to the abuse of power or being rendered powerless and voiceless (Lee, 2010; Jo, 2014).

Such shaming practices may be shaped by the dominant policy and social discourses relating to poverty. They are also induced by structural factors embedded within the delivery mechanism. Taking the former first, the underlying presumption is that both able-bodied people of working age and those with family members who are capable and obliged to support them by policy definition should be self-sufficient. Hence, they should not need to claim NBLSS (N.Park, 2002; Huh, 2009). Many of those entering the system therefore face suspicion and policed access, rather than the implementation of entitled rights. This is reflected in the extensive discretionary powers accorded to officials (Lee, 2010). Reflecting the same thinking, NBLSS is intentionally residual: it is a poor system for poor people and has failed to attract priority among the other demands on policy-makers; as a result, it is vastly under-staffed and under-resourced.

The significant lack of infrastructure, especially the limited number of welfare officers positioned in the local *dong* offices, imposes serious constraints on the quality of service provision (Kang, 2003). Although the number of staff has been increased significantly since the enactment of NBLSS in 2000, staffing levels are still largely inadequate, with officers on average being responsible for caseloads ranging from over a hundred to two hundred households (Kang, 2003). Even lower staffing ratios have been reported in parts of Seoul with, in one case, 57 officers responsible for 100,000 recipients and many more applicants (Jo, 2014).

Such under-staffing applies equally to the workfare self-sufficiency programme (Lee-Gong, 2011). The block grants made to non-governmental organisations (NGOs) implementing such schemes have not kept up with demand, and the four or five staff members attached to each local programme must typically engage in a broad set of disparate tasks, including programme development, marketing, accounting and general administration, as well as the management of an average of 22 workfare participants (Kim, 2005; SEDA, 2011).

Administrative constraints and a lack of staff resources inevitably constrain the extent to which it is possible to undertake a reliable and fair evaluation of applicants' circumstances or to provide supportive work placements, especially for those participants with limited experience and those under other social pressures (Kang, 2003). The inadequate staffing also exposes the welfare officers to a high level of stress. This, combined with working in a system that dictates strict inspection of applicants in terms of work capability, unofficial income and availability of family support, spurs the behavioural tendency of welfare officers to be driven by suspicion and a desire to limit numbers of recipients (Park, 2008). As an illustration, one of our low-income respondents retracted her application for NBLSS after experiencing a traumatising interview in which a welfare officer deliberately shamed and accused her for being an irresponsible and incapable mother and for exposing her children to poverty (Jo, 2014). The extent of such shaming seems to vary between officers. Nevertheless, 90 per cent of welfare officers included in a survey of officers' attitudes towards recipients supported maintenance of the work capability clause, a sentiment that has been interpreted as indicating distrust and even generally negative perceptions towards recipients among welfare officers (Kim and Hur, 2002).

Negative and undermining attitudes have also been reported to take place among those staff attached to local self-reliance centres who operate according to a culture of 'order and obey', wherein staff adopt 'imperial positions', 'are even more stiff than government officials', and where communication is entirely 'top-down' and 'absolutely one-way' (Lee-Gong, 2011, p 10). Such reports are particularly surprising given that they reflect a reality in organisations that had previously lobbied for the introduction of rights-based provision, as well as advocating for work initiatives based on cooperative notions of democratic member control (Kim, 2009). This suggests that organisational involvement with the compulsory workfare element of NBLSS has precipitated a shift among providing organisations from being pro-poor advocates to institutional masters (Lee-Gong, 2011). Moreover, the general lack of resources means that work programme participants are largely placed in menial occupations with limited or no training. Rather than building aspirations and promoting agency, participants talk of being deprived of hope and of feeling 'like a dolphin fed fish by a keeper' (Lee-Gong, 2011, p 16).

The attitudes of staff members are particularly salient because of the high level of discretion at their disposal and the challenges of exercising this discretion. Such challenges often involve making extremely difficult judgements about sensitive issues in face-to-face settings shaped by excessive workloads and insufficient resources (Lee and Lee, 2007). Furthermore, local officers are necessarily influenced by customs and practice that reflect the focus of the Ministry of Health and Welfare's auditing system. This system prioritises the reduction of abuse and illegitimate claims. What NBLSS recipients report is that the discretionary administrative decisions and demeanour of welfare officers reflects a restrictive approach to applicant intake (Jo, 2014). Further, the practice by staff of emotional distancing tends to turn people into numbers and statistics. Discretion also opens the possibility of the abuse of power by officials, prejudicial decision-making and the prioritisation of administrative convenience over accuracy and fairness (Lee and Lee, 2007). Participants in work programmes have to renew their work placements as they do their NBLSS claim. This typically means that they experience a period of two months' unpaid 'leave' during which their contract is reviewed and renewed. Evidence suggests that there have been instances when participants have been effectively 'dismissed' by staff simply because there has been no follow-up contact established (Lee, 2010).

While institutional ethos and staff attitudes combined with inadequate resources create conditions in which applicants and recipients of NBLSS are perhaps inadvertently subject to shaming, certain procedures make shaming explicit, possibly deliberate, and almost certainly inevitable. The requirement to approach kin to request their participation in means-testing discussed above is a case in point. More generally, applicants and recipients are frequently required to demonstrate what they cannot do rather than to document their potential (Lee, 2010). This applies particularly to the process for delineating incapacity for work. For example, NBLSS recipients report feeling humiliated after being asked to approach employers to provide them with the explicit reasons as to why they were not successful in job interviews in order to continue to receive benefit (Jo, 2014).

NBLSS recipients needing to access in-kind benefits such as discounted fees for mobile phone calls and children's school lunch funds are first obliged to visit the social welfare office to obtain an official document that displays their name, address and status of receiving benefits. This document is then to be shown or submitted to the service supplier. Recipients found it deeply humiliating to have to repeatedly request such documentation in public view in the community *dong* office, as well as the requirement to show it in various public places such as children's schools, restaurants and shops. To them, this requirement signalled publicly that they were failures, dependent on state charity (Jo, 2014).

Shame is, of course, a two-way process, and respondents' accounts of the shaming attitudes of staff and procedures may be filtered through their own personal sense of shame. The latter, however, is likely to be highly influenced by the prevalent social attitudes of those around them and to be informed, like the views of public officials, by the public discourse that is attached to anti-poverty policy-making. If, as demonstrated above, the dominant view is that poverty is primarily the result of individual failings, the encounters that take place between NBLSS officials, applicants and recipients are likely to be highly charged with a sense of shame.

Implications and recommendations

The recent history of South Korea is largely one of economic success. What was once a battlefield characterised by devastation and abject poverty, as well as driven by authoritarian governments, is now a country that has become a model of capitalist endeavour. Today, South Korea is a leading developed economy with, especially in the last 15 years, a vibrant democratic debate about appropriate models of national social welfare. Economic growth has been equated with national and ideological success, achieved through collective hard work, sometimes ruthlessly imposed, as well as through corporate and individual economic success. In the process, social values have changed, such that individuals have increasingly come to be valued according to their financial success. At the same time, the importance of familial and social obligations has declined. Poverty, once endemic, has become a sign, bearing the mark of stigma, of individual economic and of social failure.

The legacy of the initial framing of South Korea's development model is clear. Economic growth was then the anti-poverty programme. Other policies were secondary and politically viable only insofar as they were thought not to inhibit growth. Social assistance was to be residual, available only to those incapable of work and lacking the resource of family support. More recent reforms replacing state-run charity have ostensibly provided a rights-based system of provision to make ends meet for those without resources. Yet the design of the principal social assistance scheme, NBLSS, retains strong elements that reinforce the dependent status of applicants. These include, for example, obliging applicants to personally plead with kin for financial support and, for the work-able, compelling work in exchange for benefit. The legacy of charity is also evident in the under-resourcing of the system, as well as in the impossibly large caseloads, poor quality provision and overwhelming institutional focus on policing abuse rather than proactively meeting need.

The objective in this chapter was to view South Korean anti-poverty programmes through the lens of shame. It would be churlish to ignore the positive consequences of the economic success achieved in earlier times with little increase in income inequality, leading to dramatic reductions in poverty. Likewise, there have been substantial increases in the scope and, to some extent, in the generosity of social assistance benefits. Yet it is indisputable that social assistance programmes in South Korea are shaming, even shameful, in their design and delivery. Moreover, despite the current political consensus that more and more universal welfare provision is required, as claimed in the 2013 election bringing to power Park Geun-Hye (the daughter of the authoritarian president Park Jung-Hee), reform of social assistance is not yet in sight. Poverty has not been eradicated and, indeed, new forms have emerged. However, the people who experience poverty remain largely invisible, faceless and voiceless in the political debate, shamed out of existence.

Note

[1] The Han River is a river that flows through the centre of the capital city of Seoul.

References

Ahn, J. and Song, J. (2006) 'Introducing the Korean EITC: Its effects and plans', *Jae-Jung-Non-Jib*, vol 20, no 2, pp 33-71.

Huh, S. (2002) 'The social assistance system and National Basic Livelihood Security Scheme', *Korean Academy of Social Welfare*, Spring Symposium, vol 4, pp 51-69.

Huh, S. (2005) 'Evaluation of the National Basic Livelihood Security Act in its 5th year', *Welfare Archive*, vol 10, pp 21-7.

Huh, S. (2009) 'The 10th anniversary of enactment of National Basic Livelihood Security Act: The limits and tasks', *Citizen & World*, vol 16, no 12, pp 274-89.

Jo, Y.N. (2014) 'A study of poverty-shame dynamics within the life experience of people in poverty', in E. Chase and G. Bantebya Kyomuhendo (eds) *The shame of poverty: Global experiences*, Oxford: Oxford University Press.

Jung, S. (2011) 'The effects of the Korean welfare system in reducing economic hardship', Paper presented at the Society for Social Work and Research Conference, Tampa, 16 January.

Kang, H. (2003) 'The delivery of the basic social security programs: Status and issues', *Health & Welfare Forum*, KiHASA, October, pp 36-53.

Kang, S. et al. (2008) *Poverty characteristics and implications on welfare expenditure programs associated with labor supply*, Seoul, South Korea: KiHASA and KiPF .

Kim, H. (2005) 'Current situation of self-reliance programmes and direction for the future', *Labour and Society*, vol 95, January (www.klsi.org/magazine/magazine.htm?no=1284).

Kim, J. and Hur, J. (2002) 'A study on evaluation and policy development of National Basic Livelihood Guarantees', *Social Security Study*, vol 18, no 2, pp 43-70.

Kim, M. (2010) 'A change of public awareness and attitude towards the National Basic Social Security System and its implications', *Health & Welfare Forum*, KiHASA, September, pp 39-52.

Kim, S. (2009) 'The pilot project period: The beginning of the institutionalization', in Korean Association of Self-sufficiency Promotion Center, *The history and philosophy of the Self-reliance Movement*, Seoul: KASPC.

Kim, S., Lee. H. and Son, B. (2009) *Korea's poverty – New poverty, old problem*, South Korea: Han-Wool Academy.

Kim, Y., Kim, K., Kim, J., Jang, K. and Jung, K. (2007) *Social welfare in Korea*, Yang-Seo-Won. South Korea: Yangseowon.

Ku, I. (2004) 'Poverty in Korea, why it remains high? Analysis of the trend in poverty since the 1990s', *Korean Journal of Social Welfare*, vol 56, no 4, pp 57-78.

Ku, I. (2006) *Income inequality and poverty in Korea – Worsening income distribution and the need for social policy reform*, Seoul: Seoul National University Press.

Lee, H. (1999) 'The enactment background and the implications of the National Basic Livelihood Security Act', *Health & Welfare Forum*, KiHASA, October, pp 5-17.

Lee, H. and Lee, S. (2007) 'A study on influence factors of welfare bureaucrats' administrative discretion on National Basic Livelihood Guarantees', *Korean Journal of Public Management*, vol 21, no 3, pp 1-23.

Lee, H.-K. (2009) 'Emergence of the post-developmental welfare regime: A case of South Korea', Paper presented at the Annual Meeting of RC19, Montreal, 20-22 August.

Lee, S. and Ku, I. (2010) 'Evaluating the family support obligation rules in the National Basic Livelihood Security Program', *Health and Social Welfare Review*, vol 30, no 1, pp 29-61.

Lee, W. (2010) 'Depression and welfare transitions of the National Basic Livelihood Protection Program', *Korean Journal of Social Welfare*, vol 62, no 4, pp 249-74.

Lee-Gong, E. (2011) 'The role of NGOs in welfare delivery: The case of South Korea', Paper presented at the Social Policy Association Annual Conference, 4-6 July.

Lødemel, I. and Dahl, E. (2000) *Public works programmes in Korea: A comparison to active labour market policies and workfare in Europe and the US*, Preliminary report prepared for The World Bank, Oslo: Fafo.

Moon, J. (1999a) 'A study of debates on and enforcement of the National Basic Livelihood Act', *Korean Journal of Social Welfare*, vol 38, September, pp 100-25.

Moon, J. (1999b) 'Productive welfare and the National Basic Livelihood Security Scheme', *Welfare Archive*, PSPD, August, pp 18-21.

Nam, C. (2004) 'The 5th anniversary of National Basic Livelihood Security Law enactment', *Welfare Archive*, PSPD, October, pp 43-52.

OECD (Organisation for Economic Co-operation and Development) (2000) *Pushing ahead with reform in Korea: Labour market and social safety-net policies*, Paris: OECD.

Park, N. (2001) 'Poverty rate and poverty line in Korea', Conference paper, Phillipines Institute for Development Studies, April.

Park, N. (2002) 'Issues on the National Basic Livelihood Security Program', *Health & Welfare Forum*, KiHASA, May, pp 5-16.

Park, N. (2008) 'The non take-up in the National Basic Livelihood Security Program', *Social Welfare Policy*, vol 35, no 12, pp 271-95.

Park, Y. (2002) 'A study on the policy making process of the National Basic Livelihood Institution – Focused on enactment of the National Basic Livelihood Act', *Korean Journal of Social Welfare*, vol 49, May, pp 264-95.

PSPD (People's Solidarity for Participatory Democracy)/UNDP (United Nations Development Programme) (2000) *Poverty status and monitoring of Korea in the aftermath of the financial crisis*, South Korea: PSPD/UNDP.

SEDA (Social Enterprises Development Agency) (2011) *Survey on the status and working conditions of the staff in Local Self-Reliance Centres*, Seoul: SEDA, Korean Association of Self-Sufficiency Promotion Centre (KASPC).

Seo, J. (2007) *60 years of modern history of Korea*, Seoul: Yuk-sa-bi-pyung-sa.

Yeo, E. (2004) 'Family support obligation rules and those excluded from the National Basic Livelihood Security Law', *Health and Social Welfare Review*, vol 24, no 1, pp 3-29.

Yeo, Y. (2005) 'National basic livelihood security: Selection criteria, benefits rules, and problems', *Health & Welfare Forum*, KiHASA, March, pp 67-79.

FIVE

'Not good enough': social assistance and shaming in Norway

Erika K. Gubrium and Ivar Lødemel

Introduction

Norway is a thin, stretched country with a population of just over 5 million. It is one of the world's richest countries, and its residents possess among the lowest variability in living standards (The World Bank, 2011). There is a long-standing consensus among all political parties that the quality of health, education and social services should be equalised as much as possible throughout the nation. Hence, the Norwegian welfare state is built on the 'citizenship' principle, with schemes, for the most part, financed through general taxes and a tax system that is redistributive in nature (Kuhnle, 1994a, p 81). This consensus is based on a prerequisite strong work ethic and commitment to full employment, as well as the ideals of equality, social justice, social security, solidarity and social integration (Christiansen and Markkola, 2006; Halvorsen and Stjernø, 2008).

These ideals are subject to positive and negative tensions. The redistributive and integrative goals of the Norwegian welfare state are premised on an economy that maintains high employment levels and economically active people (Lødemel et al, 2001). The country's policy focus on employment and employability – crystallised as its 'work approach' – is not, however, always conducive to the broader ethical ideals listed above and may, for particular groups, work to heighten a sense of marginalisation and exclusion.

Norway's broader welfare state is characterised by a diverse array of social reforms, where eligibility is based not on class or occupation but instead on residency. Development was encouraged early on by a traditionally strong peasant/agricultural class (Halvorsen and Stjernø, 2008) joining forces with organised labour, by the relatively strong position of democratic government and by political consensus on issues related to social protection and welfare (Baldwin, 1990; Hatland, 1992). The concept of *folkeforsikring* (the people's insurance) and the principle of universal coverage entered the Norwegian policy arena well before the end of the 19th century and certainly before the universal welfare ideas of Beveridge some 50 years later (Seip, 1981; Kuhnle, 1994b).

The Norwegian Labour Party's near–hegemonic rule from 1935 until the early 1960s, along with a pragmatic post–Second World War political consensus supporting the development of a broader welfare state, ensured the rapid expansion of coverage and increased benefit levels (Lødemel, 1997a). Political disagreements swirled around early on concerning the question of whether benefits should be means-tested or universal, yet by 1960 the Labour Party had introduced a series of broad and generous social insurance schemes that were targeted at varying risk categories. Beginning with older people and then extending to 'deserving' groups such as those with a disability, the unemployed, the widowed and single parents, these were available without means-testing (Lødemel, 1997a; Halvorsen and Stjernø, 2008). Along with a redistributive tax system, the discovery and subsequent export of oil in the nation's North Sea waters since the 1970s have provided a substantial economic boost and acted as a crucial cash generator for the generous Norwegian welfare state (Halvorsen and Stjernø, 2008). Contrary to popular understanding, however, Norway is not a purely universal welfare state. While most benefits are not means-tested, most are contingent on having had a history of gainful employment (with the exception of a more basic level of benefits, including child benefit, a pension for those with congenital disabilities and the minimum/basic old-age pension). The connection between worthiness for benefits and one's employment has reflected a Labour Party emphasis on the wage earner and its aim to clarify the relationship between rights and duties (Baldwin, 1990; Hatland, 1992; Halvorsen and Stjernø, 2008).

The broad extension of generous social insurance benefits that characterises the Norwegian welfare system has also resulted in a paradox of sorts. Over the last century, broadly targeted welfare provisions have lifted (deserving) risk groups out of poverty,[1] social assistance or family dependency. At the same time, the character of the system means that those individuals *not* eligible for, or perceived as deserving of, generous benefits have been reduced to the few who are then eligible only for social assistance (Lødemel, 1997a, p 83).[2] As Norwegian social assistance is granted when all other support options in connection with loss of income have been exhausted, it is considered poverty relief. The groups making up Norway's disparate social assistance population resemble those living in relative poverty

(Halvorsen and Stjernø, 2008), and it is the social assistance claimant, therefore, that forms the focus of this chapter.

Due to these features, social assistance is considered the benefit of last resort and plays a residual role in the larger Norwegian social protection system. The paradox of a residual system prevailing under extensive institutional welfare arises from the national focus on the extensions of *alternatives* to social assistance. In this process, social assistance has remained more similar to the preceding and stigmatising Poor Law.[3] The residualism of this scheme and its 'stigma by association' are reflected in the status of claimants and in the implicit aim to pay only the minimum benefit necessary to claimants, who face negative social sanctions 'in the form of lost citizenship rights' (Lødemel, 1997a, p 269).

Scandinavian studies exploring cultural conceptions and personal experiences of poverty have reported on the psychosocial barriers – including shame and stigma – experienced in tandem with financial instability within the larger Scandinavian setting (Jönsson and Starrin, 2000; Jönsson, 2002; Underlid, 2005; Angelin, 2009). The combination of financial difficulties and the receipt of public aid may heighten this experience. Our conversations with individual claimants, in tandem with discussions with members of the more economically secure 'general public' and a review of media coverage of poverty offer a unique space within which to analyse Norway's social assistance policy for its role in heightening shame or building the dignity of claimants.

Fifteen years ago, Ivar Lødemel (1997a) began a conversation that directly connected the residual nature of social assistance in Norway with stigma and shame. Since that time, however, empirical studies within this setting have not straddled the fields of social policy and social psychology to more closely evaluate this connection. This chapter provides empirical grounding to this effort by discerning how shaming has occurred within the framing, shaping and delivery of this welfare scheme. The focus on national policy-making spans the years 2000-12 as this period has represented a revitalised public focus on poverty in Norway, a shift that has been reflected by vast reforms to Norway's labour and welfare system.

Framing policy: marginality in a generous welfare setting

As far back as the 1537 Lutheran Reformation and in contrast to most Continental European nations, the Norwegian state has restricted the role of charities and voluntary organisations in the social welfare arena (Halvorsen and Stjernø, 2008, p 11). Since the Second World War, its generous mainstream social security system has been overwhelmingly aimed at mitigating the effects of social inequalities (Esping-Andersen, 1990) and removing the significance of social origin on social mobility (Wiborg and Hansen, 2009).Yet the broader understandings of social assistance and the more personal experiences of those receiving this benefit underscore the sense of social shame that may arise from the dissonance between the standard expectation of mobility and the reality of constrained options (Gubrium, 2013a; Gubrium and Lødemel, 2014).

Our investigation of Norwegian literature suggests a larger narrative in which, following a period of urbanisation and industrialisation, new urban dwellers experienced increased means for upward social mobility and a higher standard of living.Yet modernity was also accompanied by a greater dependence on the broader labour market (Gubrium, 2013a). In modern times, shame has become an increasingly individualised phenomenon. It is associated with an internalised failure to realise social expectations and individual goals or to reach a level of personal fulfilment and potential.This has the potential of resulting in loneliness and self-blame (Frønes, 2001; Skårderud, 2001; Underlid, 2005). The presence of newer internalised shame may mean that its effect is even more crippling in its more modern incarnation and has, in this sense, acted more as a de-motivator than a motivator to participate in the workforce.

Norwegian respondents claiming social assistance linked an internalised and individualised sense of shame to their social identities as 'dependent' on last resort public benefits. This experience was mediated by the public discourse surrounding the issue of poverty. The economically secure people we spoke with frequently described the receipt of social assistance as 'not normal' given Norway's rich and generous welfare state setting, low level of unemployment and record levels of labour market participation.They placed responsibility for economic difficulties – for unemployment in particular – on the individual. Economic precariousness was described largely as a matter of unfortunate choices. Norwegian newspaper coverage, while not unduly negative, also showed a general presumption of individualised responsibility for poverty. Those portrayals of poverty that were negative were often connected with system abuse and with low levels of 'self-reliance' among welfare system claimants (Gubrium, 2014). An especially negative focus was placed on non-Western immigrant claimants who were described as not 'play(ing) by society's rules' (Herland, 2007).

Poverty in Norway is primarily a relative phenomenon and Norway might be said to represent a best-case scenario.The country's population has a median income of US$51,000 (295,500 NOK) and among the lowest levels of income inequality in international comparisons[4] (Statistics Norway, 2010). The term 'poverty' was, in fact, largely absent from policy discussions in the preceding half-century of welfare expansion. It has, however, resurged as a matter of public concern in the past two decades (Hagen and Lødemel, 2010). Despite political promises across the political spectrum to 'reduce' or even 'eliminate' poverty, poverty in Norway has, *thus far*, been 'ineradicable' (Halvorsen and Stjerno, 2008, p 103). The relational character of poverty is mirrored in the shame and social exclusion felt by those struggling economically in the midst of a rather rich majority (Gubrium, 2013a). This strain may have been further heightened with more recently increasing income disparities (Aaberge and Atkinson, 2008)[5] and a new cultural emphasis on consumption (Gubrium, 2014).

Norway's relatively high standard of living is also reflected by the fact that while the average level of social assistance cash benefit provided is comparatively high in international terms[6] (Hatland and Pedersen, 2006), the scheme is simultaneously critiqued within Norway for providing a benefit rate that is so low as to be 'nearly under the hunger line' (Aasheim, 2009). Aside from whether the benefit is too high or too low, its low level of take-up means that it remains a relatively ineffective measure for eliminating poverty (Halvorsen and Stjernø, 2008). The challenge, then, may lie in the *social* aspects of social assistance that have prevented its full or effective use.

Since the late 1990s, a Norwegian policy-making consensus has placed an explicit rhetorical focus on the social aspect of poverty, calling for strategies that will successfully integrate marginalised groups into the labour market and mainstream society. These ideas are encapsulated in Norway's broader work approach. As described below, a rights-based version of this approach has recently been directed toward social assistance, with varying psychosocial consequences for claimants.

Shaping policy: motivating troubled individuals

Population ageing and shifting family dynamics, immigration and the labour market consequences of globalisation and technology change have tested the feasibility of generous welfare provisions in the northern European Social Democratic welfare states in the past three decades (Esping-Andersen, 2000). Policy-makers have rhetorically grappled with these challenges by placing an overwhelming focus on helping troubled individuals back into the labour market. Work and work incentives have been aimed at reducing unemployment as well as minimising the dependency that has been feared to be generated by generous welfare programmes (Øverbye, 2003).

Norway's work approach also has earlier roots. Reflecting the traditional Labour Party emphasis on rights and duties, its Social Care Act 1964 made the preliminary suggestion that a work approach (*arbeidslinja*) would enable claimants to improve their qualifications and actively seek work (Hvinden, 1994). An explicit policy shift concerning the rights and expectations surrounding the receipt of social assistance, however, first took place in the early 1990s. While decisions concerning the distribution of social assistance benefits had traditionally been a matter of local discretion (Hatland, 2007), in 1991 the Labour Party-led Brundtland III administration reintroduced 'workfare' into modern Norwegian social assistance in order to motivate claimants to enter the labour market. Local authorities were, for the first time, permitted to require that claimants work in exchange for their benefits (Dahl, 2003; Lødemel, 1997b, 2001).

In contrast to the rhetorical focus on claimant integration and autonomy, studies based on surveys and interviews collected from Norwegian long-term social assistance claimants in the early 2000s linked the country's workfare approach to a range of negative social and individual repercussions. The comparatively high levels of institutionalised and general social trust found within the Norwegian population were reduced among claimants, largely due to the use of means-tested and discretionary eligibility assessment and the increased attachment of work-related conditions to the provision of benefits (Malmberg-Heimonen, 2008, 2009). These features also had the potential to decrease the mental health of social assistance claimants (Malmberg-Heimonen, 2009). In a micro-level study of the effects of social assistance receipt from a psychological perspective, long-term social assistance claimants described an overarching fear of their professional, financial and personal futures due to everyday insecurity and an inability to predict their future circumstances (Underlid, 2007). Claimants also described a sense of their own devalued status in conjunction with unpredictable and discretionary financial aid, relatively low institutional expectations and a lack of individual recognition given their categorisation as dependent 'recipients' (Underlid, 2005).

By the mid-2000s, the antagonism between Norway's welfare system and system users had become a heated matter of public debate among policy-makers, preceding a wave of reform. On the matter of social assistance, the Labour Party administration was chastised for 'having done too little for those who "sit lowest at the table"' (Editor, *Aftenposten Morgen*, 2004), as efforts to fix institutional weaknesses were associated with individual struggles. The image of passive system users was emphasised with oft-repeated suggestions that they were merely 'shuttlecocks' (*kasteballer*) being aimlessly bounced around a labyrinth of welfare agencies.

In response, policy-makers publicly expressed a sense of urgency about the need to 'fix' an unwieldy, uncoordinated, inefficient and unresponsive system that had trapped claimants into welfare benefit dependency (Reegård, 2009). They also recognised that the country's changed demographic composition and labour market requirements meant that the category of long-term social assistance claimant increasingly consisted of people with few employment-related qualifications (White Paper nr 6, 2002-03).[7] Policy-making discussions and the policies enacted by the red-green Stoltenberg II administration referred to an overall goal of social inclusion. Yet reform solutions were based on many of the same rational choice presumptions of individual agency and choice that had marked the earlier workfare approach (Lødemel and Trickey, 2001; Gubrium et al, forthcoming – 2014). The strategies applied did not, in fact, address the structural factors that limited work participation. Instead, they remained aimed at the personally constrained and motivationally challenged individual claimant who found him or herself outside the workforce (White Paper nr 9, 2006-07, pp 41-2; Stoltenberg et al, 2006).

Nonetheless, the period of reform presented an opportunity to move toward dignity building. Despite an individualised focus, Norwegian policy-makers emphasised the use of incentives in the form of the provision of enhanced programming and expectations. The move was away from workfare and toward a 'human capital' approach, with a greater focus on claimant skills and potentials (White Paper nr 9, 2006-07), this at a time of broader European movement towards punitive sanctions (Lødemel and Moreira, 2014). Norway's unique shift towards positive incentives was, in part, enabled by institutional reform involving the partial nationalisation of activation via a comprehensive 2006 work and welfare governance reform. This reform merged the formerly separate managements of the Public Employment Service and the National Insurance Service into a single entity, and partly integrated and co-localised these national services with municipal social assistance services at the local level, into common front-line municipal offices.[8]

In light of demographic and labour market challenges in the years before (White Paper nr 6, 2002-03), the merger enabled the sort of state-level work activation approach formerly accessible only to those on short-term unemployment benefits to be offered for the first time to municipal-level social assistance claimants. The new approach was encapsulated in the 2007 Qualification Programme.[9] The Programme represented a new set of support services and the provision of state benefit set at a higher level than that of basic economic social assistance. Its offer of 'more' was to more effectively move claimants into the labour market (NAV Directorate, 2011; White Paper nr 9, 2006-07). Indeed, international praise for the Programme has emphasised its encouragement of 'active citizenship' as well as its provision of 'intensive personal support' to move claimants into the labour market (Prins, 2009; Duffy, 2010).

Yet the new offer was also characterised by the use of more requirements and stricter rules for a select group of claimants (White Paper nr 9, 2006-07). Policy-maker rhetoric concerning the benefits of the Qualification Programme employed a mix of harder and softer approaches toward worklessness. Labour and Inclusion Minister Bjarne Håkon Hanssen (LP) suggested that the reform meant that claimants would no longer be able to relinquish their social responsibilities, stating that Programme participants would be subject to binding 'contracts' to force them to 'get up in the morning' and 'do their duty' (Gjerstad, 2005). Representing the tension within the red-green coalition government over the purpose of the new work approach, Socialist Left Parliamentary member, Karin Andersen, distanced herself from Hanssen's tough love rhetoric and described the Programme as a holistic measure to 'mitigate the worst impact of poverty' by 'giv[ing] everyone equal possibilities' via the 'right to' a binding welfare contract in which the duties of the welfare system would be emphasised as much as those of the claimant (Andersen, 2006).

While the rhetoric surrounding the Programme varied, there was a general consensus that it represented a new opportunity for a select group of eligible claimants. The choice to limit broader programmatic possibilities and greater social citizenship rights to a portion of the entire claimant group furthered the distinction between deserving and underserving, and created a new set of tiers within social assistance. As described below, the new distinctions of worthiness within the ranks of social assistance may result in heightened shame for claimants.

Structuring and delivery: shaming the residuum

Since the Second World War, Norway's Parliament has granted to most of its welfare system claimants 'strong' legal rights (Hatland, 2007). This includes the right to prepare for the longer term, equal provision rights across geographical location, greater autonomy and voice in obtaining provisions and the recognition that claimant needs are legitimate and that there is a social responsibility for meeting these needs (Hatland, 2007, pp 209-11). Notably, these rights do not exist within the arena of social assistance, which has largely failed to move beyond the 'weak rights' characteristic of the Poor Law era (Lødemel, 1997a). The marginalised status of social assistance with respect to the broader welfare system is strongly reflected in three ways: (1) through the system's discernment between deserving and undeserving groups, in which social assistance claimants are the least deserving; (2) through the discretionary imposition of conditions by which one can claim social assistance benefits; and (3) through the constriction of the social citizenship rights of social assistance claimants.

As a residualist welfare scheme, Norwegian social assistance is a last resort option, subordinate to the primary goal of economic growth, and is marked by strict, normatively-based and discretionary eligibility rules, as well as limited coverage (Titmuss, 1974). While a softened version of Poor Law ideology now applies, the calculus remains the same: in order to receive minimum levels of aid, claimants are subjected to conditions that are worse than those experienced by the poorest worker not receiving benefits. And this to establish the validity of a person's claim to be destitute. In Norway, the discretionary assessment of claims, heightened conditionality and restricted social citizenship differentiate the undeserving from the deserving. Policy-makers operate under the general understanding that they must carefully calculate and apply the correct incentives (or disincentives) to motivate (or force) claimants to enter the labour market. According to the social assistance claimants we spoke with, these residualist elements and this calculus have been a source of considerable shaming.

In contrast to basic social assistance, the Qualification Programme has, at least in its early years, been offered as a national alternative to municipally funded and administered economic social assistance.[10] Programme participants have been given the incentive of a higher and standardised qualification benefit and, through close cooperation with and supervision by the local labour and welfare office, they are guaranteed and expected to follow customised individual plans focused on movement back into work life. The new opportunity for broader programming and rights for social assistance claimants has, however, come at a price. Given the partial integration of the Public Employment Service and social assistance services following Norway's labour and welfare system governance reform, it is not surprising that the assumptions, aims and structure of the offer closely resemble those formerly applied to those receiving short-term unemployment benefits. The offer of 'more' is better matched to the needs and qualifications of people who are close to the labour market rather than to the complex and resource-intensive needs of long-term social assistance claimants. Many respondents described a sense of dread and internalised shame about the threat or reality of failing to fulfil the work-related expectations that would enable them to move out of the ranks of social assistance. The new distinctions that have been drawn play out at three levels: through a heightened focus on determining eligibility to rights and benefits, through the presence of work-related conditions attached to new opportunities, and through a new hierarchy that has been generated within social assistance.

Discretion and eligibility

Basic economic social assistance is a general scheme to which all of Norway's legal residents have a right.[11] Economic social assistance is a tax-free net benefit that is means-tested and granted by local authorities according to need in order to meet the basic costs of living. The high degree of local autonomy in setting benefit levels and conditions, dealing with complaints and providing activation, however, is recognised as a factor that has prevented the 'modernisation' of social assistance in Norway during the last half century (Terum, 1996; Lødemel, 1997a). These features have arguably prevented a shift to a system based on predictable and stable standards.

Similar to the UK until the 2000s and to China, India and Pakistan today (see Chapters Two, Three and Six, this volume), Norwegian social assistance is subject to a discretionary household means test. In the case of Norway, the means test is administered by the same caseworker counselling the claimant and this is significant to the claimant–caseworker interaction. One respondent described feeling "categorised" when he had applied for his benefit cheque, noting that he had had to "play a role" for his caseworker in order to be judged worthy of receiving assistance, suggesting that he was expected to look "pitiful" in order to be judged worthy of receiving help. Accessing his benefits meant demeaning himself in order to fit into institutional expectations of what it was to be a claimant. Another spoke of his reluctance to claim social assistance for fear he would have to sell his car and apartment in order to pass the means test, actions he felt would make life more difficult for his family (Gubrium and Lødemel, 2014). In general, respondents described how the determination of eligibility for the benefit had meant either emphasising that they were already living in vastly reduced circumstances or being forced to reduce their living conditions to near subsistence levels.

While the distinction between the deserving and the undeserving has long been reflected within Norwegian social assistance policy language, the Social Care Act 1964 (*Lov om sosial omsorg*), replacing the Poor Law, echoed the related idea of free choice and responsibility in its 'help to self-help' philosophy. Since 1964, the primary rhetorical focus in social assistance has been reducing dependency on the welfare state through the work approach. The early 1990s explicitly introduced the idea of distinctions made based on acceptable *need* (LOV-1991-12-13 nr 81a; Lødemel, 2001).

Since the introduction of the Qualification Programme in 2007, a further distinction within social assistance has been made through the creation of new tiers based largely on claimant employability. The Programme is targeted towards long-term social assistance claimants. It is aimed at claimants who have been judged as having severely reduced work and income ability. Yet a further eligibility criterion specifies that claimants must also possess a level of ability such that the Programme may be helpful in strengthening the possibility for participation in work life (White Paper nr 9, 2006-07, pp 34, 224). These vague and seemingly contradictory criteria have meant that their application in decision-making has varied according to the particular priorities and resources of local NAV offices (Naper, 2010). Caseworkers use the idea of employability to discretionarily divide claimants into two groups: those who are eligible to participate in the Qualification Programme and those who are not. Thus, in reality, access for claimants is more a luck of the draw than a real judgement on their ability to work.

Nonetheless, given the mix of a society that places strong emphasis on work and the complex and varied challenges faced by many of Norway's long-term social assistance claimants (Wel et al, 2006; Naper et al, 2009), the overwhelming focus on employability is likely to result in heightened shame for many of those claimants who are not deemed eligible for the new opportunities attached to the Qualification Programme. Respondents associated Programme access with their inherent employability. Those who were not eligible described a heightened sense of inadequacy and shame linked to their challenging situation. One respondent, for example, described his frustration and confusion over his rejected application. He described his long history of work experience and his current desire for a "normal job" and a "normal life", yet suggested that he had not been selected because his caseworker had felt he "wasn't qualified". He described a sense of disappointment in the fact that he would soon be placed in an unpaid position on a municipal manual labour team. His frequent emphasis on his willingness to work suggested that he understood this decision as a judgement on his moral character and his current situation.

Conditionality

Along with means-testing, the placement of conditions attached to the receipt of economic social assistance has traditionally been a part of the dis/incentive-based calculus applied to prevent long-term dependency on benefits. An early version of this approach was seen in the Social Care Act 1964, which focused on the 'rights and duties' of claimants. The Social Services Act 1991 made this principle explicit. Municipal social workers were encouraged to require claimants to participate in work-seeking activities, training or skills-building measures in exchange for benefits. For claimants on regular social assistance today, these activities remain largely unchanged from the 'work in exchange for benefit, *quid pro quo*' arrangements that began within local municipalities in the early 1990s (Dahl, 2003; Harsløf, 2008; Lødemel, 1997b).

While the specific strategies attached to Norway's work approach to social assistance have changed, the assumptions lying behind the approach remain the same. The Qualification Programme has explicitly codified a requirement that has merely been encouraged within the realm of basic social assistance since the early 1990s. The new rights and responsibilities attached to Programme participation are intended to both pressure and motivate those people 'in danger of entering a passive situation' (White Paper nr 9, 2006-07, p 224) into work. This strategy is predicated on ideas associated with paternalism and communitarianism. Claimants must receive the right mix of incentives to be motivated to enter the workforce. In doing so, they become full social participants. At the same time, they must receive the sufficient disincentives to dissuade them from staying on social assistance. An earlier national pilot study of active labour market programmes with long-term social assistance recipients had reported the mismatch between the strategies applied and the particular target group in focus (Lødemel and Johannessen, 2005). Furthermore, the presumption that claimants must be properly motivated stands in contrast to the descriptions of our respondents. Each and every one of the claimants we spoke with emphasised a keen desire to either work or to make the necessary life changes to eventually move into work. They linked the fact that they did not have the jobs that they wanted and were expected to have with a lowered self-image. One respondent expressed frustration at the meaningless and unpaid task she had been assigned of spooling thread at a factory, noting that what had been described by her caseworker as a form of therapy was really nothing more than "grunt work" and an exercise in boredom and irritation. Several others strove to hide their lack of employment from friends and loved ones due to the embarrassment and shame they felt. Respondents frequently linked their inability to access real job opportunities to a sense of frustration and hopelessness. Another respondent described his long and unsuccessful search for work, concluding that he had "given up", felt "completely empty" and did not "care any longer". The work approach had heightened his alienation from mainstream society (Gubrium and Lødemel, 2014).

Yet social assistance and the Qualification Programme apply the idea of conditionality in crucially differing ways. The focus on new duties attending engagement with the Qualification Programme have been met with new rights for participants in the form of higher, regular and standardised benefits, a broader programmatic offering and close caseworker follow-up (Odelstings Prop nr 70, 2006-07). Respondents who were engaged in the Programme were, on the whole, fairly positive about the presence of activity requirements as these were accompanied by a strong institutional mantra that they were moving towards regular, wage-earning employment (Gubrium, 2013b). Forward movement was represented to respondents in the motivational courses and internships offered through the Programme, and through higher expectations on the part of their caseworkers. One respondent noted that it was the "first time" he had noticed "any interest" in helping him to "find the right direction" (Gubrium and Lødemel, 2014). It is perhaps not surprising that respondents were positive about this activity requirement given the overwhelming focus on employment in the Norwegian welfare system and the strong work ethic dominating Norwegian society at large.

There is a mismatch, however, between the Programme's overall target group and its work-related aims. Indeed, policy-makers have been critiqued by the front-line professionals who work with social assistance claimants for the oversimplified assumption that individually targeted incentives and sanctions are the appropriate stimuli to move claimants into work, as well as for their failure to recognise the larger structural challenges claimants face (NTL, 2007). Another study has even reported concerns that the heightened focus on goals and quick solutions as opposed to more long-term holistic approaches may harm those claimants with complex and comprehensive needs (Røysum, 2012). Norway's welfare directorate has itself acknowledged professional reluctance to encourage Programme participation, suggesting that this may reflect a perceived mismatch between the target group and the programme's heavy work focus (NAV Directorate, 2012). The professionally perceived need for a more flexible approach has been

2006-07, p 12), Programme participants receive a benefit that follows the rules that pertain to ordinary income. As opposed to tax-free, non-pension-accruing social assistance benefits, the Programme benefit is taxable and counts towards the accrual of a normal pension. These features allow participants better 'security' in the short term and 'predictability' in the long term (Odelstings Prop nr 70, 2006-07, p 38; White Paper nr 9, 2006-07, p 229). While partly emphasising the individual recipient's duty to participate in and contribute more fully to society, the logistical requirements of the Qualification Programme also simulate the contours of ordinary work life, and participants engage in full-time activity on a year-long basis (White Paper nr 9, 2006-07, p 226). Furthermore, claimants engaged in the Programme receive the same holiday and leave privileges as regular wage-earning workers (Odelstings Prop nr 70, 2006-07). Finally, unlike the basic social assistance benefit, the Programme benefit is paid out by the local municipality's pay office rather than by the local welfare office.

Respondents described how these features gave them a new sense of dignity. They contrasted their identities and the expectations facing them as basic social assistance recipients with those they experienced as participants in the Qualification Programme. Many described the sense of shame they felt from peers and society in connection with claiming social assistance. Their status as social assistance claimants was demeaning: not only did they feel that society viewed them as lazy and dependent "leeches", but they also felt placed close to the bottom of welfare system hierarchy, noting their discomfort with being placed alongside people facing difficult times such as drug users, single parents and immigrants. One respondent emphasised the "shame" she continuously felt within this institutional context, describing herself as a "burden for other people". As another described it, "you have everything stolen from you; you're not a participant in society". Respondents noted that the sense of failure for not living up to their own expectations they already felt was compounded by being made to feel insignificant and inferior in the eyes of the welfare institutions from which they received support (Gubrium and Lødemel, 2014).

Respondents' sense of internalised failure and shame was supported by the paternalistic public discourse that surrounded social assistance. The duty-focused call for social assistance claimants to 'get up in the morning' has been reflected in the notion that following the Programme's prescribed activities will enable participants to begin to reclaim full social citizenship. This notion was strongly expressed by these individuals we spoke with who were economically secure and not receiving benefits. There was a general idea that labour activation would teach claimants 'the value of contribution' and to become 'active participants' (Gubrium, 2014). Indeed, for those respondents engaged in the Qualification Programme, these features were a crucial element in what they characterised as a move toward "normal". One respondent described the importance of the normalising features of the Programme, noting that the "job feeling" he received as a Programme participant made him feel that he was someone who was "contributing back to society". This had allowed him to begin to gain self-confidence and the courage to "move ahead". Many respondents echoed the notion that these features had played a crucial role in the path towards feeling better about themselves? (Gubrium and Lødemel, 2014).

Implications and recommendations

There is resounding evidence that the conversation begun 15 years ago, tying the residual nature of social assistance in Norway with stigma and shame, still bears serious consideration within the realms of policy-making and practice alike. Norway's social assistance scheme has had a residual role operating underneath a broader, more generous system of welfare provision, leaving fewer vulnerable groups within the scheme itself. Over time, group after group of 'deserving' claimants have been lifted out of this tier to be served by more rights-based social security-type benefits. This is arguably what has more recently happened with regard to those social assistance claimants who have *potentially* had the ability to work and who have been deemed eligible for the Qualification Programme. Our conversations with claimants suggest that the new possibilities tied to the Programme have improved the dignity of those who have been able to access and benefit from them.[12] Yet the presence of new possibilities for *some* has heightened the shame of the many claimants who remain on regular social assistance or for those who have not found work through participation and who must return the scheme.

The social division of welfare that existed before the Qualification Programme was the product of distinctions made based on acceptable *need*. With this new offering, however, the delineation of 'deserving' versus 'undeserving' has been shifted to one's ability to fully participate in *work*. This newly placed institutional distinction heightened the shame felt by our respondents concerning their identities as social assistance claimants. Claimants were blamed for not "playing by the rules". They focused on their own personal failings as related to their inability to find long-lasting, paid work. The shame they felt was mirrored, and perhaps heightened by, clear public and policy-making rhetoric that placed blame and responsibility for economic difficulties at the individual level.

Institutionalised and individualised notions of responsibility and deservingness in Norway date back to the Poor Law era. These notions remained with the 'help to self-help' philosophy of the Social Care Act 1964. They were heightened with the introduction of an explicit conditionality 30 years later premised on a claimant's ability to enter the labour market. Applying a macro lens, Norway's heightened work approach for social assistance claimants since 2007 can be seen as a part of the broader move towards the re/commodification of this Social Democratic welfare state (Esping-Andersen, 1990). On the more personal level suggested by our low-income respondents, the punishment for not qualifying for or attaining employment is to be left on the lowest, residual tier of a mostly generous welfare system hierarchy. This marginalised identity is often a matter of shame, personal failing and hopelessness.

The Qualification Programme has been praised at the international level for its potentially successful approach to the alleviation of social exclusion. Political rhetoric has largely focused on the Programme's provision of new rights and possibilities for eligible claimants. Indeed, the presence of the Qualification Programme has led to new rights for some claimants in the form of increased predictability and security, increased opportunities, increased social contribution and closer attention from caseworkers. Some of our respondents mirrored this enthusiasm, and described how moving into the mainstream welfare system had resulted in a new sense of motivation and self-assurance. Yet whether a programme or policy heightens shame or builds dignity depends on the particular location of the individual targeted. What is perceived as a new opportunity and a move forward for the few claimants who enter the Programme and ultimately succeed in finding employment might, by the very nature of a status hierarchy, be experienced as shaming for the majority of claimants who remain on or return to the residual tier. The findings from preliminary evaluation reports and the experiences of a majority of our respondents suggest that a move forward may be a short-lived experience even for those claimants selected for Programme participation. For the many claimants who face difficulties in working or finding work, it has introduced a new tier in which the capacity for the shaming and de-motivation of those who do not make the cut has become markedly higher. For many, having "failed again" – with a return to social assistance and an accompanying loss of economic and social rights – may heighten a sense of demoralisation.

Norway has led the way in applying a work approach to minimum protection claimants (Lødemel and Moreira, 2014). This is perhaps not surprising as the country's generous and tax-based welfare provisions are predicated, in large part, on the maintenance of high employment. Indeed, it is reasonable to expect that some effort be made to make accommodations for those individuals who are able to work. Norway's work-oriented culture also means that having a job is not just a matter of economic security. In a social sense, it is a primary arena for attaining the dignity associated with social normalisation. Most of our respondents described wanting to find work as soon as possible, equalising employment with full social participation. Given these findings, it is not the work approach, per se, that is at the heart of claimant shaming: it is the tendency to place an overwhelming focus on the individually 'challenged' claimant. It is the assumption that individual claimants 'choose' not to work, and thus need merely to be properly motivated in order to enter the labour market. As one economically secure respondent argued, perhaps policy-makers in wealthy Norway could afford to "think bigger".

Thinking bigger about the realities that claimants face, with an aim to move claimants into a realm in which they feel 'normal', secure, and recognised by the larger system, might begin the move towards an anti-poverty policy framework based on dignity. The Poor Law-reminiscent effort to weed out the undeserving claimant from the deserving does not appear to be effective at the macroeconomic or personal level. These shame-inducing distinctions would be reduced given a rate and format of economic support for basic social assistance that mirrored those used in the Qualification Programme. We recommend a state index-based, guaranteed, minimum basic social assistance benefit that is based on a national standard for a reasonable household budget. This sort of benefit would minimise the challenges and frustrations experienced by this marginalised group of claimants. Respondents in the Qualification Programme suggested that, above a certain threshold that allowed them to meet local sociocultural norms in a material sense, it was the predictability of their benefit as much as the benefit level that had served to reduce the economic and psychological anxiety that they felt. Consideration should also be given to the format of the benefit to maximise claimants' sense of social and civic participation. It was the 'whole package' of a clearer right to benefit, paid as a public sector salary, with salary-deduced rights, that provided respondents with a sense of normality and dignity. This design enabled a new sense of opportunity, hope and motivation.

Many of the respondents who were engaged in the Qualification Programme contrasted their social expectations and activities as participants with the low expectations and lack of daily structure they had experienced when claiming basic social assistance. What many found most motivating was both the availability of something meaningful to do with their time and the existence of a higher set of expectations from others and for themselves. The current opportunity of work training via internships may be useful for those claimants with the ability and skills to gain and maintain employment. Preliminary evaluations of the Programme suggest that the strategy of moving participants into work has been a potentially effective strategy, but only insofar as tasks have been shaped to the ability of the participant and only if institutional follow-up has occurred to ensure the transition of participants to longer-term work (Schafft and Spjelkavik, 2011; Djuve and Latif Sandbæk, 2012). Respondent experiences reinforce these findings. For many, engaging in internships was effective only for the short term. Many described a sense of longer-term despair and shame given inadequate regulation and enforcement on the part of the welfare administration and policy-makers to match and move them more permanently into wage-earning positions.

The overwhelmingly 'supply-side' focus on using incentives to motivate claimants to enter the labour market has resulted in the individualisation of challenges that may really lie at the system level (Djuve and Latif Sandbæk, 2012). 'Thinking bigger' may include a turn to demand-side strategies to make the labour market more welcoming to individuals with reduced working capacity or lacking broad employment experience. Provisions subsidising the continued employment of Programme interns through employer 'benefits' would encourage the broader labour market and individual employers to meet claimants half way. This is a promising strategy to ensure that Programme participants do not remain an easily exploited workforce.

Finally, building claimant dignity would mean taking serious recognition of their varying needs and goals. It would include awareness on the part of policy-makers and the public alike that what the disparate groups making up social assistance *share* is not a lack of motivation or an inherent sense of passivity. What they share is that they receive low incomes, are not fully employed, are often socially marginalised and, according to our respondents, would prefer to move ahead into 'normal' society. A dignity-building framework for Norwegian policy-making should incorporate this understanding into the policy-making process.

Notes

[1] According to the Organisation for Economic Co-operation and Development (OECD) definition of poverty below 50 per cent median income, 5.7 per cent of the total Norwegian population lived under this threshold (2009 figures) (Normann, 2011).

[2] According to Statistics Norway (2010 figures), social assistance claimants make up 2.5 per cent of Norway's population. Of this group, 39.6 per cent have received social assistance for six months or longer per year and are considered long-term recipients (www.ssb.no/sosind/tab-2011-12-05-07. html).

[3] The British Poor Law of 1834 largely influenced Norway's Poor Law of 1845. It was characterised by a level of benefits balanced between the interests of providing enough assistance to afford basic subsistence, but not enough so as to de-motivate claimants from seeking work or seeking help from private arenas (Lødemel, 1997a, p 149).

[4] Its most recently reported Gini coefficient is 0.245 (Statistics Norway, 2010).

[5] In the decades after the Second World War Norway experienced greater levels of central economic planning and progressive taxation. There was also a gradual expansion of the Norwegian welfare state and a decrease in the share of top incomes. The change in direction came at the same time as the reform of income taxation in 1992. The income share of the top 1 per cent of the Norwegian population more than doubled between 1992 and 2007, with the rise since the end of the 1980s reversing the decline that took place within the previous 40 years (Aaberge and Atkinson, 2008, pp 8-9).

[6] Compared across Europe and as measured in purchasing power parities (PPP). However, as there is no national standard for the determination of benefit levels, they vary widely (Brandtzæg et al, 2006), and accurate comparison is, therefore, difficult (Bradshaw and Terum, 1997; Kazepov, 2010; Kuivalainen and Nelson, 2010).

[7] Within the past three decades, a shift in the demographics of social assistance has taken place, and its ranks are largely made up of single parents, single people under the age of 35, unemployed non-Western immigrants, the long-term unemployed and individuals beset by a complex array of physical, substance abuse and mental health issues (Wel et al, 2006; Halvorsen and Stjernø, 2008; Naper et al, 2009; Hagen and Lødemel, 2010).

[8] Until the mid-2000s, Norway's labour market and welfare administration was the responsibility of three institutions: the Public Employment Service was responsible for public employment services and benefits to 'ordinary' jobseekers and people with work-related disabilities; the National Insurance Service managed benefits for people both within and outside the labour force, and was responsible for a range of services in relation to work and rehabilitation, family and pensions, and health-related benefits; and social assistance benefit provision was the responsibility of the local social welfare services, which was managed at the level of individual municipalities.

[9] The Programme was modelled after a precursor national programme aimed at non-Western immigrants, Norway's 2004 Introduction Programme.

[10] Earmarked national funding specifically for the Qualification Programme, along with tight internal controls and reporting, allowed Norway's Labour and Welfare Administration (NAV) to show action in its early years. Since the start-up phase from 2007-10, however, national funding has moved toward block grant funding and this change has since seen a marked reduction in the number of Programme participants at the municipal level, with tougher criteria applied for eligibility and municipalities placing higher funding priority on other areas (NAV Directorate, 2012).

[11] Furthermore, unregistered residents have a right to 'acute help' in the form of cash or emergency medical assistance.

[12] Claimant experiences with labour activation may, however, depend on a host of biographical and social particulars (see Gubrium, 2013b).

References

Aaberge. R. and Atkinson, A.B. (2008) *Top incomes in Norway*, Statistics Norway Discussion Paper no 552. Oslo: Statistics Norway.

Aasheim, A. (2009) 'Usle kommuner', *Dagbladet*, 27 August.

Andersen, K. (2006) 'Fattig midt i rikdommen', *Aftenposten Morgen*, 27 February, Commentary.

Angelin, A. (2009) 'Den Dubbla Vanmaktens Logik', Lund dissertation in Social Work, Lund: University of Lund.

Baldwin, P. (1990) *The politics of social solidarity*, New York: Cambridge University Press.

Bradshaw, J.R. and Terum, L.I. (1997) 'How Nordic is the Nordic model? Social assistance in a comparative perspective', *Scandinavian Journal of Social Welfare*, vol 6, pp 247-56.

Brandtzæg, B., Flermoen, S., Lunder, T.E., Løyland, K., Møller, G. and Sannes, J. (2006) *Fastsetting av satser, utmåling av økonomisk sosialhjelp og viklårsbruk I sosialtjenesten*, no 232, Bø: Telemarksforskning.

Christiansen, N.F and. Markkola, P. (2006) 'Introduction', in N.F. Christiansen, K. Petersen, N. Edling and P. Haave (eds) *The Nordic model of welfare: A historical reappraisal*, Copenhagen: Museum Tusculanum Press, pp 9-29.

Dahl, E. (2003) 'Does "workfare" work? The Norwegian experience', *International Journal of Social Welfare*, vol 12, pp 274-88.

Djuve, A.B. and Latif Sandbæk, M. (2012) *Fortellinger om motivasjon: Hva er gode arbeidsmetoder i NAVs AMO-kurs for innvandrere?*, Fafo-rapport 2012:27, Oslo: Fafo.

Djuve, A.B., Nielsen, R.A. and Strand, A.H. (2012) *Kvalifiseringsprogrammet og sosialhjelpsutgiftene*, Fafo-rapport 2012:63, Oslo: Fafo.

Duffy, K. (2010) 'Active inclusion: a comprehensive strategy for poverty reduction?', in D. Ben-Galim and A. Sachradja (eds) *Now it's personal: Learning from welfare-to-work approaches around the world*, IPPR Report, August, London: IPPR.

Editor, *Aftenposten Morgen* (2004) 'Fattigdom som politisk kasteball', *Aftenposten Morgen*, 14 September.

Esping-Andersen, G. (1990) *The three worlds of welfare capitalism*, Cambridge: Polity Press.

Esping-Andersen, G. (2000) 'The sustainability of welfare states into the twenty-first century', *International Journal of Health Services*, vol 30, no 1, pp 1-12.

Frønes, I. (2001) 'Skam, skyld og ære i det moderne', in T. Wyller (ed) *Perspektiver på skam, ære og skamløshet i det moderne*, Bergen: Fagbokforlaget.

Gjerstad, T. (2005) 'Jeg vil være nådeløs mot dem som nekter å skrive under på en ... velferdskontrakt', *Dagbladet*, 11 November.

Gubrium, E.K. (2013a) 'Poverty, shame and the class journey in public imagination', *Distinktion: The Scandinavian Journal of Social Theory*.

Gubrium, E.K. (2013b) 'Participant meaning-making along the work trajectory of a labour activation programme', in J.F. Gubrium and M. Järvinen (eds) *Turning troubles into problems: Clientization in human services*, London: Routledge, pp 137-154.

Gubrium, E.K. (2014, forthcoming) '"No one should be poor": Social shaming in Norway', in E. Chase and G. Bantebya Kyomuhendo (eds) *The shame of poverty: Global experiences*, Oxford: Oxford University Press.

Gubrium, E.K. and Lødemel, I. (2014, forthcoming) '(Relative) poverty in a rich welfare state: Experiences from Norway', in E. Chase and G. Bantebya Kyomuhendo (eds) *The shame of poverty: Global experiences*, Oxford: Oxford University Press.

Gubrium, E.K., Harsløf, I. and Lødemel, I. (2014, forthcoming) 'Norwegian activation reform on a wave of wider welfare state change: A critical assessment', in I. Lødemel and A. Moreira (eds) *'Workfare revisited.' The political economy of activation reforms*, New York: Oxford University Press.

Hagen, K. and Lødemel, I. (2010) 'Fattigdomstiåret 2000-2010: Parentes eller ny kurs for velferdsstaten?', in I. Frønes and L. Kjølsrød (eds) *Det Norske Samfunn*, Oslo: Gylendal Akademisk, pp 284-307.

Halvorsen, K. and Stjernø, S. (2008) *Work, oil and welfare*, Oslo: Universitetsforlaget.

Harsløf, I. (2008) *Conditionality in Norwegian welfare policies*, Policy Exchange Report, April, London: Policy Exchange.

Hatland, A. (1992) *Til Dem Som Trenger det Mest?*, Oslo: Universitetsforlaget.

Hatland, A. (2007) 'Velferdsrettigheter – et styringsmiddel under press', *Tidsskrift for Velferdsforskning*, vol 10, no 4, pp 208-20.

Hatland, A. and Pedersen, A.W. (2006) 'Er sosialhjelpen et effektivt virkemidler i fattigdomsbekjemplelsen?', *Tidsskrift for Velferdsforskning*, vol 9, no 2, pp 58-72.

Herland H.N. (2007) 'Unødig sutring om Norge', *Aftenposten*, 7 June.

Hvinden, B. (1994) *Divided against itself: A study of integration in welfare bureaucracy*, Oslo: Universitetsforlaget.

Jönsson, L.R. (2002) 'Stigma och skam', *Nordisk Sosialt Arbeid*, vol 3, pp 153-60.

Jönsson, L.R. and Starrin, B. (2000) 'Economi-skam modellen och reaktioner på arbetslöshet', *Socialvetenskaplig Tidskrift*, vol 3, pp 267-84.

Kazepov, Y. (ed) (2010) *Rescaling social policies towards multilevel governance in Europe*, Aldershot: Ashgate.

Kuhnle, S. (1994a) 'Norge I møte med Europa', in A. Hatland, S. Kuhnle and T.I. Romøren (eds) *Den Norske Velferdsstaten*, Oslo: Gyldendal, Chapter 4.

Kuhnle, S. (1994b) 'Velferdstatens idegrunnlag i perspektiv', in A. Hatland, S. Kuhnle and T.I. Romøren (eds) *Den Norske Velferdsstaten*, Oslo: Gyldendal, Chapter 1.

Kuivalainen, S. and Nelson, K. (2010) *The Nordic welfare model in a European perspective*, Work Report, Institute for Future Studies 2010:11. Stockholm: Institute for Future Studies.

Lødemel, I. (1997a) *The welfare paradox*, Oslo: Scandinavian University Press.

Lødemel, I. (1997b) *Pisken i arbeidslinjen*, Fafo Institute for Labour and Social Research, Report no 226, Oslo: Fafo.

Lødemel, I. (2001) 'Discussion: Workfare in the welfare state', in I. Lødemel and H. Trickey (eds) *'An offer you can't refuse': Workfare in international perspective*, Bristol: Policy Press, pp 295-343.

Lødemel, I. and Johannessen, A. (2005) *Tiltaksforsøket: mot en inkluderende arbeidslinje?*, HiO-report no 1, Oslo: HiO.

Lødemel, I. and Moreira, A. (eds) (2014, forthcoming) *'Workfare revisited.' The political economy of activation reforms*, New York: Oxford University Press.

Lødemel, I. and Trickey, H. (2001) *'An offer you can't refuse': Workfare in international perspective*, Bristol: Policy Press.

Lødemel, I., Dahl, E. and Drøpping, J.A. (2001) *Social policies in Norway: Processes, structures, and implementation mechanisms*, New York: UN Economic and Social Commission for Western Asia.

LOV-1991-12-13 nr 81a: *Lov om sosiale tjenester/sosialtjenesteloven*.

Malmberg-Heimonen, I. (2008) 'Sosial tillit blant langtidsmotakkere av sosialhjelp: betydelsen av fattigdom og oppvekstvilkår', in I. Harsløf and S. Seim (eds) *Fattigdoms dynamikk*, Oslo: Universitetsforlaget, pp 135-44.

Malmberg-Heimonen, I. (2009) 'The social capital and mental health of long-term social assistance recipients in Norway', *European Journal of Social Work*, vol 13, no 1, pp 91-107.

Marshall, T.H. (1950) 'Citizenship and social class', reprinted in T.H. Marshall and T. Bottomore (1992) *Citizenship and social class*, London: Pluto Press.

NAV Directorate (2011) *Sluttarapport: Implementering av kvalifersering sprogrammet 2007-2010* [*Final report: Implementation of the Qualification Program*], Oslo.

NAV Directorate (2012) *Fattigdom og levekår i Norge – Status 2012*, Rapport 1/2012.

Naper, S.O. (2010) 'Kvalifiseringsprogrammets deltakere: Hvor lang er avstanden til arbeidsmarkedet?', *Arbeid og velferd*, no 3.

Naper, S.O., van der Wel, K. And Halvorsen, K. (2009) 'Arbeidsmarginalisering og fattigdom blant langtidsmottakere av sosialhjelp i 1990 og 2005', in I. Harsløf and S. Seim (eds) *Fattigdoms dynamik: Perspektiver på marginalisering i det norske samfunnet*, Oslo: Universitetsforlaget, pp 80-110.

Normann, T.M. (2011) *Materielle og sosiale mangler. Utslag av fattigdom*, Rapporter 28/2011: SSB. Oslo: Statistics Norway.

NTL (Norsktjenestemannslag) (2007) Hearing response concerning the Qualification Program with regard to the support in the new chapter 5A in the Social Services Act, 29 March, Oslo.

Odelstings Proposition nr 70 (2006-07) *Om lov om endringer I sosialtjenesteloven*, Oslo: Norwegian Ministry of Labour and Inclusion.

Øverbye, E. (2003) 'Globalisation and the design of the welfare state', in D. Pieters (ed) *European social security and global politics*, The Hague: Kluwer, pp 145-166.

Parliamentary Response nr 148 (2006-07) *Innstilling fra arbeids- og sosialkomiteen om St meld nr 9 (2006-07), arbeid, velferd og inkludering*, Storting Committee on Labour and Social Affairs.

Prins, R. (2009) *Synthesis report: Developing well targeted tools for the active inclusion of vulnerable people*, Norway, 29-30 October, ASTRI Research and Consultancy Group (www.peer-review-social-inclusion.eu).

Reegård, K. (2009) 'Historien om NAV-reformens unfangelse', in B.R. Nuland, B.S. Tranøy and J. Christensen (eds) *Hjernen er alene: Institusjonalisering, kvalitet og relevans i norsk velferdsforskning*, Oslo, Universitetsforlaget, pp 247-62.

Røysum, A. (2012) 'The reform of the welfare services in Norway: One office – one way of thinking?', *European Journal of Social Work* (iFirst version), pp 1-16.

Schafft, A. and Spjelkavik, Ø. (2011) 'Kvalifiseringsprogrammet – sosialklientenes vei til arbeidslivet?', in T.A. Andreassen and K. Fossestøl (eds) *NAV ved et Veiskille*, Olso: Gyldendal, pp 127-47.

Seip, A-L. (1981) *Om Velferdsstatens Fremvekst*, Oslo: Universitetsforlaget.

Skårderud, F. (2001) 'Tapte ansikter. Introduksjon til en skampsykologi', in T. Wyller (ed) *Perspektiver på Skam, Ære og Skamløshet i det Moderne*, Bergen: Fagbokforlaget, pp 37-52.

Statistics Norway (2010) *Inntektsstatistikk for Husholdninger* (Income Statistics of Households), Oslo: Statistics Norway.

Stoltenberg, J., Halvorsen, K. and Haga, Å. (2006) 'De neste 100 dagene', *Dagbladet*, 25 January.

Terum, L.I. (1996) *Grenser for Sosialpolitisk Modernisering*, Oslo: Universitetsforlaget.

Titmuss, R.M. (1974) *Social policy: An introduction*, New York: Pantheon Books.

Underlid, K. (2005) 'Poverty and experiences of social devaluation: A qualitative interview study of 25 long-standing recipients of social security payments', *Scandinavian Journal of Psychology*, vol 46, pp 273-83.

Underlid, K. (2007) 'Poverty and experiences of insecurity. A qualitative interview study of 25 long-standing recipients of social security', *International Journal of Social Welfare*, vol 16, pp 65-74.

van der Wel, K., Dahl, E., Lødemel, I., Løyland, B., Naper, S.O. and Slagsvoldet, M. (2006) *Funksjonsevne blant Langtidsmottakere av Sosialhjelp*, Oslo: HiO.

White Paper nr 6 (2002–03) *Action plan against poverty*, Oslo: Norwegian Ministry of Social Affairs.

White Paper nr 9 (2006–07) *Work, welfare, and inclusion*, Oslo: Norwegian Ministry of Labour and Inclusion.

Wiborg, Ø.N. and Hansen, M.N. (2009) 'Change over time in the intergenerational transmission of social disadvantage', *European Sociological Review*, vol 25, pp 379-94.

World Bank, The (2011) *World Development Indicators database* (http://data.worldbank.org/data-catalog/world-development-indicators/wdi-2011).

SIX

Pakistan: a journey of poverty-induced shame

Sohail Choudhry

Introduction

A federal parliamentary republic of over 180 million people, Pakistan has the sixth largest population and 27th largest gross domestic product (GDP) purchasing power parity (PPP) in the world (IMF, 2012). However, its multidimensional poverty headcount stands at 49.4 per cent and it ranks 145th on the Human Development Index (OPHI, 2011; UN, 2011). Although the responsibility for policy theoretically rests with the Cabinet and individual ministers, because of a feeble and erratic democracy, it is often senior civil servants who assume the central roles in the conception, framing and delivery of policies.

This chapter begins by tracing the evolution of anti-poverty policy in Pakistan over the last 66 years to understand its role in the poverty–shame nexus. It then goes on to consider the specific psychosocial impact on beneficiaries of Pakistan's two largest ongoing cash assistance programmes, Zakat and the Benazir Income Support Programme (BISP). Research involving interviews with adults and children living in poverty and with those in economically stable positions, including nine parliamentarians (Choudhry, 2014a, 2014b, 2014c), largely supported a connection between poverty and shame (see Smith, 1776; Sen, 1983) and also suggested that shame may be largely influenced by relevant state policies. In order to investigate this finding more closely, an in-depth analysis of anti-poverty policies in Pakistan from the start of independence in 1947 until the present day was carried out. Within this time frame, a closer focus was reserved for the most recent five years, encompassing government policies introduced in the post-Musharraf era.

Historical framework: the evolution of inequality and the space for poverty-related shame

Historically, concepts such as dignity, pride and self-respect in Pakistan derive from collective religious, political and cultural traditions. Muslim minority rule over India for almost 800 years, for example, injected a certain communal pride among them that was instrumental in the demand for a separate homeland at the time of the British departure in 1947. M.A. Jinnah, the founding father of Pakistan, made a broadcast to the people of Australia on 19 February 1948 and described the collective identity of the nation in terms of 'all equal in rights, dignity and self-respect' (Dawn Archives, 2001). On the ground, however, the reality of being 'equal' was intricately rooted in a past that was hugely influenced, socially and economically, by political allegiances formed during the colonial era and by migration outcomes at the time of India's division.

Before the 19th century, there were no rights to land ownership in the areas that later became Pakistan. Instead, most farmers and peasants, under the auspices of state or tribal chiefs, cultivated tracts of land large enough to support their family. However, it was the new land tenure system of the British colonial government in the 20th century that created a system of formal land ownership by authorising the government to grant large strips of land to selected subjects of the Crown (Raulet, 1976). Over time, this policy intensified inequalities of land ownership between the more and less favoured. At the time of partition, a mass migration along religious lines between India and Pakistan also proved advantageous for the Muslim landlords on the Pakistani side of the border. Using their political and social power, they brought the abandoned land of fleeing Hindus under their control. These developments generated class divisions and inequality, even before a regular 'Pakistani policy regime' came into place. By the early 1950s, 3 per cent of the rural elite in Pakistan owned 70 per cent of all rural land (Saeed, 1982). A strong peasantry system helped these landlords acquire political electability and monopolise the corridors of power. With political power, these feudal elites, especially those belonging to the canal districts of Punjab, drew further benefit from the green revolution of the late 1950 and 1960s (Alavi, 1983). The later story of social classes, poverty and shame in rural Pakistan, by and large, is the story of this early disparity in asset distribution.

On the urban front, the industrial capitalists benefited from powerful economic incentives in the 1950s, including tax concessions and subsidies (Gardezi and Rashid, 1983). These policies helped to create the new urban capitalist elite, dependent on state patronage for survival and growth. The reduction of direct taxes on the wealthy led to the burden of indirect taxation falling heaviest on those already in poverty. The unscrupulous acquisition of land, power and patronage sowed the first seeds of resentment among the masses against the elites. With few political resources, Pakistan's 1960s military regime relied heavily on senior civil servants to follow a 'pro-growth sector policy' with little emphasis on redistribution and social protection. The national government teamed up with the powerful capitalist elite to devise policies aimed at macroeconomic growth through a number of pro-capitalist concessions, export vouchers, industrial incentives, tax holidays and other protective measures. Over time, these policies proved counterproductive by relinquishing a large portion of potential tax revenue that could have provided relief to low-income groups and taking pressure off the industrial elite to diversify into high-value products (Hussain, 2004). In the following years, this weakened the global competitiveness of exports and the market's ability to provide a sustainable livelihood for workers. Throughout the 1960s inequality increased and class distinctions sharpened, accompanied by inflation and pressure on foreign exchange.

By the end of the 1960s, inflation and inequality had already mobilised un-paralleled support for the ideal of a socialist economy championed by Z.A. Bhutto, who came to power in 1970 with a landslide majority in West Pakistan (now Pakistan). Prime Minister Bhutto favoured a mixed democratic economy aiming to gradually shift from capitalism to socialism (Gardezi and Rashid, 1983). The landslide victory of his Party under the slogan of 'bread, clothing and shelter' (*roti, kapra aur makan*) not only demonstrated the people's demand for these basic needs to be met by the state, but also created a new civic awareness of rights and welfare expectations. A review of native Urdu literature (Choudhry, 2014a) suggests that progressive intellectuals and socialist movements of the time also reinforced the negative public perception of rich elites, condemning them as shameless usurpers of national resources and exploiters of public trust and resources.

On the back of widespread public support, the Bhutto regime nationalised 31 big industrial units and introduced progressive taxation. While the state also attempted to expand welfare through the development of a larger public sector and the initiation of new social protection programmes, neither could fully bear fruit in the wake of the catastrophic economic cost of past political indiscretions. Domestically, the elitist reforms of the previous two decades had concentrated the national wealth in a few private hands unwilling to give back to the state in the form of taxes paid. The impulsive nationalisation of industry too backfired as it impeded new investment, gradually resulting in lower economic growth and higher unemployment, thus necessitating the expansion of the public sector for the political government (Hussain, 2004). Separation of East Pakistan (Bangladesh) in 1970 also opened up severe gaps in the commodity market, foreign exchange and export. As capital-intensive manufacturing became increasingly uncompetitive, the amount of debt to be paid internationally doubled, leaving little fiscal space for development and social protection initiatives. In subsequent years and after a prolonged crisis inflamed by allegations of election rigging, Bhutto's government was overthrown in 1977 by the Marshal Law of General Zia ul Haq. Bhutto was executed two years later, an act now widely regarded as the shameful judicial murder of a popular prime minister.

Externally, Pakistan had been engaged with three large-scale wars with India during the previous 25 years. The Indian nuclear test explosion of 1974 urged a nuclear development response from Pakistan, digging deeply into fiscal resources. Moreover, the Soviet occupation of Kabul involved Pakistan in a West-backed proxy war in Afghanistan, redefining the budgetary priorities in favour of national security over public welfare. Together, these factors depreciated financial commitment by the state to two of its main social programmes, the Public Works Programme and the National Development Volunteer Programme (Hussain, 2004).

Despite these setbacks, in the early 1980s the incidence and intensity of poverty in Pakistan was still no worse than elsewhere in the region, and the country's per capita gross national income far exceeded that of its South Asian neighbours, India, Bangladesh and Sri Lanka (Burki, 1988). The administrative data does suggest that the rate of absolute poverty in Pakistan, based on calorie intake, dropped from above 40 per cent in 1969 to under 20 per cent in 1988. So why, despite the elitist policies of the 1950s and 1960s, was Pakistan still in a relatively sound macroeconomic position in the 1980s? Akmal Hussain (2004) argues that the two main factors responsible for this relative stability were substantial foreign assistance received in the wake of the Afghan War and the manifold increase in remittances by expatriate Pakistanis during the late 1970s and 1980s. In addition, some cultural factors such as close communities and joint family systems also contributed to the economic ease of low-income people in the rural economy through informal collective farming and household help. The foremost welfare programme launched during this era was the official Zakat programme of 1980, which is still functional in 2012, being one of the two largest income support programmes in Pakistan.

The relatively propitious economic scenario of the 1980s faded away, however, with the withdrawal of global support after the end of the Afghan War in 1988. By the start of the 1990s, economic growth that had stood at over 6 per cent during the military regime of Zia (1977-88) began to shrink, and later averaged around 4 per cent during the democratic governments of the 1990s. The rate of poverty continuously crept upwards and the post-war Pakistan of the early 1990s presented a drastically different social and demographic picture, with three million Afghan refugees, a large number of wartime madrassa youth and a post-war social order plagued by drugs, crime, illegal weapons and poverty. Furthermore, the unprecedentedly high level of corruption that became a household story during the mid-1990s did nothing to improve the image of democratic rule. In 1996-97, the corruption carried out by top officials, amounting to the value of some US$15 billion, was estimated to have resulted in a 20-25 per cent loss of GDP (Hussain, 2004). As a consequence, there was little scope for people on low incomes to benefit from The World Bank-assisted Social Action Programme of the 1990s, which was aimed at improving their access to education, health, water supplies and sanitation. It is no wonder that the democratic decade of the 1990s, just like the 1950s, proved to be politically turbulent and economically inconsequential. While the 1950s witnessed eight governments coming to power in quick succession, ending with Ayub Khan's Marshal Law, the 1990s saw 10 unsettling government arrangements, ending with the military rule of General Musharraf.

Developments in the 21st century

With Musharraf coming to power in October 1999, 21st-century Pakistan began with a new phase of civil and military bureaucrats who already had a long history within the country's elite establishment. Aside from continuing a macroeconomic poverty reduction programme with residual income support through Zakat, the Musharraf regime introduced conditional cash transfers (CCTs) of Rs 200-350 a month, with the conditionality of school enrolment of children and 80 per cent attendance. In the absence of any examination of the psychosocial impact of these policies, it is difficult to comment whether this conditionality had any shaming elements for the recipients or their families. However, not only were recipients made to enrol in the schools, which were not always nearby, the high level of attendance expected failed to recognise the stark realities of the lives of low-income people. Conceptually, such conditions can be seen as representing a demeaning lack of trust in the recipients' own judgement of how best to spend the cash assistance for their needs. Conversely, however, conditionality may also encourage an environment of participation where beneficiaries take pride in fulfilling their end of the bargain and thereby use the assistance with better claim of right.

Post-Musharraf, social assistance (2008-) in Pakistan has been dominated by the Benazir Income Support Programme (BISP), primarily designed to provide cash transfers to low-income women. The rationale for starting a women-specific programme in Pakistan was grounded in demographic reality. In low-income countries, men are usually more likely to find mainstream jobs in the formal sector that are protected by labour laws, whereas women are more likely to depend on temporary and insecure jobs (Mitter, 1994). The cultural dictates of South Asia, still wrought by historical confusions of identity and tradition, further restrict female access to public spheres of education and employment. The consequent dependency on their male family members has long made the women of this region vulnerable and prone to the possible shame of poverty. In 1987, women on low incomes rallied in Pakistan's neighbouring region of Ahmedabad (Gujarat), India, demanding 'dignity and daily bread' (Rowbothom and Mitter, 1994). Almost two decades later, however, on the eve of BISP inception, Pakistani women fared no better in their life chances and human development. According to the Pakistan Social and Living Standards Measurement Survey (PSLM, 2008-09), only 46 per cent of the female population of the country had ever attended a school by 2008. The situation of their labour market participation was even worse, with only 10 per cent of them part of the formal labour force (FBS, 2009). It was under these circumstances that the government designated women to be the beneficiaries of BISP, which in 2012, is still the largest social welfare programme in Pakistan.

The shame of being non-entities

The low-income respondents suggested that throughout the political upheavals during 66 years of the country's history, they continuously experienced neglect and were forsaken by the state (Choudhry, 2014b). This also had profoundly adverse effects for their self-esteem. Coimbatore Prahalad (2006) associates dignity with the recognition that comes with the receipt of attention and the availability of choices. While anti-poverty policy may or may not have shaming consequences for low-income people, the poverty-induced shame is likely to be heightened if their needs are not given any attention at all. Not only would such inaction perpetuate existing shame, it might aggravate it by injecting a feeling of being a non-entity among broader societal priorities.

Policy neglect in Pakistan can take several forms. The first occurs when the state fails to involve itself in locally practiced policy-making. Since British rule, for example, the state has yielded to local customs of FATAs (federally administered tribal areas), allowing them to decide their matters according to their centuries' old law, Pukhtunwali, largely premised on the tribal traditions of pride, honour and shame (Yamane, 2011). One instance of how such neglect may translate into the shaming of low-income people can be witnessed in the tribal handling of extramarital sex incidents. Jürgen Frembgen (2006) notes that one traditional punishment in such cases has been nose mutilation, since it is the traditional bodily symbol of 'honour'. However, he finds an interesting anomaly in the application of this supposedly blind tradition: most victims of this mutilation have reportedly been married women from lower socioeconomic orders, those least likely to have any political or economic means of retaliation. Besides the physical ordeal, such mutilations bring extreme shame and stigma to those convicted. This is one example of how the absence of policy on the part of federal government and selective policy enforcement on the part of tribal elders perpetuate the shame and suffering of the most vulnerable in society.

Away from the tribal region, the mutilation of honour assumes a less visceral form in the urbanised centres of Islamabad and Lahore. Here liberal welfare policy provides the space for a form of urban Pakhtunwali, similarly targeting its victims among those living in poverty and those who are vulnerable. More broadly, a review of Pakistan's economic and welfare history sustains a story where policies primarily prioritising macroeconomic growth not only fail to provide non-stigmatising social assistance but also intensify the shaming of low-income people through neglect, inefficiency, corruption and most of all, the relinquishment of public resources to meet the interests of the elites. By creating a hierarchy in which the few exercise a great deal of power over the many, the state has generated and perpetuated social divisions and inequalities which denigrate and marginalise the poorest and most vulnerable in society. The few social assistance programmes initiated during all this period have been wrought with shaming elements, and have proven to be little help in restoring the faith and trust of most in the goodness of the state.

Shaming within policy shaping and structuring

Pakistan's two largest contemporary income support programmes, Zakat and BISP, were shaped according to the political and economic realities of 1980 and 2008 respectively. After his military takeover in 1977, General Zia was overwhelmed with the need to win popular support in his drive for legitimacy and maintenance of power. Zakat had long been an informal private charity in Pakistan, involving a tithing by affluent Muslims at a flat rate of 2.5 per cent of annual non-productive wealth. The Zia administration of the early 1980s, however, put forth the idea of an official Zakat programme with the primary objective of providing cash assistance to 'the poor' and 'the needy'. Through the Zakat and Ushr Ordinance of 1980 the state adopted Zakat as an official programme, imposing deductions from the bank accounts of all eligible Muslims every year on the first day of Ramadan. The regime tried to win additional popularity by structuring the scheme along Shari'ah lines, thereby capitalising on the religious fervour of the masses and making the new scheme impervious to political criticism. The political sensitivity of this religious identity can be demonstrated by the fact that no government in the subsequent 32 years has been able to roll back this scheme.

The nature of BISP is not, however, religious. It was, rather, conceived by the post-Musharraf democratic government of the Pakistan People's Party in 2008. The programme came about against the backdrop of global recession, which, together with the internal security and economic situation in Pakistan, pushed the inflation rate to an unprecedented 25 per cent. The elected government devised this new social protection regime in response to popular expectations arising from these circumstances. With a targeted coverage of over 5 million families during the financial year 2012-13, this programme aims to provide an economic safety net to some 40 per cent of the population that has been designated as living below the poverty threshold (representing 18 per cent of the total population).

Funding welfare and its emotional implications

With social assistance expenditure averaging less than 0.5 per cent of its GDP over the last decade, the Pakistani government has been faced with the economic dilemma of implementing a broad social protection scheme with few public resources. To date, the country has been dependent on external support to maintain even a very low level of social assistance provision for less than half of its low-income citizens. At the time of its initiation, it was proposed that BISP would have a total allocation of US$2,250 million over a five-year period, almost 25 per cent of which was expected to come from international organisations in the form of grants and loans. Unconditional cash assistance of Rs 1,000 per month (equivalent to '20-25 days of flour needs for a 5-6 member family'; see IMF, 2010) still remains the programme's central component.

The funding structure of the Zakat programme has inherently created the scope for shame. Since its inception, funding for the programme has been dependent on the contributions of wealthy Muslims and is, consequently, unstable. Enormous public sector corruption, especially in the mid-1990s, further eroded benefactor trust in the state machinery's ability to discharge their religious obligation of charity. A 1999 judgment by the Supreme Court of Pakistan, which rendered the Zakat contributions to the official scheme voluntary, added to the decline in contributions. Funds for the Zakat programme dropped from 0.3 per cent of GDP in the early 1980s to less than 0.08 per cent two decades later (The World Bank, 2007). This shrinking resource base has profound implications for recipients since declining coverage has made them uncertain about whether or not they will continue to receive support. As a consequence, many of the respondents we spoke with felt compelled to continue paying regular social homage to the relevant Zakat functionaries and their political acquaintances as a way of attempting to ensure continued financial assistance (Choudhry, 2014b). This inevitably has the psychosocial impact of placing recipients in a position where they must publicly emphasise their neediness.

Exclusionary programme characteristics

The Zakat Ordinance makes no secret of its religious motivation. Its preamble reads, 'WHEREAS Pakistan, being an Islamic State, must provide for the implementation of Islamic precepts.... AND WHEREAS Zakat ... is one of the fundamental pillars of Islam.' Of the two contradictory religious interpretations on the scope of coverage, the state follows the one that claims that non-Muslims are neither the contributors nor beneficiaries of Zakat. Section 2 of the Ordinance provides, 'It extends to the whole of Pakistan, but [as regards payment and recovery of Zakat and Ushr] applies only to Muslim citizens of Pakistan.' Christian minority respondents interviewed within our own research (Choudhry, 2014b) reported that their exclusion from the state's central income support programme for the last three decades has resulted in significant financial, social and emotional vulnerabilities, making them much worse off than their Muslim counterparts facing similar socioeconomic circumstances. According to one Christian female respondent, minorities are shame-facedly looking for informal and temporary sources of help on a day-to-day basis, unlike low-income Muslims who can at least hope to turn to the state for relatively more stable income support (Choudhry, 2014b).

Although, unlike the Zakat programme, BISP does not exclude people on religious grounds, its very origin has politically exclusionary aspects. Started in October 2008, the People's Party government named the programme after the late chair of the Party, Benazir Bhutto, who had lost her life in a Taliban assassination attack in December 2007. At that time, the People's Party had secured almost 30 per cent of the popular vote cast in the general elections. In a country with deep and bitter political rivalries, the adoption of this name instantly alienated a large majority of the population. Furthermore, the identification of eligible beneficiaries through parliamentarians resulted in the exclusion of non-political commoners, who had no access to the political leadership. Under its name and design, BISP had few chances of longevity beyond the last administration, as no government from an opposing party was likely to continue a programme exalting the name of a political adversary. The beneficiaries of the programme included in our own research were fully conscious of the uncertainty hanging over this programme attached to the 2013 general elections. Indeed, the new government has already announced plans to restructure the programme and to change its name to the Income Support Fund.

Inclusion and exclusion errors

Those we spoke with also heavily criticised both Zakat and BISP programmes for their errors of inclusion and exclusion which, they said, had resulted in the perpetuation of their poverty, uncertainty and shame (Choudhry, 2014b). The policy analysis suggests that these errors occur not only at the delivery stage but are also engrained in the policy structures and narrative. For instance, in defining the potential beneficiaries of the Zakat programme, Section 8 of the Ordinance describes it as 'assistance to the needy, the indigent and the poor particularly orphans and widows, the handicapped and the disabled, eligible to receive zakat under Shariah....' Clearly, the phrase 'eligible ... under Shariah' seems exclusionary, but it is also vague as no further explanation of eligibility is provided here. In effect, whether or not someone is deemed to be eligible for assistance is left to the discretion of those responsible for programme delivery. As a result, according to a World Bank study, only 43 per cent of the total Zakat expenditure reached the poorest 40 per cent of the population (The World Bank, 2007). This leaves open the question of how the remaining funds have been used.

As for BISP, the original targeting mechanism of beneficiaries through parliamentarians was an unparalleled recipe for enhancing the shame of prospective recipients. Each parliamentarian was allowed to recommend up to 8,000 people from their political constituency, who, after a verification of citizenship, were given a monthly income supplement of Rs 1,000. With no objective protocol for identification, all applicants were left at the mercy of their elected representatives. The fact that the programme was meant for only female beneficiaries further complicated the shaming structures of the eligibility process. In Pakistani culture, women, especially those from the lower social classes, are restricted to their homes and limited in terms of participation in public life. This left potential applicants mostly unable to follow up their welfare applications without the involvement of male family members. It severely limited the possibility for parliamentarians, especially male parliamentarians, to gain even a glimpse of potential beneficiaries, much less to determine a good sense of their true economic circumstances and thus offer informed recommendations. This knowledge gap led to necessary reliance on intermediary agents who mediated between parliamentarians and potential beneficiaries. Hence, those women who wished to access benefits had to mobilise male family members to convince these agents that they were eligible for and in need of support. The added fact that such appeals either entailed bribes or informal recommendations and pleading heightened the demeaning nature of the eligibility process. One woman we spoke with described how she had had to 'beg' several times before her uncle followed up her benefits case with the secretary of her Member National Assembly (MNA). Another respondent reported providing free cleaning for four months at the house of a relative of someone who could help her application for assistance (Choudhry, 2014b).

Under heavy domestic and international criticism of this identification method, the government started a poverty scorecard survey in 2010, thus shifting to a more technical approach. At the time of writing, some 27 million households (over 90 per cent of the country) had been surveyed, identifying 7.15 million eligible families. Only parts of the tribal areas were still outstanding. Despite having its own shortcomings of design and execution, discussed in the following section, the survey has already rendered 1.1 million families earlier identified by parliamentarians as ineligible.[1] These inconsistencies confirm large-scale political misuse of authority in the initial identification process of BISP.

Shaming through policy delivery

With respect to the delivery of Zakat and BISP, shame emerges as a significant feature, which has severely constrained the effectiveness of these programmes in assisting those in greatest need. To start with, beneficiaries of both Zakat and BISP programmes complained about the excessive procedural formalities involved in the welfare process (Choudhry, 2014b). Considering that 40 per cent of the population (PSLM, 2010-11) has never attended a school, it is no wonder, that low education attainment has an impact on the uptake of welfare benefits. Several respondents described how the shame of illiteracy or ignorance made them reluctant to personally pursue their applications in government offices. Illiteracy in Pakistan has a long political history, especially given the feudal propensity to keep low-income people ignorant of their rights and hence politically silent. Such ignorance also renders the economically marginalised people dependent on their political patrons, who happily use this control to maintain the status quo of creed and class as well as further their political pursuits.

Zakat eligibility and delivery

The have/have not distinction within the Zakat programme and its increasing bureaucratisation have arguably transformed a discreet traditional system of 'giving alms' to one that publicly names and shames both recipients and donors. An analysis of the principal Zakat programme, the Sustenance (*Guzara*) Allowance, highlights the potential sources of shaming associated with its design. The Zakat contributions are only mandatory for people whose possessions are over a certain threshold of wealth, equivalent to 85g of gold or 585g of silver. According to the religion, the eligible recipients (*Mustahqeen*) include the destitute, widows, disabled people and orphans. A centuries-long understanding of Zakat has effectively divided the population along two lines: those who are required to give Zakat and those who are eligible to receive it. In practice, the scheme reflects two contradictory premises: the religious doctrine of discreetness in giving and receiving charity on the one hand, and the heavy state emphasis on documentation on the other. As a consequence of this contradiction, with the 1980 state policy intervention in Zakat, *Mustahqeen* who had previously been hidden in society, often only known to their private benefactors, became publicly visible. As reported by those recipients we spoke with (Choudhry, 2014b), the new Zakat policy had made them subject to more procedures, lowered the likelihood of an approved application and subjected them to longer waits and queues outside the Zakat offices.

The discretionary and religious aspects of eligibility determination for the Zakat programme are both shaming components at the point of delivery. The lack of any systematic targeting mechanism means that eligibility for the programme is determined at the discretion of state officials. The religious doctrine of rightful eligibility causes a second tier of scrutiny. Within this context, it is easy for unsympathetic eyes to scrutinise the recipients of Zakat in the public domain according to their own understanding of eligibility. The state-led Zakat programme has not only rendered suspected misusers of Zakat guilty of fraud, but also of a major sin, something that is highly shameful in a largely orthodox society. Zakat recipients who were interviewed as part of our own research, suggested that this pressure put great strain on rightful recipients who became very self-conscious of public scrutiny and their uncertain image in the eyes of the wider society (Choudhry, 2014b). Hence the identity of Zakat recipients has become inherently stigmatised. Indeed, one World Bank study found that 21 per cent of Zakat recipients complained of having been victims of stigma (The World Bank, 2007).

Ironically, the early 'nationalisation' period of Zakat has also created shaming structures affecting potential benefactors. First of all, compulsory deductions from the saving accounts of wealthy Muslims amounts to making a moral judgement both about their faith and their commitment to voluntarily pay their Zakat, as advised in the religion. Second, a long-time tradition before the movement of Zakat into a publicly administered benefit had the payment of Zakat prioritised towards those needy personally known to the benefactor. Many Zakat-payers, therefore, do not wish the government to deduct their Zakat amount from their bank accounts and disperse it to unknown beneficiaries. Finally, widespread administrative corruption further minimises trust by Zakat-payers in the government. Given these factors, it is not uncommon for Zakat-payers to opt to maintain control over their Zakat money and the selection of beneficiaries. This is achieved by the withdrawal of savings a few days before the deduction date or by providing a false declaration of their faith or sect to avoid at-source deductions. Both of these methods can, however, involve embarrassing interactions with bank personnel as their intention to pay Zakat privately can easily be misconstrued as unwillingness to pay Zakat at all, deemed to be morally shameful. The manner in which this policy creates explicit structures of shame for the non-poor is nowhere better reflected than the description of official procedure for the refund of erroneous Zakat deductions in the Ordinance:

> Provided further that, where for any reason Zakat or Ushr is collected on compulsory basis from such a person *and he does not wish to leave it in the Zakat fund as Sadaqah* [non-obligatory religious charity] *or Khairat* [donation or benevolence] *in the name of Allah as a manifestation of the unity of the Ummah and claims refund* ... the amount so collected shall be refunded to him in the prescribed manner. (emphases added)

Here the language connects the tithing of Zakat to an individual's moral conduct and religious beliefs, and in this sense it does not merely shame, but also emotionally blackmails potential contributors. Furthermore, in terms of delivery, the Ordinance debars non-Muslim citizens from being part of the administrative body of Zakat delivery (Section 19A). And even for Muslims, the Ordinance imposes additional shaming devices, such as placing pre-requisites that among others require that body members be 'known to be pious', 'offer five times prayers daily' and have sound moral integrity (Section 18[4]). It is on account of such design flaws, coercion and shaming techniques that the official Zakat programme has never fulfilled its potential of becoming a successful public–private welfare venture, and funding is gradually drying up.

BISP eligibility and delivery

While not overtly applying the moralistic framework of religion to shame potential system misusers, BISP does have eligibility and delivery mechanisms within distinctly shaming moralistic overtones. The beneficiary 'family' unit of BISP refers to an 'ever-married woman older than 18 years'. The measure's categorisation of such women further hints at the dominant social taboos. A beneficiary may be either: (1) living with her husband and unmarried children; (2) divorced and living with her unmarried children; (3) divorced and living alone or with her parents/relatives; or (4) a widow living alone, with her unmarried children and/or with her parents/relatives (BISP website www.bisp.gov.pk). It is interesting to note that according to cultural expectations, these categories make no mention of a single mother who has never been married. As well as being a grave religious violation, this 'excess' would be a matter of great shame and stigma. For once, policy itself shies away from addressing this otherwise relevant issue, thereby acknowledging the element of shame associated with out-of-wedlock children and perpetuating the poverty and shame of such families, however few.

The introduction of a poverty survey in order to achieve a fairer distribution of BISP also appears to have provided instead a legal framework for political nepotism. The proxy means-testing method used for this survey has the potential to yield substantially inaccurate results in an economy reeling from the unsettling shocks of natural calamities (earthquakes and floods) and the ongoing 'war against terror'. Proxy means-testing within this context may not account for the recent dynamics of transitory household poverty. Together with low administrative capacity and high corruption, the scorecard survey also remains open to political interference at the design and execution stages.

Further, the eligibility cut-off score itself has been set in such a way that it is most beneficial to the geo-political constituency of the ruling alliance. While a survey of households shows that families in the Sindh province (the political stronghold of the ruling party) represent 1 out of every 2.6 deemed eligible for benefits, whereas families in the Punjab, whose opposition party Muslim League (N) is running the provincial government, represent only 1 out of every 5.6 listed as eligible. Such an outcome does not mesh, however, with an earlier poverty headcount, conducted by The World Bank on the basis of national datasets (PIHS, 1998-99, 2001-02; PSLM, 2004-05, 2005-06), in which Punjab and Sindh were reported with similar longitudinal trends of headcount poverty (The World Bank, 2006). Even in 2010-11, that is, when the BISP survey was taking place, the official poverty statistics reported for the two provinces were almost alike (Planning Commission, 2012). It is not difficult to imagine how a politically motivated poverty survey may have subjected low-income people to the humiliation of uncertainty and injustice. According to a government official involved in the survey, the element of personal discretion during the survey process meant that low-income people felt they had to 'plead, beg and run from pillar to post; to get themselves enrolled on the list of beneficiaries (Choudhry, 2014c).

Finally, while the 'family' unit of beneficiary is defined as consisting of 'a woman who has ever been married', the survey is conducted on the basis of households, taking overall assets into account without reference to who owns what. It is possible that in a joint or extended family system in Pakistan, there could be several women within a household who fulfil the definition of a family – for instance, a wife, a mother and a widowed sister of a man living in the same household –

yet in entirely different economic circumstances. While some of these family members may be in need of benefits and some not, a survey on the basis of household fails to make this differentiation. The exclusion of some people from benefits despite being eligible is likely to be as shaming as the inclusion of those above the threshold who would like to have the social recognition of 'not being poor'.

The locus of blame

Despite feeling the shame of poverty, many respondents of the study noted that they were not ashamed of receiving benefits, as they did not consider them responsible for their socioeconomic situation (Choudhry, 2014b). Most were not able to refer to specific current or past policies, yet they blamed structural causes such as state policy, "the system", "government" and "big guns" for reducing them to the condition they were in. Hence, they were justified in receiving the "meagre compensation" that they were getting from the state. Living in a society with a legacy of policies patronising the rich and the privileged for six decades, it is not surprising that some respondents also described the general propensies of the rich as "shameless". One respondent summarised the sentiment by saying that "it is the rich who should be ashamed, not the poor." The sense of exploitation further exasperated their anti-rich sentiment and displaced a sense of shame with feelings of aggravation and anger. Going a step further, one respondent justified the perpetration of petty crimes such as shoplifting or purse snatching by explaining how these were committed by the "oppressed poor" against the "oppressing rich". Given these rather rebellious accounts, one wonders how it is that such an exclusionary political and economic system can run unchecked and why people on low incomes have so far not engaged in coercive collective action to change their condition.

The truth of the matter is that despite resentment, marginalised people seem to have few options to alleviate their feelings of frustration, shame and distress. This is where Sen's (1983) notion of capabilities comes in to play. In Pakistan, poverty has eliminated any options to demand changes to one's situation without risking the little one currently has. Rather, the strategies to counter poverty-induced shame are more defensive in nature. These included borrowing money to keep up appearances on social occasions such as weddings or when dealing with native cultural expectations such as providing a dowry. Clearly the attempt to deny one's true condition takes its toll in an economic and psychosocial sense. This effect is spurred on by a range of events, including through the shame of borrowing to the consequences of repayment default. The low-income people we spoke with described having to resort to desperate measures in order to change their condition, ranging from selling drugs to prostitution and from engaging in anti-social behaviour to committing crimes (Choudhry, 2014b). Hence, despite significant resentment against the rich alongside a desire to improve their condition, in the absence of an enabling social and political environment, people on low incomes found themselves unable to overcome the obstacles entailed.

At the time of writing, the most recent policy developments had maintained elements of shaming within them. In his budget speech of June 2012, Finance Minister Dr Hafeez Sheikh informed parliament that targeted food and essential items subsidies would be provided to low-income people through state-operated Utility Stores. Formed in 1971, Utility Stores have grown to over 6000 branches across Pakistan and the opening of another 2000 is in the pipeline. The intention has been that holders of BISP cards receive a ten per cent concession on selected food items. In the past, Utility Stores have attracted long queues of people waiting for their turn to receive the subsidised food and other items. Such queuing up creates public visibility, which can be humiliating and may heighten internalized shame over one's impoverished condition. Another budget announcement for the fiscal year 2012-13 was the proposal for publicising the names of the taxpayers on a government website and issuing them with special acknowledgment cards facilitating access to important government forums: the offices of Immigration, Airports, Passports, among others. While instigated with a view to encouraging compliance with taxation laws, this initiative has introduced a new structural disadvantage for people who are below the tax threshold. Of no fault of their own, people on low incomes have been excluded from the preferential treatment extended to the wealthy on the sole basis of their money. Already experiencing the pinch of poverty, this discrimination has likely further exasperated poverty-induced shame and inferiority.

Ironically, there is little willingness on the part of policy-makers to take responsibility for ongoing policies. Members of Parliament belonging to both the ruling party and the opposition with whom we spoke admitted that there were considerable welfare policy and delivery flaws. Yet they unanimously placed blame on the "system" and the civil service, suggesting their helplessness in the face of a powerful bureaucracy (Choudhry, 2014c). The civil servants we spoke with blamed an outdated system of civil service recruitment and lack of expertise within a particular civil service sector, leading to a severe lack of capacity for informed policy-making. Indeed, with a weak political leadership, the strong civil bureaucracy seldom faces any checks and balances with respect to the motive, conception, design and delivery of policies. However, it is not difficult to imagine the ordeal of a civil servant drafting a shame-sensitive anti-poverty policy without any prior theoretical, comparative or empirical knowledge of this realm. As a result, short-term political priorities, administrative and financial expediencies, common sense and impulse become the cornerstones of new policy in the making.

Implications and recommendations

The dignity of those receiving welfare has never been a cornerstone concern of anti-poverty policies in Pakistan. Not only has the political will never been present, class divisions alongside a feudal mindset, successive turbulent regime changes, low capacity and the short-sightedness of policy-makers favouring short-term political gains have all played a role in perpetuating policies that have sacrificed the dignity of low-income people in favour of other considerations. Over time, such policies have reinforced the sense of shame that is attached to the experience of poverty and have extended the economic marginalisation of low-income people into social and political domains. Although impoverishment will always theoretically contain an element of internal shame, it is nonetheless possible to craft policies in such a way that the element of external shaming is minimised for those receiving welfare benefits.

As discussed earlier in this chapter, the shame of poverty can only effectively be addressed if anti-poverty policies are sensitive to its existence. To start with, the cash provision components of both Zakat and BISP must be made less stigmatising. For Zakat, the obvious way is to revert it back to its original status as a private charity. This would ensure ease of access, compassion, better selection and discreetness. Alternatively, Zakat revenues can be made part of the overall welfare budget of the country, so that individuals receiving cash assistance from these funds are not identifiable as Zakat *Mustahqeen*, nor schemes made from these funds regarded specifically as Zakat schemes. The stigma associated with BISP primarily originates from the alleged non-eligibility of its recipients, who are generally regarded as political beneficiaries. A non-political targeting mechanism can greatly help to restore the image of the programme. BISP, however, has a commendable strength in its Smart Card initiative, which enables its beneficiaries to use cash points to withdraw their welfare money thus minimising the shame of human interaction in such transactions. Considering that some 4.3 million BISP beneficiaries are due to receive Smart Cards by June 2013, it is fully possible for Zakat and BISP to operate using the same Smart Card system for a relatively shame-free disbursal of cash assistance.

Both Zakat and BISP programmes must also be more inclusive on religious and political measures, respectively. For Zakat, the most straightforward inclusion option is to adopt the religious interpretation that allows non-Muslims to be Zakat beneficiaries. However, if this proves difficult in the face of religious opposition, the state can simply supplement Zakat contributions by adding proportionate state funding for non-Muslims. Factually, it would mean adding only 5 per cent of state funds to the pool of contributions by wealthy Muslims (since the percentage of non-Muslims in the total population is about 5 per cent). While BISP has been attached to a partisan identity, the new government's decision to move to an uncontroversial name (Income Support Fund) may allow low-income people from the opposite political spectrum to claim programme benefits. The severe political interference and nepotism marking the income support component of BISP might be reduced by gradually moving the bulk of programme funding to capacity enhancement and skill-building initiatives.

Finally, it is important to maximise the sense of co-ownership, responsibility and accountability of prospective programme beneficiaries. This might be most enhanced if the livelihood and microcredit initiatives associated with BISP were run as community-based programmes, with ongoing business advice and guidance provided by the state to increase chances of success and to protect participants from the shame of default. In rural areas, community-based rural support programmes already have a strong history of successful outcomes. Further expansion of these would not only strengthen the agricultural base of the economy, but also arrest the trend of mass migration to urban centres. Furthermore, those programmes with a track record of success that have also aimed to enhance capacities and skills should be further expanded in order to sustain long-term assistance and to provide exit strategies to the income support beneficiaries.

While important, reform of Zakat and BISP is only the first corrective step in the wake of the enormous shaming magnitude of poverty and welfare benefits currently existing in Pakistan. More enduring responses must address the breakdown of social trust that has attended vast poverty. This is only possible with the establishment of a national inclusive growth programme having the support of all political parties, providing longevity through future political regimes. All social safety nets, capacity-building and social provision programmes of the country may be aligned with the advice of the programme. Its guiding principle should be co-ownership and co-responsibility that are shared among local authorities, communities and individuals. Practically, it would mean working closely with carefully segmented small communities and neighbourhood organisations to enable them to empower low-income members in an inclusive and dignified manner. The nature of activities can range from providing missing health, education, water supply and sanitation facilities to creating sustained employment through area-suitable cottage industry and other small-scale entrepreneurial ventures. While the current livelihood programmes of Zakat and BISP can clearly be merged with such a system, even the income support components can be better utilised for providing short-term assistance to the individuals involved in appropriate skill enhancement programmes.

Lastly, the state needs to ensure that competent policy-makers are at the helm of welfare policy and delivery. Pakistan must not keep suffering from policy-making that revolves around the whims of uninformed senior civil servants. Pending the evolution of the political process to a stage where more educated and enlightened politicians are able to find their way to the ministries, it is essential to build the capacities of the civil service. The most viable way of achieving this might be to follow Ishrat Hussain's proposed formula of creating specialised streams and concentrations of expertise within the civil service (NCGR, 2006), placing mid-career civil servants in one specialised area and then building up this specific expertise for the rest of their careers. This can be supplemented by bringing relevant experts from the academic, voluntary and private sector on board to devise policies that ensure inclusive social welfare without casting negative shaming effects on the psychosocial wellbeing of intended beneficiaries.

Note
[1] The BISP website and chair of BISP's Panel interview with Jang and *The News* was published on 12 November 2012 and is available at www.thenews.com. pk/Todays-News-13-18787-Farzana-Raja-recounts-achievements-of-BISP

References
Alavi, H. (1983) 'Elite farmer strategy and regional disparities in agricultural development', in H.N. Gardezi and J. Rashid (eds) *Pakistan: The roots of dictatorship: The political economy of a praetorian state*, New Delhi: Oxford University Press, pp 291-309.

Burki, S. (1988) 'Poverty in Pakistan: Myth or reality', in T.N. Srinivasan and P.K. Bardhan (eds) *Rural poverty in South Asia*, New York: Columbia University Press, pp 69-88.

Choudhry S. (2014a) 'The wealth of poverty-induced shame in Urdu literature', in E. Chase and G. Bantebya Kyomuhendo (eds) *The shame of poverty: Global experiences*, Oxford: Oxford University Press.

Choudhry S. (2014b) 'Tales of inadequacy from Pakistan', in E. Chase and G. Bantebya Kyomuhendo (eds) *The shame of poverty: Global experiences*, Oxford: Oxford University Press.

Choudhry S. (2014c) 'How best to shame those in poverty; Perspectives from Pakistan', in E. Chase and G. Bantebya Kyomuhendo (eds) *The shame of poverty: Global experiences*, Oxford: Oxford University Press.

Dawn Archives (2001) 'Justice-III' column, by Ardeshir Cowasjee (http://archives.dawn.com/weekly/cowas/20010909.htm).

FBS (Federal Bureau of Statistics) (2009) *Labour Force Survey 2008-09*, Twenty Eighth Issue, Islamabad: Government of Pakistan, Statistical Division.

Frembgen, J.W. (2006) 'Honour, shame, and bodily mutilation. Cutting off the nose among tribal societies in Pakistan', *Journal of the Royal Asiatic Society of Great Britain and Ireland*, vol 16, pp 243-60.

Gardezi, H.N. and Rashid, J. (eds) (1983) *Pakistan: The roots of dictatorship. The political economy of a praetorian state*, New Delhi: Oxford University Press.

Hussain A. (2004) 'Institutions, economic structure and poverty in Pakistan in South Asia', *Economic Journal*, vol 5, no 1, pp 69-102.

IMF (International Monetary Fund) (2010) *Pakistan: Poverty reduction strategy paper*, IMF Country Paper No 10/183 (www.imf.org/external/pubs/ft/scr/2010/cr10183.pdf).

IMF (2012) *World Economic Outlook database*. (www.imf.org/external/pubs/ft/weo/2013/01/weodata/index.aspx).

Mitter, S. (1994) 'On organising women in casualised work', in S. Rowbotham and S. Mitter (eds) *A global view in dignity and daily bread*, London: Routledge, pp 14-52.

NCGR (National Commission for Government Reforms) (2006) *Report of the NCGR on reforming the government in Pakistan* (www.ncgr.gov.pk/).

OPHI (Oxford Poverty and Human Development Initiative) (2011) *Country briefing Pakistan* (www.ophi.org.uk/wp-content/uploads/Pakistan2.pdf?cda6c1).

PIHS (Pakistan Integrated Household Survey) (1998-99) Islamabad: Government of Pakistan, Federal Bureau of Statistics.

PIHS (2001-02) Islamabad: Government of Pakistan, Federal Bureau of Statistics.

Planning Commission (2012) *Annual plan 2012-13*, Government of Pakistan (www.pc.gov.pk/annual%20plans/2012-13/chapter-14_poverty_alleviation_and_millennium_development_goals.pdf).

Prahalad, C.K. (2006) *The fortune at the bottom of the pyramid: Eradicating poverty through profits*, Pearson Education Inc, published as Upper Saddle River, NJ: Wharton School Publishing.

PSLM (Pakistan Social and Living Standards Measurement) (2004-05) Islamabad: Government of Pakistan, Statistical Division, Federal Bureau of Statistics.

PSLM (2005-06) Islamabad: Government of Pakistan, Statistical Division, Federal Bureau of Statistics.

PSLM (2008-09) Islamabad: Government of Pakistan, Statistical Division, Federal Bureau of Statistics.

PSLM (2010-11) Islamabad: Government of Pakistan, Statistical Division, Federal Bureau of Statistics.

Rowbothom, S and Mitter, S. (1994) *Dignity and daily bread: New forms of economic organising among poor women in the third world and the first*, London: Routledge.

Raulet, H. (1976) 'The historical context of Pakistan's rural economy', in R.D. Stevens et al (eds) *Rural development in Bangladesh and Pakistan*, Honolulu: University of Hawaii Press, pp 198-213.

Saeed K. (1982) 'Public policy and rural poverty: A system dynamics analysis of a social change effort in Pakistan', *Technological Forecasting and Social Change*, vol 21, no 4, pp 325-349.

Sen, A. (1983) 'Poor, relatively speaking', *Oxford Economic Papers*, vol 35, pp 153-69.

Smith, A. (1776) *An inquiry into the nature and causes of the wealth of nations*, Oxford: Clarendon Press.

UN (United Nations) (2011) *Multidimensional Poverty Index (MPI)*, Human Development Reports Office, MPI Country Briefings (http://hdr.undp.org/en/statistics/mpi/).

World Bank, The (2006) *A validation exercise on the official poverty estimates for 2005-06* (http://siteresources.worldbank.org/PAKISTANEXTN/Resources/Poverty-Assessment/361361-1216396471531/PAK_OPL.pdf).

World Bank, The (2007) *Social protection in Pakistan: Managing household risk and vulnerability*, Technical Report 35472-PK, Human Development Unit South Asia Region.

Yamane (2011) 'The rise of new madrisas and decline of tribal leadership within the FATA', in S. Keiko and F. Adelkhah (eds) *Pakistan in the moral economy of the madrasa*, Abingdon: Routledge, pp 11-31.

SEVEN

Separating the sheep from the goats: tackling poverty in Britain for over four centuries

Robert Walker and Elaine Chase

Blaming and shaming: early ideological roots

The UK is a comparatively small, highly centralised state that operates a first past the post-electoral system.[1] This, combined with strong party loyalty, typically provides ministers with largely unfettered authority to reform policy while in government. The electoral system has also delivered comparatively long spells of government, often lasting two or three five-year terms. This means that it is not unheard of for substantive policy programmes to be implemented and then radically reversed by opposition parties subsequently entering government with a mission and mandate for reform. This said, the potential for inchoate and reactive policy-making is partially mitigated by a stable civil service with a constitutional duty to critique policies proposed by ministers before assuming responsibility to implement them.

Perhaps more remarkable, however, is a legacy of social policy with respect to poverty that is traceable back to at least 1552. The comparatively early decline in the political influence of religious institutions in Britain meant that civil bodies, initially under the oversight of Justices of the Peace, took responsibility for meeting the needs of people experiencing poverty. These both reflected and helped to create a mindset that prioritised poverty relief above the more modern goals of social cohesion and egalitarianism. This would, in the late 19th and early 20th centuries, shape the broader development of welfare policies in other European countries (see, for example, Chapter Five, this volume). It also meant that, with the exception of the National Health Service (NHS), the universalist, insurance-based policies introduced as part of the post-Second World War settlement were to prove less durable than in continental Europe. While governments of the political left and right have since implemented policies premised on different ideological assumptions, they have for the most part unquestionably accepted a division between 'the poor' and the 'non-poor' and the need to differentiate among 'the poor' on moral grounds.

Himmelfarb (1984a, 1984b) argues that in Medieval England giving alms to 'the poor' was a religious duty that drew no moral distinctions among them. Such distinctions emerged later with the 1601 Elizabethan Poor Law, which categorised the 'impotent poor' alongside two groups of 'able-bodied poor' – those who *could* not work, the unemployed, and those who *would* not work, the 'rogues and idlers'. These distinctions essentially coined the 'deserving'–'undeserving' dichotomy. It has since both dominated political and public discourses surrounding poverty and created space for shame to emerge as a central component of policy. Indeed, the *Oxford English Dictionary* (OED, 2012) defines the word 'deserving' with reference to the 'deserving poor'.

Yet while the Elizabethans, via this 'could not'–'would not' distinction, explicitly recognised factors affecting people's ability to work which may have been outside of their control, the Victorians in the 1834 Poor Law later confounded the two groups of able-bodied poor. Those in need were divided into two homogenised groups: the 'impotent' poor, those who were too young, too old or too sick to work, and the 'able-bodied' poor, considered to be the 'master evil' in their consumption of available provisions (HMSO, 1834, p 279). The 'workhouse test' denied help to the able-bodied unless they were so destitute as to be willing to accept accommodation under strict work-based regimes in conditions worse than those experienced by the poorest, independent worker. It was designed to avoid ambiguity by differentiating the pauper – the able and therefore undeserving – from the simply poor (HMSO, 1834, p 262), and in essence was inherently shaming. The 1830s was a period of economic recession in the midst of industrial transformation, with high unemployment and prevalent begging and crime. Lacking knowledge of the cyclical and structural nature of unemployment, reformers explained increased demands on the Poor Law system in terms of a lax administration that had demoralised 'the poor' and that had encouraged them to live at the community's expense (Bruce, 1968). The mantra has been sustained within political and media commentary on welfare policy ever since. Furthermore, a review of a selection of British literature spanning some one hundred years, together with an analysis of British social realist films (Chase and Walker, 2012a), demonstrates how these assertions have infiltrated cultural values and norms over time and become inculcated in the public psyche. Those living in poverty and the lower social classes have, it seems, always been systematically derided, criticised and labelled as unworthy by those with greater wealth and status.

Not only have these assumptions heightened the stigma and shame experienced by recipients of aid throughout history, they provide the ideological backdrop to four more recent periods of welfare reform in Britain: the 'Fowler reforms', legislated for in the Social Security Act 1986 under the Conservative government led by Margaret Thatcher; the Jobseekers Act 1995 (The Crown, 1995) introduced by John Major's Conservative government; the labour market reforms of the *New²* Labour government under Tony Blair; and the Welfare Reform Act (The Crown, 2012), a flagship policy of the Conservative-Liberal Democrat Coalition government and the brainchild of Iain Duncan Smith, at the time of writing, Secretary of State for Work and Pensions.

This chapter traces the ways in which shame and stigma have been challenged or exaggerated in the framing, structure and delivery of these different eras of welfare policy. The focus is deliberately on policies relevant to families with dependent children and the ways in which recipients have experienced these policies. Particular attention is paid to the framing and structure of Universal Credit, which has yet to be implemented, and to the logic and delivery of the New Labour reforms, which are comprehensively evaluated. The Fowler reforms and Jobseeker's Allowance are discussed as they introduce important concepts and rationales relevant to these later reforms.

Blaming and shaming: solidification of concepts

The Fowler reforms, 1985/86: responding to the 'burden' of social security

The Fowler reforms were instigated on the back of comprehensive reviews of housing benefit and social security, which concluded that the British social security system had 'lost its way' (DSS, 1985, p 1). The system, it was claimed, had generated both an *unemployment trap*, where people found 'themselves worse off in work than if they were unemployed' (DSS, 1985, p 1) and a *poverty trap*, whereby the system design meant that disposable family income barely rose, and indeed sometimes fell, as gross income increased. The reforms, led by a right-of-centre government under Margaret Thatcher, left a profound legacy in terms of how issues of poverty were subsequently framed politically, and the sorts of policy responses believed to be effective.

Framing of policy: meeting genuine need

The rhetoric surrounding reform generated the idea of social security spending as 'a burden' and the need to roll back the state. Moreover, it pitched the interests of one citizen – the benefit recipient – against another – the taxpayer, fundamentally ignoring the reality that they were often one and the same person. It also diverted attention to the 'responsibilities of the individual' rather than the state, to make 'sensible provision for themselves' (DSS, 1985, p 1). The implication of this premise was that any spending increases were due to people not making sensible provision for themselves, thus applying the concept of 'undeserving' to benefit recipients as a whole.

The reforms established the leitmotiv of disincentives that has since dominated discourses surrounding benefits, above all those emphasising unemployment and poverty traps (Weale, 1985). Reliance on neo-classical economic theory convinced the government that 'shirking', although morally wrong, was nevertheless rational for those whose income was more on benefit than when working. Furthermore, the importance that the government attached to disincentives in shaping their reform was not justified by empirical evidence, which would have indicated that the effects on actual behaviour were minimal (Collard, 1985). Rather it referred to survey evidence of the general public who perceived it as unfair that low-income families who were out of work received more support than those on similar incomes who were working (Weale, 1985, p 327). Thus, the Fowler era illustrated the emergence of an important dynamic in policy framing: increased engagement with selective public opinion cited as factual justification for policy irrespective of a lack of empirical evidence concerning its validity.

The Fowler reforms introduced a common income test for the major means-tested benefits, simplified the main social assistance benefit under a new name (Income Support) and, in order to incentivise working, increased the generosity of means-tested benefits for in-work families with children through Family Credit. The previous social assistance benefit had provided personalised financial assistance under a rights-based framework of regulation. While the new Income Support retained the principle of entitlement rather than discretion, it moved to assessing categorical rather than individualised need. Allowances were calculated for families, those aged over 60 and 80, people with disabilities, lone parents and dependent children. In making these changes, the government was prepared to accept 'an element of rough justice' to simplify administrative systems which, it anticipated, would lead to more streamlined services with fewer delays (DSS, 1985; Heathcoat-Amory, 1985).

More than anything, however, the Fowler reforms firmly legitimised a culture of shaming those receiving benefits. They facilitated the reintroduction of discretion at the expense of legal entitlement, supported a discourse that prioritised personal responsibility over social rights, and allowed the idea to take root that recipients of social security were themselves a burden and not always in genuine need. In terms of structures, the aspirations were towards integration and simplicity in order to ensure the maximisation of work incentives and efficiency in the delivery of benefits.

Jobseeker's Allowance, 1995: making the right way clear

The same emphasis on simplicity, cost-effectiveness and individual responsibility was subsequently reiterated almost a decade later in the White Paper (HMSO, 1994) preceding the Jobseekers Act of 1995. The Act likewise reflected an overarching concern with the issue of providing the proper incentives to keep people in work.

As in the Thatcher era, the stimulus for reform under John Major's Conservative government was a severe rise in unemployment. The White Paper (HMSO, 1994, para 1.5) explicitly stated its policy objectives as: ensuring that people understood and fulfilled the conditions of benefit receipt; better value for money; incentivising the return to work; and better service delivery to recipients. However, whereas the Fowler reforms had offered unemployed people a carrot – more money in work than when unemployed – the Major reforms introduced the stick of lower out-of-work benefits and increased conditionality.

A key component introduced by the Act was that payment of the benefit became conditional on signing a Jobseeker's Agreement. This not only required jobseekers to demonstrate that they were 'available for and actively seeking work', as had been the case since the introduction of Unemployment Benefit in 1911, but also that they were available 'for any work that they could reasonably do' (HMSO, 1994, para 4.3). Furthermore, answering the 1994 White Paper claims of loopholes that enabled recipients to legally evade work, the Act included further sanctions. Thus, benefits could be refused or reduced when the unemployed person's behaviour (and indeed appearance) was judged to 'actively militate against finding work', only to be re-instated if the recipient could demonstrate *hardship* (Strickland, 1996). Ministers were unequivocal in asserting the taxpayer's 'right to expect the commitment of unemployed people to make every effort to get back to work' (HMSO, 1994).

At the time, the Low Pay Unit, a lobby supported by academics, suggested that the ministerial belief that claimants would rather remain on benefit than take work vacancies, was 'profoundly mistaken', as was the conclusion that 'greater coercion was necessary in order to reduce employment' (Wheatley, 1994, 23). However, with the exception of a single Liberal Democrat spokesperson who suggested that the reforms were 'all stick, no carrot', the strong opposition party critique of the Act mostly focused on the extent of benefit cuts rather than on the shift towards greater conditionality. Indeed, 'the "tough love" doctrine of mutual responsibility' was heartily applauded by the press (see Bassett, 1994). Popular right-wing newspapers focused approvingly on ministers' use of the word 'workshy', while middle-of-the-road papers carried a number of articles reflecting the view that the introduction of workfare was a positive development (see, for example, Deans, 1994; Wood et al, 1994). Likewise, remarks by government officials were interpreted positively as evidence that Jobseeker's Allowance would help 'prevent the emergence of an underclass excluded from the opportunity to work and dependent upon welfare' (Reid, 1994, p 28). These same iterations of policy serving to prevent *dependency* and to disincentivise the *workshy* have become ever more prominent in contemporary media discourses in relation to welfare and poverty (Chase and Walker, 2012c), and appear firmly embedded in public perceptions of those in receipt of benefits (Chase and Walker, 2012d).

The incoming Labour government retained Jobseeker's Allowance in 1997. Official evaluations concluded that Jobseeker's Allowance had had modest effects on unemployment rates, most notably in areas with the least unemployment, but that the deterrent effect was marginal since the majority of unemployed people claiming benefit were eagerly committed to finding employment (Kellard and Stafford, 1997; McKay et al, 1999; Smith et al, 2000), a finding confirmed from our own research with people living on low incomes (see Chase and Walker, 2012b). Indeed, only a third of employment support advisers believed that penalties were effective in enforcing compliance with benefit rules (Rayner, 2000).

One important structural development accompanying Jobseeker's Allowance was the attempt to separate policy-making from implementation through the establishment of executive agencies to deliver public services at arm's length from ministers. These worked according to prescribed budgets and a set of performance targets with respect to clearance times, accuracy, customer satisfaction, financial management and financial control (McKay and Rowlingson, 1999). The first four targets were concerned with efficient delivery but equally spoke to benefit recipients' interest in receiving the right benefit as quickly as possible. Moreover, reflecting the focus on service, the Benefits Agency had shortly before begun to use the term 'customer' to refer to benefit claimants since, even though they could not shop around and had no customer's right of exit, the Agency's ethos was to shape their 'business' around the needs of users, as far as financial constraint allowed.

The rhetoric of 'customers' aside, targets on accuracy sprung primarily from concerns with financial control and the issues of fraud and abuse. In 1992, in a speech given to the Conservative Party Conference, the Secretary of State made reducing fraud a personal crusade, noting: 'Be in no doubt, this government and this Secretary of State will not tolerate fraud.... I've set a target of £500 million and I mean to get it back' (Peter Lilley, as cited by McKay and Rowlingson, 1999, p 158). The ensuing anti-fraud policy effort included investment in computer technology and benefit payment cards as well as publicity campaigns encouraging the public to report suspected fraudsters via a free and confidential 'hotline'. A legacy to these initiatives is the ongoing media and political obsession with the notion of welfare 'fraud' and the need to name and shame 'fraudsters' (see Chase and Walker, 2012c).

The crystallisation of blaming and shaming

New Labour, 1997-2010: welfare is a constraint

Whereas the earlier Conservative governments had sought to cut back on government and the welfare state, the incoming New Labour government believed that expenditure on social security – or 'welfare' as it increasingly came to be called – was a constraint on what government could achieve (Walker and Wiseman, 2003). Welfare limited the money available for government spending on more worthy sectors such as education and health. It also, New Labour argued, lessened the flexibility of the labour market and inhibited the creation of new wealth that could be used for further social investment. Welfare was not only a burden: it was a burden that prevented progress.

Welfare reform became an important element in New Labour's economic agenda, aiding the development of a modern economy with a flexible labour market that would enhance Britain's international competitiveness. Some in the Party's leadership also shared a strong ideological and indeed moral agenda with many of their Conservative predecessors, and were thus motivated by a belief that welfare dependency was rife and debilitating, and that instilling a sense of responsibility among benefit recipients must be prioritised (Walker, 1998).

Welfare reform to modernise the economy

New Labour's principal objective in 1997 was to modernise the economy and with it, the welfare state. Strategic goals focused on macroeconomic stability and growth; a flexible and adaptable labour market; investment in education and skills, including lifelong learning; moving people from 'welfare to work' around a framework of 'rights and responsibilities'; and 'making work pay' through the introduction of a National Minimum Wage and a tax and benefit system to promote 'work incentives' (HM Treasury, 1997, p 41).

Yet beneath the positive packaging, the underlying motivations were similar to those of the outgoing Conservative government: individual social security schemes were said to have established barriers to employment, promoted long-term 'dependency' and encouraged 'abuse of the system'. While the Conservatives viewed social security expenditure as a consequence of people being idle, New Labour took the same idea and presented it as the cost of keeping people idle, a symbol of previous economic failure. In this presentation they drew political license for reform from campaign focus group research, which reported on public negativity towards social security claimants and a demand for increased spending on health and education (Mattinson, 2010).

Whereas the Conservative government had avoided using the term 'poverty', New Labour presented employment as the solution to poverty, drawing attention to the sustained increase since 1979 in the number of 'workless households' and the prevalent 'low pay – no pay' cycle (HM Treasury, 1997). Aside from those that were work-related, however, anti-poverty policies themselves were fairly muted until in March 1999 the then Prime Minister, Tony Blair, declared the government's commitment to eradicating 'child poverty' within a generation – 20 years (Blair, 1999). Bold though this aspiration was, and despite the lack of an official definition of poverty at the time, it was prevented from being vacuous by the commitment to publish an annual poverty audit against which progress could be assessed. As almost the last gesture of the Labour government, the target was enshrined in legislation in the Child Poverty Act 2010, leaving the incoming government with a daunting task and much incentive to change the definition of poverty (DWP/DfE, 2011).

In other words, Labour effectively adopted the view of the preceding Conservative government in its emphasis on failure to work as a major cause of poverty and the proposed solution of welfare system reform. Since old welfare policy had 'encouraged dependency, lowered self-esteem and denied opportunity and responsibility in almost equal measure' (Blair, 1997), modern welfare policy was to be premised on the notion of promoting opportunity and personal responsibility.

Rights and responsibilities

New Labour was much influenced by its close working relationship with the US Clinton administration and its perception that the idea of public expenditure needed to be made more acceptable to middle-class taxpayers. The idea that political support for welfare could be increased by imposing greater conditionality was taken up in the Labour Party manifesto as a promise of a 'modern welfare state based on rights and duties going together' (Labour Party, 1997). Like Margaret Thatcher and John Major before him, Tony Blair, among others, was of the view that welfare had become a problem rather than a solution, destroying the work ethic and other family values (Walker, 1998). Indeed, Frank Field, New Labour's first minister for welfare reform, unambiguously described welfare as 'the enemy within' which 'erodes the wider moral order of society' (Field, 1997, p 20).

Blair promised wholesale reform, based on enlightened self-interest that would itself lead to moral regeneration. Reform was predicated on work (or workfare) as a condition of citizenship and 'communitarian' principles of obligations and duties (Deacon, 2002; Griggs and Bennett, 2009). Even in the Party manifesto, employment was juxtaposed against responsibilities and against the threat of an emergent 'have-not class, unemployed and disaffected from society' (Labour Party, 1997).

Reflecting these ideas, New Labour's first Green Paper on welfare reform, *New ambitions for our country: A new contract for welfare* (DSS, 1998), established the concept of rights linked to responsibilities through a contract between the state and recipients of support. While such a notion might have led to an expansion in insurance-based benefits, the trend during Labour's period in office was instead towards increased means-testing and stronger and more widely applied conditionality, thus widening the scope for shaming those failing to comply.

Structure: work and making work pay to combat poverty

Apart from the introduction of a minimum wage, New Labour's strategy to address poverty was essentially to adopt the same two-pronged approach as the previous Conservative government, subsequently labelled as 'welfare to work' and 'making work pay'. Added to this was the surprising last-minute focus on tackling 'child poverty'.

Welfare to work

Jobseeker's Allowance had been a cornerstone of the former Conservative government's welfare to work strategy, providing co-located job placement and social assistance provision with the enforcement tools of explicit conditionality and sanctions. To these New Labour added a series of 'New Deal' activation programmes for various groups of working-age benefit recipients. Whereas the Conservatives had shied away from an explicit workfare focus, New Labour embraced it as one of a set of pathways that jobseekers might follow: a subsidised job, self-employment, full-time education or training, work in the voluntary sector or on environmental task forces. Now 'clients', rather than 'customers', were guided down appropriate pathways by newly trained personal advisers, and a system of sanctions was applied in the event that clients failed to participate: two weeks of full Jobseeker's Allowance benefit lost for the first breach, rising to a maximum of 26 weeks for those with repeated breaches.

By the turn of the 21st century the UK had two mandatory and four voluntary New Deal programmes (for lone parents, disabled people, the partners of unemployed people and those aged over 50). This same period also saw the introduction of Employment Zones, employment programmes for long-term unemployed people living in areas geographically targeted as having very high concentrations of worklessness. As the Conservative-Liberal Democrat Coalition came to power in 2010, the Flexible New Deal was being introduced to replace these programmes, while rhetorically applying the same key activation principles: strengthening rights and responsibilities; personalising and tailoring services to the needs of claimants and employers; adopting a local approach to tackling worklessness; and promoting a partnership approach to service delivery involving public, private and third sector organisations (DWP, 2010a).

Incremental change aside, during the first decade of the 21st century there were four developments that profoundly changed the social contract underpinning British social security provisions. All sought to further activate the 'inactive' and reduce the number receiving support without seeking work. The first was the 2001 introduction of mandatory work-focused interviews (WFIs), expanding compulsion (and therefore the possibility of sanctions) to groups other than the traditional unemployed, including lone parents and new recipients of the disability and illness-related Incapacity Benefit. The second was the development of Pathways to Work, a mandatory multi-component programme designed to help Incapacity Benefit recipients to enter and retain work. The third was the replacement of Incapacity Benefit with the more work-oriented Employment and Support Allowance; and the fourth, the movement of lone parents from rights-based Income Support to conditional Jobseeker's Allowance. These changes radically reduced the numbers of people presumed to be deserving of support relative to those who were not.

Making work pay

Apart from the introduction of a National Minimum Wage in April 1999 and tax and National Insurance reductions for 1.5 million low-paid workers (HM Treasury, 2000) a year later, the key component of New Labour's policy to make work pay was the introduction of the Working Families' Tax Credit (WFTC), a refundable tax credit that was acknowledged to be a wage subsidy.

In many respects WFTC was more like the benefit it replaced (Family Credit) than a true tax credit. It was calculated on the basis of household rather than individual income (the UK income tax system is individualised) and paid fortnightly for renewable periods of six months. The preferred mode of delivery was through employers, emphasising to workers the true benefit of working while arguably reducing the stigma attached to the claiming of benefits. As a concession to women's and anti-poverty lobbies, claimants were allowed to opt for the benefit to be paid separately to the non-working parent with care of the children. Being a tax credit rather than a benefit, WFTC was not initially counted as public expenditure, and appeared as a reduction in government spending while actually increasing family incomes substantially. A second generation of tax credits was introduced in 2003 and revised again in 2005.

If tax credits did increase the incomes of families supported by low-waged work and made them more able to actively participate in society, they arguably will have lessened the shame attached to poverty. Indeed, take-up was higher in contrast to earlier in-work benefits, suggesting either that the stigma of applying was less, possibly because many more people were eligible and claiming, or that relative need was greater due to rising wage inequality. Nonetheless, the system still meant increasing numbers of people having publicly to admit that they could not earn enough to provide adequately for their families without help from the state.

Tackling child poverty

Space prohibits full discussion of the agenda to eradicate child poverty announced in March 1999 (Blair, 1999). Suffice to say that, because child poverty was viewed as a product of parental worklessness and increased the chances of children experiencing worklessness later in life, the agenda was a supply-side labour market policy said to offer immediate and intergenerational benefits (HM Treasury, 1999). Equally, the focus on children was a pragmatic political device to circumvent negative attitudes towards a focus on tackling poverty and to build support for an anti-poverty agenda.

Relevant policy papers emphasised the need to address the underlying causes of poverty: low family incomes, the transmission of poverty from one generation to the next and neighbourhood influences. In addition to family income measures discussed earlier, the wider social and 'cultural' causes of poverty were to be countered through high quality services, which would harness the power and expertise of voluntary and community sectors to break the 'cycle of deprivation'. Despite the facade of universalism captured in the title of key policy documents such as *Every Child Matters* (DfES, 2003), the policy structures in practice tended to be heavily targeted, focusing on deprived neighbourhoods and 'dysfunctional families' experiencing 'multiple problems', and therefore divisive. They were also exclusionary, frequently emphasising personal failings rather than structural constraints (Garrett, 2007; Hoyle, 2008). An exception to this generalisation was Sure Start, comprising over 500 local programmes and providing a wide range of family services in disadvantaged communities, which became the flagship policy of such interventions. Having begun as a policy tightly targeted on areas of deprivation, Sure Start moved towards more universal provision only to be subsequently criticised as having been hijacked by more affluent beneficiaries.

If the focus on child poverty was forced on government by a collective antipathy to 'the poor', New Labour's own rhetoric did nothing to counter this. Instead, the mostly targeted structure of service provision reinforced the idea that it was for the inadequate or unfortunate few who could not cope, and that children needed to be protected from adults who were poor and often poor at parenting.

Delivery and recipient perspectives: responsibilities, few rights

Reforms in the delivery of benefits under New Labour led to a more target-driven approach to governance; greater use of private and voluntary sector resources; the increased application of communication technology; and greater utilisation of customer satisfaction surveys and research.

The creation of Jobcentre Plus and the merger of the employment and social security departments into the Department for Work and Pensions in 2001 resulted in the largest public service delivery department in the UK, with over 20 million 'clients'. Most of those of working age were obliged to participate in regular WFIs, fortnightly in the case of unemployed claimants. By 2010, over 50,000 adviser interviews were being conducted in Jobcentre Plus offices each working day (DWP, 2010b).

What claimants sought were simple rules and procedures making it readily possible to understand benefits, their eligibility to them and the steps that they needed to follow to access them (Kellard and Stafford, 1997; Stafford et al, 1997). They appreciated good communication, being kept informed and avoiding the necessity of having to repeat personal circumstances when providing information to agencies. They disliked delays or having to queue. They laid great stress on being treated with respect, as reflected in the demeanour and behaviour of staff and in attractive décor, clean premises and privacy.

Departmental strategies partially mirrored these aspirations and, in fact, customer satisfaction surveys revealed that 75 per cent of customers were satisfied, overall, with the service received (Thomas et al, 2009). By 2011, 88 per cent of recipients were reporting satisfaction with the service, but it is difficult to establish whether this was true improvement or due to a new system of measurement (Howat and Pickering, 2011). The key to dissatisfaction, however, was perceived lack of support and being treated unsympathetically by staff; feeling pressured to apply for unsuitable jobs; lack of allocated time, privacy and continuity of advisers; and inadequate tailoring of support to personal needs and circumstances. Equally, while customers understood the broad principles guiding the sanctions regime, they found the basic conditions of Jobseeker's Allowance unclear, particularly problematic for customers with English as a second language, low literacy levels or learning difficulties.

Our own research, involving in-depth interviews with people on low incomes (Chase and Walker, 2012b; Walker et al, 2012) echoed the concerns raised in previous research. With a few exceptions, where particular benefits advisers were described as helpful and supportive, participants typically described encounters within job centres as frustrating and soul destroying. Being treated as a group, or 'just a number', having to explain circumstances over and over again to different people, having to constantly complete forms, being made to feel small and people 'not bothering to get to know you as a person' were repeatedly iterated as examples of how the process of claiming benefits became dehumanising. One participant, a single mother with two children, for example, commented: "If you check my work record, you can see that I haven't always claimed benefits ... and I just thought 'if you checked that, you wouldn't make me feel so bad about sitting here'." Another woman, also a single mother, took issue not only with the fact that those working at the employment office "look at you like you're crap", but also resented the personal restrictions on her when she entered the office, such as having to turn her phone off, not being allowed to wear a 'hoodie' or being sanctioned for being five minutes late when caring for a small baby. Many people alluded to the awkwardness and stigma attached to being in receipt of benefits, one man, for instance, commenting: "I feel like I'm sponging."

The perceived regulation and inflexibility of the benefits system and the threat of sanction provided further layers to people's sense of aggravation. One woman described the six-monthly review meetings she was obliged to attend while being on Income Support. Currently with a four-year-old attending school part time and a four-month-old baby, she resented the fact that she still had to attend 'back to work reviews' when the logistics of her returning to work in her current circumstances were prohibitive.

New Labour and the policing of poverty

Labour belatedly returned the word 'poverty' to the political lexicon, embedding it in legislation, and attempting to reduce it primarily through increased employment and reduced worklessness. If benefits were a means of tackling poverty, some among the New Labour leadership also saw welfare dependency as a cause of poverty. Moreover, New Labour did not directly challenge the public's largely individualistic view of the causes of poverty (for example, 63 per cent attributed child poverty to parents not wanting to work; see Park et al, 2011), or its negative view of welfare, but rather made use of them in the mantra of 'rights and responsibilities'. In return for the continued provision of state help, Labour portrayed itself as requiring and policing active commitment from welfare recipients. This carefully matched demands by taxpayers sounded out in focus groups and sounding off in the popular press. Furthermore, extending increased benefit conditionality to groups, such as people with disabilities, that had, even under the Poor Law, been considered 'deserving', New Labour both pandered to popularist views in the hope of electoral gain and ratcheted up the stigma felt by all those needing to be reliant on state welfare. Labour's legacy was to confound the social problem of poverty with the political problem of increased spending on welfare and to add further confusion in the public's mind as to what was cause and what was effect.

Universal Credit: welfare as the problem

At the time of writing a new wave of welfare reforms borrowing from the rhetoric of New Labour are underway in the UK. Under the Welfare Reform Act 2012 and beginning in 2013 a large number of benefits embracing in-work and out-of-work, insurance-based, means-tested and citizenship benefits are to be combined into a single Universal Credit. This is to be complemented by a single Work Programme, merging the programmes established by New Labour and delivered by largely private sector providers operating on a payment-by-results basis. The official website (DWP, 2012a) claims that the scheme 'ensures value for money for the taxpayer by … paying service providers from the benefits saved from getting people into work.'

It is too soon to determine how well Universal Credit and the Work Programme will achieve their different objectives and promote the wellbeing of 'recipients', as they are once again being called. At this stage, we primarily limit our reflection to policy-maker framing of reform.

Framing: the rising cost of welfare dependency and poverty

The White Paper introducing the rationale for Universal Credit returned to a focus on the flaws of the pre-existing welfare system, including inefficiency, complexity, limited incentives for working and vulnerability to fraud and error (DWP, 2011, p 7). These issues, it concluded, had 'failed to convince many people to make the transition into work' (p 8). Yet it was the system's alleged role in the creation of 'welfare dependency' for which it came under greatest criticism, as it had the effect of 'trapping individuals, families and whole communities in the very condition it was supposed to alleviate' (p 12).

The notion that poverty stems from unemployment, or more specifically, from choosing not to work, fundamentally continues to polarise poverty discourses in the UK. The emphasis on individual failings, rather than structural causes, accounting for poverty generates a symbiotic cycle of media furore and political rhetoric. Hence the prominent and hugely pervasive view that welfare *dependency* and poverty are intertwined, and that the root cause of poverty is not working. This view generates an echo across political and media discourses and is fed back via the public's response to these ideas in the form of letters and opinion pieces.

Analysis of a random sample of media coverage of issues of poverty and welfare in the UK over five years (2007-12) revealed that people in receipt of state benefits, and particularly out-of-work welfare benefits, were regularly the target of stigma and vilification (see Chase and Walker, 2012c). Besides being blamed for their circumstances, those in receipt of benefits frequently became pawns in the political crossfire. The idea of New Labour having created welfare machinery responsible for entrapping people on state benefits was a repeated analogy. The systemic shaming of the unemployed as 'not wanting to work' was continually echoed over time and space.

Importantly, these same themes, and indeed the same language, were reiterated by participants within focus groups made up of people not currently living in poverty in the UK (see Chase and Walker, 2012d). Despite identifying early on in the group discussions some of the prominent structural causes to poverty, participants tended to move quite quickly to a range of individual or micro-factors accounting for poverty in the UK. While some identified factors such as family commitments and personal difficulties in entering the workplace, discussions soon frequently turned to certain deficiencies among those living in poverty: an unwillingness to work; a lack of 'work ethic' (often said to be inherited from previous generations); a lack of capabilities; and limited aspirations in life – what one person described as "a poverty of aspiration". Others asserted that people living in poverty often had a propensity to not take responsibility for themselves. They were said to have developed a skewed sense of wanting "rights without responsibilities".

These assertions are, of course, reminiscent of those attached to reforms as far back as the Poor Law Amendment Act 1834. The difference is perhaps in the now explicit notion that many people have chosen to remain on benefits, implying that they are in fact defrauding the authorities and are engaged in criminal activity – claiming irrespective of need – and are therefore not genuinely poor but 'paupers'. Again, the theme of *welfare fraud* is one that is heavily planted in both media and political discourses. Indeed media shock stories, rather than empirical evidence, are often shown to generate political response by ministers. Benefits allegedly contribute to a 'broken society', with 'welfare dependency' creating an 'underclass' in which people choose not to work, choose to defraud the authorities, choose to service their addictions and to exist as a burden on society (Chase and Walker, 2012c).

What is more, such ideas are made explicit in the language used by ministers to justify the more recent reforms. In a pre-election speech in 2010 entitled 'A new welfare contract', Prime Minister David Cameron outlined the electoral reason for prioritising welfare reform:

> For far too long in this country people who can work, people who are able to work, and people who choose not to work, you cannot go on claiming welfare like you are now. I have lost count in this election campaign of the number of people who've told me how angry it makes them. One person said to me, "I get up at six, I go to work at seven, and I walk past house after house where the curtains are closed and I know that person isn't going to work, even though they could go to work. Why should I pay my taxes so that someone else can choose to live on welfare?"

Speaking at the launch of the White Paper in 2010, *Universal Credit: Welfare that works*, Iain Duncan Smith, Secretary of State, detailed the social rationale for the reforms – worklessness creating 'a semi-permanent underclass' – and the source of his analysis, personal observation:

> As I travelled to many of Britain's poorest communities I concluded that tackling poverty had to be about much more than handing out money. It was bigger than that. I could see we were dealing with a part of society that had become detached from the rest of us. People who suffer high levels of family breakdown, educational failure, personal debt, addiction – and at the heart of all of this is intergenerational worklessness. Only in understanding this can poverty be defeated.

Later, on the second anniversary of the 2010 election, Duncan Smith reaffirmed the attack on worklessness, describing it as having become 'ingrained', having generated a 'cultural pressure' to conform to this lifestyle and as associated with the perception that 'taking a job is a mug's game' (Duncan Smith, 2012). Moreover, analysis of other ministerial speeches reveals the extent of the government's concern that worklessness, along with dependency, engenders a sense of hopelessness and low expectations and 'breeds intergenerational poverty' (DWP, 2011, p 1), contributing to a divided, 'broken' society.

Ministers in the Thatcher and Major Conservative governments, despite wanting to limit social security expenditure, were circumspect in their language, hinting at abuse by reference to 'genuine need', but limiting aggressive negativity to their campaigns against fraudsters. Now it seems, after more than a decade of New Labour's rhetoric on worklessness and responsibilities, ministers feel more able to use and be informed by the language of the streets.

Structure: simplicity and clear signals

As proposed, Universal Credit is said to be simple to understand, to minimise work disincentives and to always ensure that it pays to work. Its fundamental logic is that people choose to work purely on the basis of financial incentives and that this has fuelled the belief that Universal Credit will end unnecessary worklessness and welfare dependency. In further pursuit of this goal, a new claimant contract has been put in place, tougher penalties for fraud introduced, and 'abuse' is to be 'driven out' of the Social Fund system by giving greater power to local authorities (DWP, 2012b).

If the new system of Universal Credit successfully delivers the correct benefits to recipients efficiently and on time, the reforms might indeed serve to dignify claimants with the quality service that is demanded by 'customers' (DWP, 2011, p 38). However, the scope for greater shaming is very real. Reductions in benefit may lead to people being either unable to adequately feed and house themselves or face the added indignity of indebtedness. The replacement of the national Social Fund to cover exceptional needs with a discretionary local authority provision risks a return to a Poor Law scenario. Thus, we may return to a time in which the interests of the prosperous are often prioritised over the needs of people living in poverty, who are literally a financial burden on the community and forced to beg for public charity by proving themselves to be more deserving than the next poorest person.

Implications and recommendations: the making of a class apart

Arguably more than any other advanced economy, the British welfare state prioritises poverty relief over other social policy objectives such as social cohesion. It makes poverty the principal route of access to social security provision while additionally drawing moral distinctions between those who are 'deserving' and 'undeserving'. Recipients are repeatedly shamed by the presumption of their un-deservingness in the political rhetoric surrounding the rationale of welfare provision, and in the design and delivery of related services. Welfare policy has increasingly focused on the presumed personal inadequacies of individuals and communities, effectively ignoring wider structural causes of poverty and diverting political and public discourse away from them.

Indeed, the belief that personal failure more than anything accounts for poverty and that those experiencing it are less worthy than others, appear to be notions that have become culturally embedded. Earlier work on the cultural representations of poverty and shame through literature and film (Chase and Walker, 2012a), an analysis of media portrayals of poverty and welfare (Chase and Walker, 2012c) and focus groups discussions with the general public about their perceptions of the causes of poverty and of those experiencing it (Chase and Walker, 2012d) have all demonstrated the pervasiveness of these same assumptions. Such findings have clear implications for anti-poverty policy in the UK.

As demonstrated, despite the ostensible goal of welfare policy in the UK being poverty relief, structural reforms to welfare have largely been driven by concerns with benefit cost, welfare dependency, incentives and abuse. These concerns appear to have usurped the importance of reducing poverty – which increased from 15 per cent in 1984 to over 21 per cent in 2010[3] (Cribb et al, 2012). Subsequent reforms have sought to make clear the financial incentives of work by holding down the value of certain out-of-work benefits and increasing the generosity and scope of income-tested wage supplements alongside the increased use of activation programmes. The result has been to substantially increase the numbers of people subject to means-testing, and the associated risk of stigma. The number with an unconditional citizenship right to benefits and the freedom to seek work opportunities without explicit bureaucratic control and the threat of sanction has been reduced. Policy reform has sought to engineer and control a change in people's behaviour and in so doing has served to erode their autonomy, along with their sense of agency and self-respect. In the attempt to curtail the growth of a phantom behavioural underclass, policy has created a welfare class with reduced citizenship rights and subjected to greater policing of their behaviour.

Unsurprisingly therefore, and despite survey findings indicating high 'customer' satisfaction among service users, when asked directly, benefit recipients often describe systems as dehumanising and their treatment as demeaning. The danger is that over time they begin to internalise the policy rhetoric, reiterated by the media (Chase and Walker, 2012b), that they are members of 'a class apart' and assumed to be undeserving until they can prove otherwise. With the odds of changing their circumstances stacked against people in poverty, such policies are more likely to sap and undermine self-confidence and agency than they are to facilitate exit from poverty.

Our analysis suggests that, in order to shift anti-poverty policies from being shame-inducing to dignity-promoting, policy reform should start with a critical evaluation of its framing. As indicated earlier, consecutive governments, almost irrespective of political persuasion, have all served to legitimate talk of social security as a burden and to juxtapose the claims of those on benefit against the interests of taxpayers, explicitly dividing into two competing groups the population that post-war policy-makers had sought to unite through National Insurance. Talk of genuine poverty has continuously raised suspicions of false or fabricated poverty and propagated beliefs that benefits create disincentives to work, encourage negative role models for children and perpetuate intergenerational poverty. Employing the explicit language of rights and responsibilities, the dominant rhetorical presumption is that benefit recipients are not fulfilling their responsibility to work. Hence, the idea that the right to benefits – not just for the unemployed, but also for lone parents and people with disabilities – should be conditional on job search and job readiness. At the time of writing, under the Liberal-Conservative Coalition government, these stigmatising notions are more pronounced than ever. Unless politicians, the media and the public are sensitised to the ways in which these unfounded assumptions are deployed to justify policies that fail to address the structural causes of poverty and only serve to shame and undermine the dignity of those in receipt of benefits, then we can only assume path dependency in how such policies are framed for a further 500 years.

Notes

[1] An electoral system in which the candidate with the most votes wins and all votes cast for other candidates count for nothing.

[2] 'New' Labour refers to a period in the history of the British Labour Party from 1994 to 2010, led by Tony Blair and Gordon Brown.

[3] Measured as 60 per cent of median equalised income after housing costs.

References

Bassett, P. (1994) 'Tories and Labour take up battle stations over jobs', *The Times*, 25 October.

Blair, T. (1997) 'The 21st century welfare state', Speech to the 'Social policy and economic performance' Conference, Amsterdam, 24 January.

Blair, T, (1999) 'Beveridge revisited: a welfare state for the 21st century' in R. Walker (ed) *Ending child poverty: Popular welfare for the 21st century?*, Bristol: Policy Press, pp 7-34.

Bruce, M. (1968) *The coming of the welfare state*, London: Batsford.

Cameron, D. (2010) 'A new welfare contract', Speech, Tuesday 20 April.

Chase, E. and Walker, R. (2012a) *Portrayals of poverty and shame in British literature and contemporary film*, Working Paper (http://softinnovators. com/spi/content/united-kingdom). Unpublished report.

Chase, E. and Walker, R. (2012b) 'The co-construction of shame in the context of poverty: Beyond a threat to the social bond', *Sociology*. vol 47, no 4, pp 739-754.

Chase, E. and Walker, R. (2012c) *'It must be true – I read it in the news!' Representations of UK poverty in British national newspapers 2006-2012*, Working Paper (http://softinnovators.com/spi/content/united-kingdom). Unpublished report.

Chase, E. and Walker, R. (2012d) *The role of society in shaming people living in poverty: Views and perceptions of the general public*, Working Paper (http://softinnovators.com/spi/content/united-kingdom). Unpublished report.

Collard, D. (1985) 'Social security and work after Fowler', *Political Quarterly*, vol 56, no 4, pp 361-73.

Cribb, J., Joyce, R. and Phillips, D. (2012) *Living standards, poverty and inequality in the UK: 2012*, IFS Commentary C124, London: Institute for Fiscal Studies.

Deacon, A. (2002) *Perspectives on welfare: Ideas, ideologies and policy debates*, Buckingham and Philadelphia, PA: Open University Press.

Deans, J. (1994) 'Big earners meet the workshy in welfare cash war', *Daily Mail*, 24 October.

DfES (Department for Education and Skills) (2003) *Every Child Matters*, Cm 5860, London: The Stationery Office.

DSS (Department of Social Security) (1985) *Reform of social security (vol 1)*, Cmnd 9517, London: HMSO.

DSS (1998) *New ambitions for our country: A new contract for welfare*, Cm 3805, London: DSS.

Duncan Smith, I. (2010) 'Universal Credit: Welfare that works', Speech at launch of the White Paper, Thursday 11 November.

Duncan Smith, I. (2012) Leonard Steinberg Memorial Lecture, Policy Exchange, Westminster, London, Wednesday 9 May.

DWP (Department for Work and Pensions)/DfE (Department for Education) (2011) *A new approach to child poverty: Tackling the causes of disadvantage and transforming families' lives*, Cm 8061, London: DWP and DfE.

DWP (2010a) *Flexible New Deal*, London: DWP (www.dwp.gov.uk/ supplying-dwp/what-we-buy/welfare-to-work-services/flexible-new-deal/).

DWP (2010b) *An analysis of the productivity of the Department for Work and Pensions 2002/03 to 2008/09*, London: DWP.

DWP (2011) *Universal Credit: Welfare that works*, Cm 795.7, London: DWP.

DWP (2012a) The Work Programme, 'Helping people to find and stay in work', London: DWP (www.dwp.gov.uk/policy/welfare-reform/ the-work-programme/).

Field, F. (1997) *Reforming welfare*, London: Social Market Foundation.

Garrett, P. (2007) '"Sinbin" solutions: The "pioneer" projects for "problem families" and the forgetfulness of social policy research', *Critical Social Policy*, vol 27, no 2, pp 203-30.

Griggs, J. and Bennett, F. (2009) *Rights and responsibilities in the social security system*, Occasional Paper No 6, London: Social Security Advisory Committee.

Heathcoat-Amory, D. (1985) *Hansard*, House of Commons Debates, 18 June, vol 81, pp 187-269.

Himmelfarb, G. (1984a) *The idea of poverty*, London: Faber.

Himmelfarb, G. (1984b) 'The idea of poverty: England in the early Industrial Age', *History Today*, vol 34, no 2, pp 23-30.

Howat, N. and Pickering, E. (2011) *Jobcentre Plus customer survey 2011*, DWP Research Report No 775, London: Department for Work and Pensions.

Hoyle, D. (2008) 'Problematizing *Every Child Matters*', *The encyclopaedia of informal education* (www.infed.org/socialwork/every_child_matters_a_critique.htm).

HMSO (1834) *Report from His Majesty's Commissioners for inquiring into the administration and practical operation of the Poor Laws*, London: HMSO.

HMSO (1994) *Jobseeker's Allowance*, White Paper, Cm 2687, October, London: HMSO.

HM Treasury (1997) *The modernisation of Britain's tax and benefit system: Employment opportunity in a changing labour market*, Pre-Budget Publications, Number 1, London: HM Treasury.

HM Treasury (1999) *Tackling poverty and extending opportunity*, The modernisation of Britain's tax and benefit system, Number 4, London: HM Treasury.

HM Treasury (2000) *Tackling poverty and making work pay – Tax credits for the 21st century*, The modernisation of Britain's tax and benefit system, Number 6, London: HM Treasury.

Kellard, K. and Stafford, B. (1997) *Delivering benefits to unemployed people*, DSS Research Report No 69, London: The Stationery Office.

Labour Party (1997) *New Labour, because Britain deserves better*, Election manifesto, London: Labour Party (www.labour-party.org.uk/manifestos/1997/1997-labour-manifesto.shtml/).

McKay, S. and Rowlingson, K. (1999) *Social security in Britain*, Basingstoke: Macmillan.

McKay, S., Smith, A., Youngs, R. and Walker, R. (1999) *Unemployment and jobseeking after the introduction of Jobseeker's Allowance*, DSS Research Report No 99, London: The Stationery Office.

Mattinson, D. (2010) *Talking to a brick wall: How New Labour stopped listening to the voter and why we need a new politics*, London: Biteback.

OED (*Oxford English Dictionary*) (2012) *The definitive record of the English language* (www.oed.com).

Park, A., Clery, E. and Phillips, M. (2011) *British Social Attitudes 28*, London: NatCen Social Research (http://ir2.flife.de/data/natcen-social-research/igb_html/index.php?bericht_id=1000001&index=&lang=ENG).

Rayner, E., Shah, S., White, R., Dawes, L. and Tinsley, K (2000) *Evaluating Jobseeker's Allowance: A summary of the research findings*, DSS Research Report No 116, London: The Stationery Office.

Reid, P. (1994) 'Hopeless, helpless and lawless.... Danger signals from the underclass. A moral dilemma the Chancellor must not ignore', *The Mail on Sunday*, p 28.

Smith, A., Youngs, R., Ashworth, K., Mckay, S. and Walker R. (with Elias, P. and McKnight, A.) (2000) *Understanding the impact of Jobseeker's Allowance*, DSS Research Report No 111, London: The Stationery Office.

Stafford, B., Kellard, K. and Horsley, E. (1997) *Customer contact with the Benefits Agency*, DSS Research Report No 65, London: The Stationery Office.

Strickland, P. (1996) *Jobseeker's Allowance*, Research paper 96/5 (16 January), London: House of Commons Library, Education and Social Services Section.

Thomas, A., Coleman, N., Turtle, J., Bone, S., Bassett, C. and Mason, J. (2009) *Jobcentre Plus customer satisfaction research: Findings from quantitative and qualitative research*, London: DWP Research Report No 657, London: Department for Work and Pensions.

Walker, R. (1998) 'The Americanisation of British welfare: A case-study of policy transfer', *Focus, Journal of the Institute for Research on Poverty*, University of Madison–Wisconsin, vol 19, no 3, pp 32-40.

Walker, R. and Wiseman, M. (2003) 'Making welfare work: UK activation policies under *New* Labour', *International Social Security Review*, vol 56, no 1, pp 3-29.

Walker, R., Chase, E. and Lødemel, I. (2012) 'The indignity of the Welfare Reform Act 2012: Why the ILO matters for UK antipoverty programmes', *Poverty*, vol 143, pp 9-12.

Weale, A. (1985) 'Mr Fowler's psychology: reform of social security', *Political Quarterly*, vol 56, no 4, pp 321-30.

Wheatley, J. (1994) *The Jobseekers' Bill (Bill 5 of 1994/95)*, Research Paper 94/129 (15 December), London: House of Commons Library, Education and Social Services Section.

Wood, N., Sherman, J. and Prynn, J. (1994) 'Dole system to be replaced by "workfare"', *The Times*, 25 October.

EIGHT

'Food that cannot be eaten': the shame of Uganda's anti-poverty policies

Grace Bantebya Kyomuhendo and Amon Mwiine

Introduction

Over the past 25 years, the varying approaches encompassed within Uganda's anti-poverty effort have been touted as a best case model in the developing world (Hickey, 2011). Uganda is a land-locked country lying astride the equator in east central Africa. It is closely linked by economic and colonial history to Kenya in the east, Tanzania in the south, South Sudan and the Democratic Republic of Congo (DRC) to the north and west respectively, and Rwanda in the southwest. Agriculture is the mainstay of the economy, contributing 31 per cent of the gross domestic product (GDP), 85 per cent of exports and employing at least 77 per cent of the active labour force (MFPED, 2004; UBOS, 2007). This agricultural influence has resulted in an economic system dependent on rain-fed crops and livestock farming. As Uganda has yet to develop and adopt irrigation and water harvesting technologies to any significant extent that could reduce the country's dependence on rain-fed agriculture (UNDP, 2005; UBOS, 2010), the country's economic health has been subject to the vagaries of weather and climate.

With a per capita GDP of US$1,457 in 2003 (UNDP, 2005) and a per capita income of US$334 in 2005 (UNDP, 2005), Uganda was and remains ranked among the poorest countries in the world. Rural poverty has been influenced by a combination of factors, including the slow growth of the agricultural sector and low prices of agricultural products; decreasing soil fertility and crop yields; malnutrition and a heavy disease burden including HIV/AIDS, malaria and tuberculosis; gender inequalities in access to productive resources; and a lack of focus on the poorest in public sector investment to support agriculture.

Endemic corruption is also a key challenge that pervades all aspects of life. Said to be a legacy of colonial rule, it arguably impeded Uganda's economic development in the decades of autocratic rule following independence (Ruzindana, 1997). During the era of democratic reform, the Museveni government and its National Resistance Movement (NRM) promised 'clean government', both in its push to be elected in the mid-1980s and post-election in an effort to appeal to international donors. Corruption, however, has since remained a serious problem (Flanary and Watt, 1999; Akello, 2012; Izama, 2012). International aid was withdrawn in 2012 in response to rampant violations (Ford, 2012).

Given these challenges, the reduction of poverty and vulnerability has been both an integral part of Uganda's national development strategy and yet has also met stumbling blocks in the translation of national promises into local practices. Indeed, significant success has been attained over the past decade. The percentage of Ugandans living in poverty decreased from 56.4 to 24.5 per cent between 1992/93 and 2009/10. While this success means that over 23 million Ugandans lived above the poverty line[1] in 2010, more than half were classified as insecure non-poor (UBOS, 2010). These households were able to meet their basic needs, but also had consumption levels that were below twice the poverty line and remained insecure and vulnerable to falling into absolute poverty.

Although Uganda continues to assess poverty situations using a poverty line, considerations such as vulnerability, social isolation and humiliation are dimensions likely to capture the hardships endured by specific groups as well as or better than lack of income (Sen, 2000; Webster and Pederson, 2002). While poverty has material and non-material dimensions, development partners and policy-makers working in Africa tend to address the material aspects of poverty due to their tangibility.

This chapter focuses on one of poverty's non-material dimensions: the putative nexus that exists between poverty and shame. Scholars recognise that poverty-induced shame excludes people living in poverty from access to opportunities and equal participation in mainstream development processes (Sen, 2000; Webster and Pederson, 2002; Chase and Bantebya Kyomuhendo, 2014). This chapter focuses on the role that anti-poverty policy may play in this nexus. We trace the effects of key anti-poverty measures that have been implemented in Uganda, analysing how the framing, structuring and delivery methods associated with each either moderate or exacerbate the poverty–shame nexus.

Uganda's anti-poverty policy-making efforts have been shaped in the last 15 years under two primary strategic frameworks: the Poverty

Eradication Action Plan (PEAP) 1997, which in the past five years has increasingly been displaced by the 2010 National Development Plan (NDP). The PEAP era reflected public policy cooperation between government and development partners, and applied a gender focus to the improvement of social service delivery in the areas of education, health and sanitation. It also saw a shift in government focus from rehabilitation to poverty eradication. Two of the policies analysed in this chapter – universal primary education (UPE) and the Plan for Modernisation of Agriculture/National Agricultural Advisory Services (PMA/NAADS) – have been key components of the PEAP approach.

The NDP represents a new framework paradigm that has responded to the promise of economic wealth. This promise is tied to the anticipated exploitation of oil reserves and follows the publicly touted success of the PEAP era.[2] Public discussions have also, however, focused on a number of structural bottlenecks threatening to undermine further development. Hence, the primary policy emphasis has shifted away from poverty reduction and towards economic transformation and wealth creation, with a special focus on addressing development constraints. While the sustained reduction and eventual eradication of poverty remain, they are now second to transformation, and the NDP focuses on binding constraints across administrative, infrastructural and behavioural realms. The third policy measure analysed, Prosperity for All (PFA) (or *Bonna Bagaggawale*), represents this new approach.

While the approaches and objectives concerning development policy have changed over the years, what they share is a failure to consider the potential for shaming given the presence of social norms and practices concerning poverty. This potential is also inherent in the design and provision of programmes and benefits. Our presentation of the three anti-poverty measures discussed in this chapter takes this crucial element into consideration. The chapter analysis draws from policy documents relating to the three policy measures described above. Our analytic focus on policy and shame is further informed by fieldwork exploring the experiences of individuals living in poverty and public discourses and perceptions concerning poverty.

The discussion is separated into three sections. We begin with a focus on the framing or broader socioeconomic and cultural context circumscribing Ugandan social policy-making over the past 15 years. This section describes a marked shift in approach represented by the replacement of PEAP with the NDP as the dominant approach. The second section deals with the structuring, shaping and delivery of the UPE and PMA/NAADS programmes, belonging to the PEAP approach and of the PFA, subsumed under the newer NDP approach.

Within this section, we focus on the discourses, design elements and delivery practices connected to PEAP programmes that create or ameliorate poverty-induced shame and impact on the agency of those living in poverty. The PFA approach is fairly new and has not, as of yet, been highly researched. Thus, our evaluation of PFA is limited mostly to the feedback received in conversations with local community members, and is posed as a reflection on the possible shaming nature of this reform. The third section discusses the implications that these policy approaches have on the lives of those targeted for poverty alleviation. The analysis ends with a set of recommendations for formulating policy that work toward building the dignity of Uganda's most vulnerable.

Framing policy: shifting priorities

While absolute poverty in Uganda has persisted, there has been a significant decrease across all regions of the country. In 1990, the lack of a hand hoe or animal hide was perceived as a key indicator of poverty. In 2011 the lack of an ox plough or mattress was the corresponding indicator. Likewise, those perceived to be poor in 1990 lacked access to education and healthcare. Today it is the quality of these services rather than access to them that is at issue. The reduction of absolute poverty should, however, be interpreted with caution. The marked improvement does not reflect a unified reality across the country. Between 2005/06 and 2009/10 the largest improvements in welfare took place in the country's central and eastern regions and in the West Nile sub-region. Poverty figures, however, vary dramatically: while 77 per cent of the population of the capital city of Kampala is middle class, 76 per cent live in absolute poverty in the north eastern segment of the country (Republic of Uganda, 2012).

The trend also fails to consider the increasing importance of relative poverty (Republic of Uganda, 2012), especially in Uganda's urban areas. Income inequality throughout Uganda increased significantly in the period between 1992 and 2010, especially within Uganda's urban areas (Republic of Uganda, 1992b, 2009). The 10 million Ugandans who currently live above twice the poverty line and are thus categorised as 'middle class' are distinct in a number of respects. In addition to lower vulnerability and a lower threat of risk than is faced by those living closer to the poverty line, Uganda's middle class devotes a higher proportion of its total consumption to expenditure on education and has fewer and more highly educated children. Middle-class households are marginally more likely to run a business and to draw wages from non-agricultural-related income (Republic of Uganda, 2012). These differences mean that, unlike much of Uganda's population, the middle class is less likely to be subject to the variable circumstances that are attached to a reliance on subsistence agriculture. This security is reflected in the fact that middle-class parents possess the resources to push for quality education for their children.

Poverty reduction through the PEAP approach

The politics of development in Uganda have been an instigator and result of these macroeconomic changes. The PEAP approach prevalent in the early 1990s to early 2000s was, in part, driven by two elements. The first was Uganda's insecure economic status during this period. The country held a place on the HIPC (Heavily Indebted Poor Countries) list[3] and its domestic budget was supported largely through appeals to donors that focused on poverty reduction and the Millennium Development Goals (MDGs) (Hickey, 2011).

Second, a no-party presidential election system meant politicians easily gained votes when applying a clientelist approach of the promise of radical and populist reforms in primary education and health, as well as smaller-scale agriculture. The PEAP approach was said to be a showcase for poverty reduction-oriented policy-making in the developing world (Hickey, 2011). Reflecting the heavy focus on poverty reduction, the Museveni government set up the Poverty Action Fund in 1998 in order to channel resources from HIPC debt relief to key sectors associated with this aim. The virtual fund became an integral part of the national budget and instrumental in translating the PEAP priorities into public expenditure. Political interventions were, however, typically developed and proclaimed from the top, and the promises attached to a policy frequently looked quite different at the ground-level implementation phase. The story we tell below illustrates several of many cases in which policies were introduced without consideration given to infrastructural and social realities. While these policies were framed by optimistic language and good intentions, on the ground the promises attached were difficult to live up to.

Structural transformation through the NDP approach

The mid-2000s saw changes to the Ugandan economy and political system that reflected and encouraged a new development strategy. The 2010 NDP approach was initiated as the country shifted to multi-party politics in 2006. It also reflected a political will, most notably by President Museveni and his NRM party, to gain more national autonomy over Uganda's development policy agenda (Hickey, 2011). The discovery of oil reserves and the subsequent move by the country off the HIPC list has further encouraged an earlier focus that Museveni had placed on 'modernisation' and structural transformation. This new rhetorical emphasis has been designed, in part, to appeal to potential investors in the country's future oil ventures, notably China, whose aid has been prioritised for activities related to infrastructural development and business (Lee, 2007).

These changes have resulted in a broader policy-making shift from priorities placed on poverty alleviation to that of building the middle class. Interest in appealing to investors, in particular China, has further encouraged the focus on modernisation (Whitfield, 2009, as cited in Hickey, 2011). As in China, the shift in focus to modernisation has been matched by a new rise in income inequality and relative poverty, especially marked in urban areas (see Chapter Two, this volume). It is clear that absolute and relative poverty still represent huge problems for much of the Ugandan population. Modernisation and building the middle class is not a solution to the deep economic difficulties faced by the vast majority, and holds the potential to widen the gap between the economically secure and poor even further.

The shift in focus is reflected in language associated with the PFA programme emphasising 'productivity' and 'prosperity' over 'poverty eradication'. It is reflected in the choice to target support to 'productive' larger-scale farmers. The de-prioritisation of people living in poverty is also mirrored in the government's replacement of the former PEAP goal of reducing poverty to 10 per cent by 2017 with that of attaining middle-income status by the same year (Republic of Uganda, 2010, as cited in Hickey, 2011). Finally, unlike the PEAP, the NDP does not equally prioritise the development pillars of growth, higher incomes and quality of life, but rather, creates a new hierarchy of fiscal priorities. Placed at the top of this hierarchy are 'productive' priority areas such as production, employment and infrastructure (roads and energy). At the bottom are social sectors (water and sanitation, health and nutrition, education and sports). Where the PFA does maintain spending on these sectors, it does so by upgrading the focal points within them, for example, by shifting emphasis from primary education to higher education and from small-scale farming to larger agribusinesses. This new hierarchy is further reflected in severely reduced fiscal expenditures towards the PFA as well as in stagnated spending on primary education and health (Hickey, 2011). Hence, this shift has resulted in the creation of new tiers of opportunity for some (the better off). However, as described below, it has also marginalised the concerns of the most vulnerable and resulted in heightened shame for these groups.

Structuring and delivering policy: two development approaches

PEAP and poverty reduction

The story of the two PEAP era policies described here provides insight into the limitations of short-term thinking and top-down delivery that circumscribed anti-poverty policy-making from the 1990s onwards. These limitations, we will show, along with a lack of infrastructure to support policy efforts, have resulted in heightened shame for many of those targeted for poverty reduction.

Shaping and structuring UPE

UPE was a flagship measure introduced under the first PEAP in 1997 and still remains. This populist reform was aimed at reducing poverty through the development of human capital among the majority of Ugandans. The aim of the policy was to promote citizenship, along with moral, ethical and spiritual values; to promote scientific, technical and cultural knowledge, skills and attitudes; and to eradicate illiteracy and equip children with the basic skills and knowledge to contribute to national development (Republic of Uganda, 1992a). The official goal was to provide basic access to quality and affordable education for all Ugandans, helping to secure the goals stated within the PEAP Education for All (EFA) campaign and the MDGs by 2015 (Republic of Uganda, 2006). Basic access meant the provision of a minimum level of necessary facilities and resources, and parents retained responsibility for providing exercise books, pens, uniforms, school meals and transport. UPE also decentralised school management, giving local governments the responsibility to recruit teachers, construct classrooms and inspect schools (Avenstrap et al, 2004). Finally, the government chose to implement UPE only in government-aided primary schools, thereby hoping to shift the focus of targeting from certain families to certain schools. This indiscriminate targeting of government-aided primary schools in both rural and urban settings, however, would end up posing unique constraints for children from poor families (Republic of Uganda, 2006).

The measure initially offered free primary school tuition to a maximum of four children in households determined eligible according to local discretion. Placing an emphasis on gender parity and inclusion, at least two subsidised students per family were to be girls, and priority was given to disabled children (Kisubi, 2008). The result was a near doubling in primary school enrolment, from 2.9 million to 5.3 million between 1996 and 1997. In 1997, without concern for potential infrastructural limitations, the government broadened its commitment from four children per family to *all* primary school-aged students. This move reflected a shift in targeting criteria from financial need to citizenship, a move that some critics perceived as an appeal to voter populism, with vested political connotations for the incumbent government (Kisubi, 2008). The political promise was to achieve UPE for all children aged 6-12 by 2000 (Kisubi, 2008).

The programme was a success in terms of increasing access to education. The effect on the poorest quintile was particularly marked – school access almost as high as that of the richest quintile, and the total enrolment ratio rose from 68 to 123 per cent in the first year of UPE and to 240 per cent in the first six years (Deininger, 2003; Avenstrup et al, 2004). The radical increase in enrolment during these first years was not, however, matched by a matching outlay of increased resources, resulting in 'access shock' (Avenstrup et al, 2004). With this came overcrowded schools, multiple school shifts, teacher and material shortages and a rise in 'over-age' students. Academic standards plummeted. Furthermore, pupils had to do without school essentials, much less those 'extras' that had not been covered by government funding (Avenstrup et al, 2004).

Open access to primary schools and the complete elimination of school fees, a key source of financing in conjunction with the ensuing access shock, resulted in the need to increasingly depend on the unreliable and untimely remittance of funds from Ministry of Education headquarters in Kampala (Avenstrup et al, 2004). This situation was particularly untenable for rural UPE schools. While the government had committed itself to implementing the UPE programme in all government-aided primary schools, the responsibility for managing and supervising the schools had been delegated to district councils in 1997 (Republic of Uganda, 1997). The amount and efficiency of fund disbursement was especially problematic in rural areas, where the release of funds tended to be particularly delayed (Kisubi, 2008). Hence, while the decentralised UPE framework has been credited with a dramatic increase in primary school enrolment, public primary education services are still dogged by concerns over financing, equity, quality and the need for curriculum reform (Bashaasha et al, 2011).

In a nutshell, lack of infrastructural support and of detailed planning or baseline data posed key implementation challenges undermining the benefits of universal access. Other ad hoc features of UPE such as the automatic promotion of pupils irrespective of performance, abolition of school uniforms and a school lunch programme reflected the pressures and constraints in government efforts to deliver UPE. For the pupils coming from poor families, however, these pressures would manifest themselves in unique ways.

Shaming through UPE delivery

Reflecting the PEAP focus on poverty reduction, the UPE programme emphasised the elimination of unequal access to primary education in order to provide greater opportunities to children coming from poor families. The application of this strategy without proper infrastructural back-up, however, led to the attachment of a poverty label to UPE schools, as resulting access shock included a drop in academic standards. This heightened prevalent public scepticism with regard to financing and educational quality in the schools. While the adults we spoke with were all defined as poor or economically insecure, many refused to accept poverty as an innate identity and found the label 'painful'. The fact that children were expected to attend UPE schools that served the 'poor' heightened this experience and was found detestable and shameful by pupils and parents alike (Kyomuhendo Bantebya and Mwiine, 2014a, 2014b).

UPE schools were not only burdened with the quality issues and stigma tied to access shock; the presence of students from widely diverging economic statuses within the same school heightened the feeling of relative deprivation experienced by pupils from families with fewer economic resources. The premise that poverty was universal and hence all families were 'deserving' of public aid was fundamentally flawed since middle-class families had been comfortably able to afford to pay for their children's education, both in government-aided and in private schools (*Bukedde* Newspaper, 2002; Kisubi, 2008). As of 1997, all children were indiscriminately targeted for the schools, resulting in a mix of children from various economic statuses within the same school. The rural families we spoke with described the shaming effects of relative deprivation. In urban areas where private schools were established, middle-class parents were able to access a presumably higher quality education option and thus steer their children away from public schools. In the rural areas, however, there were few private schools. Middle-class families who could otherwise comfortably afford tuition and other fees for their children had no option but to keep their children enrolled in the now lowly ranked UPE schools. Despite accessing free tuition from government, poorer students often had to do without school basics including a uniform, lunch and scholastic materials such as mathematical sets and pens.

For pupils from more economically vulnerable families, the stark differences between them and their better-off peers triggered negative, internalised feelings of shame, inadequacy, low self-worth and frustration. For these pupils, the government-aided primary schools were experienced as new and unavoidable arenas of poverty-induced shaming. Many felt ashamed, angry and sad at their inability to meet these material standards, in comparison to their better off peers. Material differences were reflected in social disparities, and many also noted that the shame they felt drove them to keep to themselves (Kyomuhendo Bantebya and Mwiine, 2014a).

The government did not stop at failing to consider many of the provisions that would better integrate students from families of all income levels. It further exacerbated the shaming of pupils from poorer families by distinguishing between them and pupils from better-off families. A case in point was the contentious decision by the Museveni government to prohibit school administrations from charging lunch fees, which would have enabled the schools to offer a lunch programme. After headteachers started charging lunch fees at several schools, the government response was prompt and explicit. While on a tour to monitor the UPE implementation in Busoga (Eastern Uganda), President Museveni threatened that headmasters who flouted his directive would end up in jail (*Bukedde* Newspaper, 2002). He boldly stated that the middle-class parents who insisted that their children must have lunch at school should move their children to private schools instead of forcing poor parents to pay for meals (Kisubi, 2008). This policy not only failed to provide a school lunch option for children from poorer families (via subsidies), it also used these pupils as the rationale for failing to provide a lunch programme at all. The children we spoke with described the experience of going a full school day without lunch as not only physically disorienting, but it also heightened their shame, especially when they compared themselves with their better-off peers who carried prepared lunches to school (Bantebya Kyomuhendo and Mwiine, 2014a).

The depreciation of standards and heightened division in rural schools between pupils of differing economic backgrounds led to a quickly eroded image of government-aided UPE schools. Attached stigma was reflected in the degeneration of public perception of the schools as representing the promise of *Bonabasome* (EFA) to the reality of *Bonabakone* (illiteracy/mediocrity for all – literally, 'food you cannot eat'). For pupils who had no alternative but to be enrolled in UPE schools, it was this derogatory and undignified public perception that was particularly shaming (Bantebya Kyomuhendo and Mwiine, 2014a).

Shaping and structuring PMA/NAADS

PMA/NAADS was introduced four years after UPE implementation and within the wider framework of the PEAP and the set of priorities related to agriculture and rural development. PMA was announced in 2000 as a multisectoral strategy to 'eradicate poverty through a profitable, competitive, sustainable and dynamic agricultural and agro-industrial sector' (MAAIF, 2006). It aimed to transform poor subsistence farmers into progressive commercial entrepreneurs. It remains a cross-sectoral framework for guiding the development of policies and investment plans to enable rural groups living in poverty to improve their livelihoods in ways that are sustainable. In particular, it focuses on raising farm productivity, increasing the share of agricultural production that is marketed, and creating on and off farm employment (NAADS Act 2001; MAAIF, 2006).

PMA has an ambitious agenda of policy and institutional reform and investments in seven intervention areas, including agricultural extension through the NAADS programme (MAAIF, 2000; MFPED, 2004). In conjunction with PMA, NAADS was put in place in 2001 to increase the efficiency and effectiveness of extension services. The NAADS Act 2001 provided the mandate to develop a demand-driven agricultural service delivery system for poor subsistence farmers. NAADS has employed a public–private approach to empower farmers to demand and control agricultural advisory services (Benin et al, 2007), and was expected to have a positive impact on the adoption of modern agricultural production technologies and practices. The government's announced objectives associated with the introduction of PMA were meant to increase income and enhance the quality of life of poor subsistence farmers. This effort would be realised through programmes to increase their productivity and share of marketed production; to improve their household food security; to provide gainful employment through agro-processing factories and services; and to promote the sustainable use and management of natural resources (Benin et al, 2007). PMA stated that NAADS would promote an 'efficient extension service' for 'smallholder resource-poor farmers' in the interest of the 'public good'. Following this, national expenditures targeted to this group were to increase (Benin et al, 2007).

The processes and outcomes tied to NAADS were full of good intentions. It was to be structured to take into consideration the particular needs, constraints and resources of economically vulnerable farmers in order to generate practical options for improvement. Farmer participants within NAADS were to be 'empowered' as active 'partners' in the improvement of their situation (Namara, 2009). Emphasis was placed on how the work programme and activities of agricultural advisers would be determined by the farmers themselves (Namara, 2009). Informed by this conceptual framework of active partnership and empowerment, and in response to the poor performance and low stakeholder support of the existing Unified Extension Service, NAADS was conceived as a national programme that would operate using a decentralised demand-driven and private sector-oriented approach (MAAIF, 2000). Its objectives included the development of appropriate farmer-controlled institutional structures and processes for managing NAADS at all levels (NAADS Act 2001; MAAIF 2000).

The decentralised nature of NAADS is reflected in an elaborate structure and implementation framework spanning every local and regional government administrative structure, farmer institutions and forums. The stakeholders involved are farmer organisations, local governments, the private sector and non-governmental organisations (NGOs). The collective nature of farmer groups is to be a means for increasing the voice of participant farmers. Farmer forums – assemblies of farming group leaders – are the mediators between the demands of the farmer groups that are formed and the NAADS committee. This leader group also supervises the implementation of NAADS at grassroots level. The services offered to participating farmers are to include improved technologies, trainings and microcredit offerings (savings and credit cooperative organisations (SACCOs)) (NAADS Act 2001; MAAIF 2006).

Shaming through PMA/NAADS delivery

The rhetoric associated with PMA/NAADS has been considerably focused on addressing the plight of poor subsistence farmers in rural settings, seeking to transform them into self-sustaining progressive farmers. Its focus on empowerment is not, however, well matched with its rigid structure and top-down approach. The NAADS committee, and not the farmers themselves, control group formation and the committees tend to prefer better-resourced small farmers rather than those who are more economically vulnerable. This mode of operation limits social mobilisation and cohesion, and the preconditions for group formation further serve to alienate subsistence farmers living in poverty. This focus on improving the income of farmers with some resources does not take the social aspects of poverty into consideration.

The NAADS and non-NAADS farmers we spoke with described how the most vulnerable were least likely to gain access to resources through the programme. Those registering for groups expressed frustration, anger and cynicism about the programme's processes. They described NAADS as a programme that was actually designed to benefit the rich and as lacking the necessary capacity to address even the most basic needs of subsistence farmers living in poverty. For these poorer farmers, NAADS merely helped 'those who already have money'. One farmer described the irony in being told that he had not been chosen to receive livestock as he himself 'did not have the capacity' to make good use of this offering. The participating farmers also cited cronyism and nepotism when it came to determining who should access benefits, noting the need to bribe coordinators in order to be registered for the programme. Many farmers had lost hope after being on the waiting list for improved crop and animal husbandry inputs for years. Some saw themselves as worse off than their non-NAADS counterparts (Bantebya Kyomuhendo and Mwiine, 2014a).

Again, suggesting a mismatch between policy intent and practice, the farmers experiencing poverty with whom we spoke also described NAADS group meetings as specific arenas of heightened shaming. Many noted that poor farmers were not allowed to speak during meetings, and if they did speak, they were often openly ridiculed and put down by their better-off counterparts (Bantebya Kyomuhendo and Mwiine, 2014a). In fact, many of the wealthier farmers we spoke with also openly acknowledged the challenges faced by poor farmers in accessing NAADS resources and benefits. These farmers cited the programme's complex design in declaring that NAADS was 'not meant for' and, in fact, its lofty promises were 'a mockery to', those people experiencing poverty. Wealthier farmers cynically questioned how, for instance, a landless and illiterate peasant farmer could benefit from the agricultural innovations and technologies offered to a select number of programme participants, much less bribe NAADS officials to register in the first place (Bantebya Kyomuhendo and Mwiine, 2014b).

As opposed to the oft-frustrated NAADS participants we spoke with, poorer farmers not participating in NAADS expressed their content with remaining unregistered, noting that they did not see any benefit to doing so. These respondents described feeling spared the plight of their counterparts who had adopted NAADS, as they had not had to endure the same shame, discrimination and frustration. They asserted that NAADS was, indeed, not well matched to the realities and wellbeing of the rural poor, who live from hand to mouth and often subsist on casual labour. The programme was meaningless in terms of the economic focus on agricultural yields and production efficiency, and adoption instead only served to bring to the fore one's poverty and hitherto hidden shame and lack of agency (Bantebya Kyomuhendo and Mwiine, 2014a).

Hence, as with UPE, the implementation of NAADS did not serve in the longer term to promote the dignity of the most economically vulnerable. Rather, like UPE, this programme heightened the shame that poorer people attached to their impoverished circumstances. Both policies were focused on poverty reduction through the provision of equal opportunities, rather than equal outcomes. As such, they did not prioritise meeting the particular needs of their more economically vulnerable targets in order to ensure that promises matched implemented reality. While both programmes were designed to release these groups from chronic poverty, instead they created a new space in which to experience the constraints of their poverty, heightening poverty-induced shame.

The NDP: structural transformation and modernisation

Given the system resource challenges represented by the PEAP approach, the shift to infrastructure building and larger production of the NDP has arguably offered the promise of a more sustainable long-term path to poverty reduction (Hickey, 2011). The NDP approach is reflected in the 2005 programme, PFA, or *Bonna Bagaggawale*. Reflecting the NDP focus on structural transformation, the basic framework for the programme focuses on production, value addition, marketing and microfinance.

Shaping and structuring the PFA

The return of political pluralism in Uganda prior to the general elections in 2006 created an increased incentive for the incumbent government to more broadly re-engage with and redefine development policy as a means of mobilising electoral support (Hickey, 2011). The language was of PFA rather than mere poverty reduction. This shift has not merely been discursive, but has been facilitated through a shift in budgeting towards NRM manifesto priorities. Thus, rather than the laborious process of allocating budgetary resources to pro-poor sectors of public expenditure, goals are to be realised through more direct measures, most notably through fiscal support for new microfinance programmes for 'productive' farmers (Hickey et al, 2011).

Despite the promise of a more sustainable long-term path to poverty reduction, the fact that the foundation for the PFA lies in an election manifesto and its launch was hasty has deprived the programme of well-articulated structuring and implementation mechanisms. Six years into PFA, its implementation has remained patchy without much evidence of economic and structural transformation on the ground. In our research we encountered only one consistently implemented component of PFA in the community-based SACCOs, which typically provide small loans to individuals.

Shaming through PFA delivery

The challenge of obtaining credit and servicing the loans attached to SACCOs was a strong thread running through our conversations with individuals living in poverty. Those respondents who had been rejected for a loan noted that this was due to lacking collateral, and described a resulting sense of dejection and shame. One more well-off respondent described the challenge of not having enough collateral, asking how it was possible that a person 'who cannot even afford salt' could access a loan. This respondent also described the frequency of discrimination against poorer registrants, noting: 'when a poor man turns up, they size him up and send him away!' (quoted in Bantebya Kyomuhendo and Mwiine, 2014a, 2014b).

PFA credit organisations were also decried as schemes for fleecing the hapless, vulnerable and ignorant. For those farmers we spoke with who had managed to access loans, failure to make payments subjected them to humiliating experiences such as the confiscation of property and personal belongings, prosecution and incarceration or penalisation in the form of increased interest rates. After bad experiences, respondents described their decisions not to avail themselves again of a SACCO loan, one noting: 'I'd rather remain poor but free.' As a result of difficult experiences with SACCOs, many of the people we spoke with described their increasing inclination to borrow instead from local revolving funds (nigina)[4] or friends and relatives where the risks of exposure to poverty-induced shaming was minimal (Bantebya Kyomuhendo and Mwiine, 2014a, 2014b).

The promise of wealth creation and social transformation was in the end degraded to public association with the exacerbation of poverty, hopelessness and above all, shame. The failed nature of Bonna Bagaggawale was, in fact, so deeply engrained in the public's eye that this term also came to be used to refer to cheaply manufactured commodities, such as plastic sandals, primarily associated with impoverishment. Other cynics renamed the programme *Bonna Baavuwale*, literally, 'Poverty for All' (Bantebya Kyomuhendo and Mwiine, 2014a, 2014b).

Implications and recommendations

A number of anti-poverty policies have been formulated and implemented in Uganda since the 1990s. Analysis of the programmes encountered in our research with individuals affected by the UPE, PMA/NAADS and PFA suggest that, contrary to their promising objectives, they have not provided an effective means for individuals living in poverty to be empowered, much less to fully escape the stigmatising effects of poverty. In fact, there is evidence to show that while these policies have been explicitly framed in a manner seeking not only to address poverty, but also to promote human dignity, their structuring and delivery fall far short of attaining this noble objective.

A common feature shared by these initiatives is that they were quickly introduced to capture the interest of the citizens and to win political favour, without proper documentation for implementation and a focus on whether the necessary infrastructure existed. These policies therefore reflect a tendency within Uganda wherein policy-making and politics are frequently based on political rather than economic calculations. As a result economic analyses are typically not done or are set aside in favour of specific political aims (Hyden, 2006). Further, there has been little attempt to consider lessons learned from past efforts or the feasibility or future consequences of reform. These features of policy-making have resulted in the implementation of programmes that do not reflect the needs and realities of their economically vulnerable target groups.

Our analysis has shown that the anti-poverty policies do not attend to the role of poverty-induced shame, and more specifically, its insidious effects in the structuring and delivery of the policies/programmes. In the case of UPE, for instance, the programme's goals of providing equitable access to quality and affordable education, as well as of promoting citizenship and knowledge/skills were noble. Yet they did not consider the broader implications of a massive influx of pupils of many socioeconomic backgrounds into one school, with only minimal support provided. The policy's structure, especially the subsequent shift in focus from a targeted group of recipients to universal provision, was likely calculated to appeal to a wide array of the electorate in rural areas. Yet 'access shock' and stigmatising rhetoric by government officials emphasised the disparities existing between children from economically secure and challenged families. For the latter category of children, who could not afford the scholastic basics that would allow them to fit in with the broader student body, material disparities degenerated into negative psychosocial emotions such as shame, low self-worth, anger and frustration. These responses culminated in these pupils choosing social disengagement in an attempt to avoid further shame. The UPE schools, far from being centres of teaching and learning excellence, became virulent arenas of poverty-induced shame, a scenario that is in direct contrast to the goals and objectives of initial policy.

Furthermore, our conversations with the individuals targeted for relief have revealed the crucial implementation challenge posed by endemic graft and corruption at the level of implementation, wherein the distribution of inputs has been regressive in so far as those who possess resources have a natural advantage over those who do not. For example, PMA/NAADS has been introduced to increase market-oriented production via a strengthened extension delivery service and empowerment of local small land farmers. As with the UPE, NAADS has blurred the definition of who is eligible for programmatic benefits. The focus on extension has failed to consider the wide gap in resources between poor and better-off rural farmers. Its noble framing notwithstanding, the targeting of the 'economically active poor' rather than the most vulnerable subsistence farmers has created tensions among the targeted recipients. This is reflected in onerous requirements for participation – the ownership of land and livestock and other permanent assets and the demonstration of community leadership experience (social capital), among others – that have made this service largely inaccessible to the most vulnerable. In reality, the offer of new opportunities has created new categories of 'deserving' and 'undeserving', and has excluded those who are poorest and most in need. The view of poor farmers that PMA/NAADS is a programme designed to benefit the already rich and the sense of alienation that follows is further emphasised by their lack of voice in group meetings. The focus of PMA/NAADS has been overwhelmingly focused on the income aspect of poverty, at the expense of crucial social aspects of anti-poverty work. Policy-makers would do well to place priority on the issue of poverty-induced shame.

As with programmes falling under the PEAP approach, the promises attached to the NDP approach have not been supported by clear strategies to realise these goals. Furthermore, given the corruption and broad social disparities marking the Ugandan policy-making context, the goals themselves fail to consider the challenges associated with human capital building and economic redistribution. Rather, at this point, the programmes offer a hierarchy of 'deserving' and 'undeserving' in which people living in poverty are least deserving and the strategies for development are aimed primarily at the more highly resourced.

The PFA (*Bonna Bagaggawale*) policy/programme reflects the newer NDP development approach, in which poverty alleviation remains a rhetorical focus, yet has been dominated by new priorities placed on production, microfinance, marketing and processing. There is scant evidence of poverty alleviation remaining in the implementation process. Again, the social dimensions of poverty, including the poverty-induced shame that characterises the real-life experiences of the rural poor, have been deliberately ignored. Instead the programme's associated microfinance institutions have tended to act as profit-maximising institutions, with the result that the terms and conditions for accessing credit have been impossible, especially for the most vulnerable. Our conversations with poorer community members reveal that the process of loan recovery has subjected them to untold misery, ridicule, shame and indignity. In response, they have shunned the very institutions that were established to avail them with credit and working capital on fair terms. For the rural poor it has been far better to live in a vicious cycle of poverty than to get entangled in a vicious cycle of poverty-induced shame.

While introduced under the umbrella of varying approaches, the UPE, NAADS and PFA programmes have all shared a reluctance to consider the realities and socioeconomic limitations faced by the children and adults living in poverty in rural Uganda. The enduring question thus is whether it is possible to shame-proof these programmes to render them appealing to these groups.

The evidence presented suggests that the design and announcement of anti-poverty policy should be preceded by adequate baseline research and planning. Our respondents described deep social challenges related to poverty and consideration of the social dimensions of poverty that should guide the planning and implementation phases of policy-making. The policy-making tendency in Uganda has been to rhetorically focus on poverty, and yet programmes have been designed to target individuals living in less severe poverty (as with NAADS) or to not target at all (as with UPE). In spite of the high levels of severe poverty in the country, the newer NDP approach has shifted focus to modernisation and structural transformation, with disastrous consequences for those most vulnerable. Initiatives like the PFA have cast out those living in poverty and at best represent a false promise of something more. The reality of deep absolute and widening relative poverty in Uganda suggests that anti-poverty policy must take into consideration the needs of those living in the most severe poverty and hardship. The ways in which the multiple needs of the most economically vulnerable can be met should be considered a priority issue of anti-poverty policy design. This sort of consideration means a shift in focus from providing equal opportunities in terms of baseline support to providing for equal outcomes through comprehensive and socially sensitive measures.

Finally, the deep corruption that pervades Ugandan policy-making at all levels must be tackled head on, yet this problem currently appears to be intractable. The creation of farmers groups by NAADS was a promising approach to build a collective voice for programme participants. Yet this sort of 'induced participation' strategy reflects a large-scale, policy-driven approach that is marked by bureaucratically managed development interventions. A broad survey of this approach in development work has documented its general ineffectiveness and the compounding of corruption by entrenched elites at the local level of government (Mansuri and Rao, 2013). Indeed, its top-down nature and the mechanisms surrounding group formation and function benefit the resourced most and emphasise to poorer participants that they lack voice and leverage.

As corruption is a facet of Ugandan life that runs from national policy-making down to local service provision, efforts to shore up the grassroots formation of collectives by the economically vulnerable – if also matched by greater accountability at the level of management and bureaucracy – may be a more effective means for them to improve the economic leverage and security of the most vulnerable. This strategy may be the best hope for maximising social resources and for offering a mechanism for real empowerment for the dispossessed. It would require the incorporation of Uganda's rural poor into the decision-making process. The inclusion of the country's most vulnerable into the democratic processes guiding their economic recovery is an important step towards building real dignity.

Notes

[1] The poverty line signifies the minimum consumption below which individuals are considered to live in absolute poverty. It reflects the cost of consuming 3,000 calories per day based on the standard food basket for the poorest 50 per cent of the population.

[2] The new approach also reportedly reflects a return to multi-party politics and the declining influence of traditional aid donors (Hickey, 2011).

3 This list reflects a group of developing countries with high levels of poverty and debt, making them eligible for special assistance from the International Monetary Fund and The World Bank.

4 In the local Luganda language, *nigina* literally means 'feel good' and also refers to gatherings where women pool resources and form revolving funds in which members may periodically benefit by way of receiving cumulative material and cash from members.

References

Akello, J. (2012) 'Uganda: Name, shame the corrupt', *The Independent*, Kampala, 4 December.

Avenstrup, R., Liang, X. and Nellemann, S. (2004) 'Kenya, Lesotho, Malawi and Uganda: Universal primary education and poverty reduction', Conference paper presented at 'Scaling up poverty reduction: A global learning process', Shanghai.

Bantebya Kyomuhendo, G. and Mwiine, A. (2014a) 'Needy and vulnerable but poverty is not my identity: Experiences of the poor in Uganda', in E. Chase and G. Bantebya Kyomuhendo (eds) *The shame of poverty: Global experiences*, Oxford: Oxford University Press.

Bantebya Kyomuhendo, G. and Mwiine, A. (2014b) 'Poverty the invisible "shadow": Views of the better off and the Media in Uganda', in E. Chase and G. Bantebya Kyomuhendo (eds) *The shame of poverty: Global experiences*, Oxford: Oxford University Press.

Bashaasha, B., Mangheni, M. and Nkonya, E. (2011) *Decentralization and rural service delivery in Uganda*, IFPRI Discussion Paper, Washington, DC: International Food Policy Research Institute.

Benin, S., Nkonya, E. and Okecho, G. (2007) *Assessing the impact of the National Agricultural Advisory Services (NAADS)*, Uganda Rural Livelihoods, Washington, DC: International Food Policy Research Institute.

Bukedde Newspaper (2002) 'Mugalekere abanaku – RDC Asabye abagagga okugya abaana mu masomero ga UPE' ('Leave UPE schools for the poor – Resident District Commissioner advises the rich people to take their children out of UPE schools and leave them for the poor'), 7 January.

Chase, E. and Bantebya Kyomuhendo, G. (eds) (2014) *The shame of poverty: Global experiences*, Oxford: Oxford University Press.

Deininger, K. (2003) 'Does cost of schooling affect enrollment by the poor? Universal primary education in Uganda?', *Economics of Education Review*, vol 22, no 3, pp 291-305.

Flanary, R. and Watt, D. (1999) 'The state of corruption: A case study of Uganda', *Third World Quarterly*, vol 20, no 3, pp 515-36.

Ford, L. (2012) 'Uganda vows to "beat these thieves" in bid to reassure aid donors', *The Guardian*, 20 November.

Hyden, G. (2006) *African politics in contemporary politics*, New York: Cambridge University Press.

Hickey, S. (2011) *Beyond the poverty agenda? Insights from the new politics of development in Uganda*, Manchester: Institute for Development Policy and Management, University of Manchester.

Izama, A. (2012) 'Uganda: Oil, corruption and entitlement', *The Guardian*, 1 October.

Kisubi, A. (2008) *Critique and analysis of universal primary education (UPE) in Uganda in general and suggestions for improvement in particular local areas*, Presented at the Houston, Texas Busoga Twegaite Annual International Convention, May 22 – 26th, 2008.

Lee, M.C. (2007) 'Uganda and China: Unleashing the power of the dragon', in M. Lee, H. Melber, S. Naidu and I. Taylor (eds) *China in Africa: Current African Issues*, vol 35, pp 26-40.

Ministry of Agriculture, Animal Industry and Fisheries (MAAIF) (2000) *National Agriculture Advisory Service Programme master document of NAADA Task Force and Joint Donor Group*, Kampala, MAAIF.

MAAIF (2006) *Draft report of the performance evaluation of the National Agricultural Advisory Services (NAADS) ITAD*. Kampala, MAAIF.

Mansuri, G. and Rao, V. (2013) *Localizing development: Does participation work?*, Policy Research Report, Washington, DC: The World Bank.

Ministry of Finance, Planning and Economic Development (MFPED) (2004) *Poverty eradication action plan, 2004/5-2007/8*, Kampala: MFPED.

Namara, B. (2009) 'NGOs, poverty reduction and social exclusion in Uganda', *Institute of Social Studies*, no 4, pp 43-80.

Republic of Uganda (1992a) *Education Policy Review Commission report*, Kampala.

Republic of Uganda (1992b) *National Household Survey*, Kampala.

Republic of Uganda (1997) *Decentralisation policy*, Kampala.

Republic of Uganda (2004) *PEAP (Poverty Eradication, Action Plan), 2004/05-2007/08*, Ministry of Finance, Planning and Economic Development, Kampala.

Republic of Uganda (2006) *Education sector policy overview paper*, Kampala.

Republic of Uganda (2009) *National Household Survey*, Kampala, Uganda.

Republic of Uganda (2010) *Uganda national development plan: Growth, employment and socioeconomic transformation for prosperity*, Kampala: National Planning Authority.

Republic of Uganda (2012) *Poverty status report: Reducing vulnerability, equalising opportunities and transforming livelihoods*, Kampala: Ministry of Finance, Planning and Economic Development.

Ruzindana, A. (1997) 'The importance of leadership in fighting corruption in Uganda', in K.A. Elliott (ed) *Corruption and the global economy*, Washington, DC: Institute for International Economics, Chapter 7.

Sen, A. (2000) *Social exclusion: Concept, application, and scrutiny*, Manila: The Asian Development Bank.

UBOS (Uganda Bureau of Statistics) (2007) *Statistical abstract*, Kampala.

UBOS (2010) *Uganda National Household Survey 2009/2010, Republic of Uganda*, Kampala.

UNDP (United Nations Development Programme) (2005) *Uganda human development report linking environment to human development: A deliberate choice*, Kampala.

Webster, N. and Pedersen, L. (eds) (2002) *In the name of the poor: Contesting political space for poverty reduction*, New York: Zed Books.

Whitfield, L. (ed) (2009) *The politics of aid in Africa*, Oxford: Oxford University Press.

NINE

Shame and shaming in policy processes

Sony Pellissery, Ivar Lødemel and Erika K. Gubrium

In the first chapter of this volume, Erika Gubrium showed how novel concerns in the current global stage have inspired our research on the relationship between shame and anti-poverty policy. As the volume by Chase and Bantebya (2014) demonstrates, shame is closely linked to poverty regardless of the existence and nature of anti-poverty policies. And where such programmes are in place, an encounter with officialdom is only one of many arenas where a poor person is reminded of his or her inferior status. Still, as the preceding chapters have demonstrated, and as we summarise here, policies and programmes have the potential to either *heighten* or *lessen* the shame that people feel as a result of living in poverty. For example, shame can be heightened for an applicant at the point of the determination of eligibility for an anti-poverty measure, if only for having to admit to or demonstrate their poverty. If an applicant is treated without respect and dignity, this feeling is likely to be heightened further. In other situations, policies can lessen the feeling of shame, provided that applicants and recipients are met by officialdom in a respectful way and if, in fact, the benefits and services received alleviate poverty or offer new opportunities for self-reliance.

This chapter attempts to draw conclusions by comparing very diverse country contexts and different types of policy measures. It therefore faces the challenge of applying an appropriate methodology. But how does one compare heterogeneous social policies in hugely different national contexts? The broad design of this research has followed a maximum difference approach (explained in chapter 1) (see Walker, 2014) in order to explore the possibility of a universal connection between poverty and shame. However, the comparison of policies themselves is more elusive. When the impact of policy – with a particular focus on poverty-induced shame – is in question, it is difficult to disentangle causality attributed to policy rather than context. For instance, how does one compare the personal impact of education policy in Uganda with that of a human capital-based work activation programme in Norway?

The purpose of this chapter is not to compare these diverse contexts and policies in order to establish that one national setting or policy is more or less shaming than another. The point of comparison is theoretical generalisation, with a focus on identifying the policy mechanisms that may potentially heighten or lower the shame of individuals living in poverty. All the cases in this volume assume multiple causal paths to the same outcome (Ragin, 1997). Conclusions are drawn by interpreting the interactivity of functions, by comparing and contrasting cases (Stake, 2005). As a first step towards this, in the next section we summarise the unique country contexts and the specific policies that we have focused on in order to understand policy-induced shame. Following this, we compare and contrast the cases according to three moments in the policy process – framing, shaping/structuring and delivery – in order to draw general conclusions.

Worlds of difference: policy contexts and offerings

The policies in focus within each of the seven settings vary widely and reflect great variability in policy-making climates and macroeconomic situations. Those selected for representation in this volume have all been publicly managed and financed. All have been introduced on a national level. While settings vary dramatically – in terms of political climate, fiscal resources and cultural understandings of the role of welfare and of the state in welfare provision – the ways in which anti-poverty policies may induce shame are visible across these settings. Furthermore, the inclusion of highly variable settings enables us to identify potential shaming mechanisms, by identifying the shared factors that emerge. This method also allows a preliminary conversation concerning the translatability of policies, the ability to engage in successful policy learning from one site to another.

A review of policies targeted towards individuals living in poverty suggests that the settings in the global South that are undergoing economic modernisation and/or building national welfare states have perhaps drawn inspiration from more established welfare states in the North. Policy-makers in the South, grappling with a range of definitions, normative influences and regional needs, have prioritised several of the recent and earlier residualist tendencies of the North that have been targeted towards low-income groups: distinguishing between the categories of 'deserving' and 'undeserving', imposing conditions by which one can claim benefits and limiting or decreasing social citizenship rights for benefit recipients.

A changing notion of poverty is perhaps most marked in a setting such as China, described in Chapter Two. China has quickly moved from a planned to a planned, yet market-based, economy. In Communist-era China, social provision followed a model of occupational welfare, where services were guaranteed via the employment contract/system, the so-called 'iron rice bowl' (*danwei*) model. All working-age urban residents were assigned long-term jobs in state-owned or collective enterprises. References to urban poverty during this period were primarily limited to a small minority of 'households in difficulty'. A concern with the 'new urban poor' – represented in part by those who have been released from lifetime-guaranteed positions at formerly state-owned enterprises – has, however, emerged since the opening of the Chinese economy in the 1980s. With an aim to preserve stability and harmony, the national government has introduced the *dibao* system (officially, the Minimum Standard of Living Scheme, MSLS) in 1999. This provides minimum relief via residual social assistance and has been targeted towards those who are unemployed. Rhetorically, the system has aimed to be, as Premier Li Peng has stated, 'an effective program that costs little but is beneficial to social stability'. With modernisation and advanced capitalism and the growth of consumerism and individualism, poverty has increasingly come to have been seen – if not rhetorically, than at the point of delivery – as a personal failing, open to shaming because it is considered to be indicative of socially and economically dysfunctional behaviour.

In settings such as India and Pakistan, massive corruption and social inequalities have led to a fragmented focus on the poverty issue. Chapter Three demonstrates that India's social protection schemes have also been subject to nepotism and corruption. Furthermore, they have adhered to shifting definitions of poverty over time. In this hierarchical society where societal rules are more pervasive (and persuasive) than state-created rules, and where responsibility for these schemes has been at the regional and state levels, the definition of 'poor' has been regionalised and driven by the clout and interests of certain identity-based groups. Widely varying definitions of poverty over time and across the land have resulted in people feeling cheated by newly introduced eligibility criteria and by the potential for corruption. The welfare programmes introduced in India and Pakistan are susceptible to corruptive forces taking place, particularly in the targeting process. For instance, in India, the food subsidy programme, the Public Distribution System (PDS), diverts over 70 per cent of grain to private markets rather than to intended claimants. India's Employment Guarantee Scheme (NREGA), which provides 100 days of manual labour to individuals from rural households, is also hugely affected by targeting errors. The corrupt and fragmented nature of delivery that characterises these services has led to varying experiences of shaming.

The South Korean experience of anti-poverty policy-making presented in Chapter Four is very close to the Chinese story. A move away from Confucian values was reflected in the individualistic policy focus of Park Jung-Hee. Following huge economic success through the 1960s and 1970s, South Korea stabilised a welfare model that prioritised economic growth over welfare provisions. The National Basic Living Security Scheme (NBLSS), with its 'productive welfare model' has introduced a work capability criterion to determine eligibility to a minimal level of social assistance benefits. Such a criterion does not fit a target group that includes younger claimants who seek, but cannot find, work, and a large number of much older claimants who are unable to work. Furthermore, the maintenance of the more traditional approach of making the receipt of public support conditional on the substantiated lack of family support has the potential to shame not merely the individual claimant, but also the whole family. While the scheme represents a modernisation of social assistance, it has maintained a tradition of family subsidiarity whereby family members may be approached to provide for the applicant (before eligibility is established).

A prosperous economy combined with the broad extension of generous social insurance benefits has resulted in two paradoxes within the generous welfare state setting of Norway (Lødemel, 1997). It is broadly understood that social mobility has vastly increased in Norway with the rise of the welfare state in the 20th century, with the country ranked at the top of international comparisons and the themes of social mobility and egalitarianism a strong part of the Norwegian public discourse for the past century. Indeed, broadly targeted welfare provisions introduced since the Second World War have lifted 'deserving' risk groups out of social assistance or family dependency into various social insurance schemes. At the same time, as Chapter Five describes, the character of the system has resulted in the paradox that those individuals *not* eligible for the relatively generous social insurance benefits are mostly the very marginalised, many of whom are beset by a complex range of social and physical issues. Furthermore, the presence of a strong set of welfare protection offerings, linked with a focus on employability to shore up the system, has resulted in a heightened focus on the role of individual actions in determining one's status. This might be likened to the shame experienced by those who have not achieved success amidst new wealth in market-driven China and South Korea. In Norway, however, it is the seemingly endless possibility for social mobility predicated on the presence of a strong welfare state that has translated into a heightened sense of shame for those who have not fared so well. The human capital-based Qualification Programme offers the possibility of a way into the labour market for a select group of social assistances recipients. Increased benefit levels and new programme offerings are attached, however, to one's ability to work, leaving the most vulnerable on the outside.

Pakistan's story, presented in Chapter Six, has been one of the shaming of low-income people via general policy neglect by ruling parties. A long period of colonial rule led to massive inequalities and a system of nepotism. This was followed by a period in which 'pro-growth sector policies' benefited capitalist elites and increased income inequality, with almost no national focus on redistribution and social protection. While the promise of change was attached to a democratic socialist backlash in the 1970s, vast inequalities remained. Yet a parallel stream of consciousness began to develop among low-income people, wherein the rich were cast as shameful and the focus was on welfare rights. This alternate possibility was not, however, realised due to a succession of wars and resulting fiscal weakness. It was not until the 1980s that a series of discretionary and charity-based minimum social protection schemes were put into place in a system that has been heavily marked by corruption. Pakistan's current Benazir Income Support Programme (BISP), aimed at low-income women, offers limited assistance on the basis of political and administrative selection to around 18 per cent of the population. According to BISP estimates, some 40 per cent of the population remain below the poverty line. Coverage by an older assistance scheme, Zakat, is religion-specific and has decreased over recent years.

Welfare residualism has had a long history in Western welfare reform and can be traced back to the ideas encapsulated in the UK's early Poor Laws. The 1834 Poor Law 'workhouse test' denied help to the able-bodied unless they accepted accommodation under strict work-based regimes in conditions worse than those experienced by the poorest, independent worker. Drawing on individualised notions of responsibility and causality for poverty, the forced subsistence and limited social rights provided by this 'self-acting test' was designed to be dreadful for the recipient; its purpose, after all, was to limit fraud and establish the validity of a person's claim to be destitute. As Chapter Seven illustrates, these themes still heavily inform policy-making and rhetoric concerning individuals living in poverty to this day. The new Universal Credit scheme forwarded by the Liberal-Conservative Coalition government in the UK takes to an extreme the notions of individual responsibility and cost-effectiveness that resurged in the Conservative era of the 1980s and early 1990s. It has drawn strongly from the 'rights and responsibilities' discourse of New Labour in the late 1990s and 2000s. In so doing, it has crystallised the shaming elements of heightened conditionality, suspicion and stigma attached to any person claiming benefits.

In contrast to the six settings described above, Chapter Eight describes Uganda's story as one of unintended consequences. Uganda was and is still considered among the poorest countries in the world. The reduction of poverty and vulnerability has been an integral part of its national development strategy, and significant success has been attained over the past decade. The universal public education (UPE) reform has offered the promise of a universally targeted and empowering scheme for the country's youth, but has been undermined by lack of a solid infrastructure and hasty decision-making. The National Agricultural Advisory Service (NAADS) has been introduced to increase market-oriented production for the 'active poor' in rural areas via a strengthened extension delivery service, and empowerment of local small land farmers, with a specific gender focus. The income aspect of poverty has been prioritised over the social aspects and the most vulnerable have been excluded from this new opportunity. In a similar way, the new Prosperity for All (PFA) programme is one that best serves those claimants with some resources, leaving the most destitute to choose between the possibility of facing severe sanctions for lack of resources or remaining in their current situation.

Throughout the chapters, the strategies of strict eligibility, conditionality and restricted social citizenship have differentiated the 'undeserving' from the 'deserving'. This distinction, according to our respondents, has been a key source of shaming. While the format, level and strategy behind the calculation of benefits vary from setting to setting, these elements have great significance for the respondents' sense of wellbeing.

Shame/shaming at three policy moments

Typically, research focusing on the impact that policies may have on recipients studies this at the point of delivery (Spicker, 1984; Lister, 2004). We are interested in the wider policy process for two reasons. First, keeping in mind that 'social services are used to impose sanctions as well as to confer benefits upon their clientele' (Pinker, 1971, p 144), the framing and shaping of policies sets, first, the stage and, later, the rules and resources that determine what will be delivered and how. Second, these earlier stages of the policy process have in themselves an impact on people. In the framing of policy an atmosphere of othering and blaming will have a different impact on the climate surrounding those targeted by the discourse compared to one of inclusion, and perhaps compassion.

Framing policies

To date, no nation has arrived at a system of generous and equal benefits and services to all groups in society. Imbedded in the struggle over limited resources, the provision of welfare is always subject to political debates and conflict. The debates differ, however, with regard to the nature of need addressed and the target group of the policy in question. Where the policy is likely to bring benefits to all (for example, a universal old-age pension), the struggle is likely to be focused on economic concerns and priorities. In other policy areas, normative questions are more likely to dominate the debates. While this can be seen in policies targeted at, for example, disability and single parenthood, social assistance and other anti-poverty measures everywhere stand out as those that are surrounded by normative debates, be it prior to their inception or in the context of reform. For example, commenting on European experiences, Bradshaw and Terum (1997) argue that social assistance debates are always about behaviour.

The importance of the normative is compounded by the fact that while many target groups (older people, civil servants) are well organised and benefit from the vocal support of strong interest by society, those living in poverty have much less voice. Shame may further prevent these individuals from attempting to express themselves in public fora. Cultural and political milieux (rather than economic foundations) shape the acceptance of normative frames into policies (Campbell, 1998). For instance, the diagnosis for the reasons of poverty and proposed solutions are influenced by the level to which society places value on the distribution of wealth, and therefore to the legitimacy the state derives in carrying out this distributive role.

While always normative, the values attached to anti-poverty policies may, however, be rooted in discourses ranging from the positive and compassionate to those that portray people living in poverty as idle, feckless and in need of corrective measures. In the following we are concerned with how discourses (those relating to the nature of poverty and its manifestations, as well as those that place accountability) and how the broader goals guiding the policy-making process have an impact on the subsequent shaping and delivery of policies.

Table 9.1 provides an overview of many of the instances wherein policy framing has the potential to shame anti-poverty measure recipients. Norway and India represent two extremes on a policy-framing continuum of shaming potential. Norwegian egalitarianism has accorded prime responsibility to the state for redistribution. Within this generous welfare setting, poverty is an exception. The 'abnormality' of experiencing poverty may intensify the sense of loneliness and frustration for this small section of the population. In contrast, India is characterised by rampant poverty, a hierarchical society and a disconnect existing between policy-making elites and the common people. The weak Indian state relies on society for its structures of redistribution. A disconnect between policy-makers and the common people is shared by the post-colonial settings of Pakistan and Uganda. This disconnect has two implications. First, continual policy neglect and the lip service that characterises rhetorical pro-poor statements (particularly at election time) reinforce a political system in which policy goals are linked to electoral success rather than to making substantive societal changes. Thus, historically poor social groups (lower castes in India, women in Pakistan and small farmers in Uganda) continue to be vulnerable to societal forces despite sizeable financial allocations for their betterment. Second, the idealist policies that elites formulate are not realistically translatable to country contexts, leaving people still vulnerable to societal forces. Such policies create unintended consequences, with benefits most often skewed towards those who are less vulnerable to begin with. A striking example of this unintended consequence is the highly stigmatised character of Uganda's UPE schools, whose initial goal was to raise the human potential of the nation's poorest children.

Compared to the post-colonial experiences of anti-poverty policy framing in India, Pakistan and Uganda, two other case countries – China and the UK – provide another contrasting story. China has made a dramatic transition from a planned economy (with the objective of a classless society) to a market economy (with competition as the predominant strategy). This is also reflected in a transition in values. While the values of Confucianism remain, the modern values of an achievement society are now equally important. National policy has also undergone a transition: from the *danwei* system, where the state authority ensured a set of comprehensive social protection measures, to *dibao*, which aims to relieve the urban poverty that arose in the context of market liberalisation. In contrast, the UK is a story of historical continuity. Policy framing in this setting has continued a long tradition

Table 9.1: Anti-poverty policy framing: effect on shaming across seven settings

Setting	Policy evidence	Shaming potential
China	Structural transition from planned economy to market economy created 'new urban poor'; social security, decoupled from employer, became the responsibility of provincial governments; aim of national social assistance scheme (*dibao*) was to bring social stability in the context of the creation of a new vulnerability	Recognition of new poverty and the aim of achieving social stability promises progressive approach to citizens
India	National political leaders and technical experts framing the policies are disconnected from the common people; clientelist announcement of policies to gain votes	Poor people treated as vote banks, leading to depersonalised introduction of welfare doles
Norway	A generous welfare state where most are doing well and with increased cultural focus on consumption; problem of long-term reliance on social assistance due to poor capital formulation gives shape to the Qualification Programme	Small section of population who continue to remain on social assistance are likely to be perceived as 'unfit' for human capital formation
Pakistan	Policy neglect of people in poverty reduces them to a non-entity; non-expert ministers creating policy results in policy discussions that are not necessarily well informed or effective	Policy neglect of the poorest sections means they are left to rely on societal mechanisms to redress deprivation
South Korea	Close link made between welfare objectives and economic growth; departure from Confucian thinking with the emergence of individualist industrialism; economic growth prioritised over redistribution	The individual is blamed for inability to participate in the market to escape from poverty
Uganda	Given the pervasiveness of poverty and rent-seeking aims, politicians have long made calls for poverty reduction via populist policies; in more recent times, there has been an increasing national policy-making focus on achieving economic prosperity through productive investments	In the drive for economic growth, the concerns of marginalised populations have not been taken care of, exposing them to market logic
United Kingdom	The tendency to classify poor as 'deserving' and 'undeserving' since Elizabethan Poor Law; since 1985, both Conservative and Labour governments focused on policy as 'poverty traps' and as creating long-term 'dependency'	Individual claimants held responsible for their welfare and for holding back national economic prosperity

of holding individuals primarily responsible for poverty, a legacy that spans the Poor Law of 1601 to the Welfare Reform Act 2012. Individual responsibility for poverty has resulted in a pre-occupation with distinguishing 'deserving' from 'undeserving'. Although contrasting in terms of level of continuity, the efficiency concerns of the anti-poverty policies in both countries are strikingly similar. In China this is manifested as the description of *dibao* as 'a program that costs little' and in the UK, Universal Credit as 'giving value for taxpayers' money'. The exposure of the individual to shaming in the global North (as well as in modern China and today's South Korea) is in contrast to the experiences in Pakistan, Uganda and India, where family and community values provide a shield to shame reaching the individual.

Shaping and structuring policies

In addition to the ideational underpinnings that frame policies, while engaging in the shaping and structuring of anti-poverty measures, policy-makers are pulled in two directions. First, they must consider the fiscal pressure that a new anti-poverty policy will bring. Second, they must consider the political ramifications of introducing a policy. Seen from these two dimensions, the seven settings present a variety of lessons. Table 9.2 provides an overview of instances in which the structure of policies has resulted in the potential to shame anti-poverty measure recipients.

All of the settings in the global South reported evident fiscal pressure. Although welfare entitlements in these countries are very low, the scale of poverty is at such a high level as to make fiscal pressure real. While the total proportion of gross domestic product (GDP) spent on social security in low-income nations tends to be marked lower than that in Organisation for Economic Co-operation and Development (OECD) nations (Weigand and Grosh, 2008; Dornan and Porter, 2012), their expenditure on *anti-poverty programmes* as a proportion of total social security spending is much higher than that in OECD nations (Walker, 2012). In countries such as Uganda and India, the political benefits of engaging in the poverty alleviation effort were huge, and so, despite great fiscal pressures, anti-poverty programmes were rolled out. The result has been that available resources have had to be thinly spread. In China, the level of support provided by the *dibao* benefit is only sufficient to relieve *absolute* poverty. In Pakistan and China, limited funds have resulted in limited coverage.

In settings within both global South and North, the mechanisms introduced to establish fiscal control have resulted in the shaming of measure recipients. For instance, in Uganda, the limited agricultural resources that have been made available for distribution under the NAADS programme has meant that programme managers strategically classify applicants as to who has 'capacity' to generate income by rearing

Table 9.2: Anti-poverty policy structuring and its effect on shaming across seven settings

Setting	Policy evidence	Shaming potential
China	*Dibao*: limited coverage concentrated in urban areas; minimal benefit level only targeted at the very poor and only relieves absolute poverty	Vulnerability of populations like migrants are unaddressed; given prosperous urban growth, addressing only absolute poverty shames recipients experiencing relative poverty
India	BPL: sets the standard for who is 'poor enough' to receive benefits and services NREGA: the design is manual labour made available through self-targeting PDS: subsidised food grain for people in poverty	The designs of both programmes assume poor quality benefits/work are acceptable for those who are living in poverty
Norway	Workfare approach remains for social assistance: the Qualification Programme offers 'more' to some, yet applies a 'tough love' approach focused on individual motivation, with worth tied to employability	Heightens the marginalised distinction of those who fail to move up to the new higher tier of social assistance and for whom the new offering is not useful or meaningful
Pakistan	Exclusionary design of Zakat and BISP programmes, in addition to the low funding available for programmes, leads to low and biased coverage	Minority groups are excluded from Zakat benefits; the discretionary nature of BISP is not well matched to all-female target group
South Korea	NBLSS designed as a benefit made available from the state if the family cannot provide; work orientation and preoccupation with moral hazard requires people to continually update recipient status	Low take-up of NBLSS by those who do not want to shame or be shamed by their own family
Uganda	UPE: focus shifted from financially needy families to all families NAADS: targeted at 'economically active' farmers PFA: services targeted at 'productive' farmers	Resource constraints; poverty does not find policy space; unless engaged in 'productive' spheres, poor people face punitive sanctions
United Kingdom	Workfare programmes: 'activate' those who must depend on public funds Tackling child poverty: with the exception of the Sure Start programme, the emphasis is placed on parents' individual failings Universal Credit: merges 'undeserving' and 'deserving' benefit recipients into one category – all face increased conditionality and lower benefit levels	Introduction of stringent conditions, aimed at reducing the number of people receiving benefit; policy structure mirrors preoccupation with policing individuals to reduce system dependency

livestock (in the section on delivery, below, we discuss the issues related to discretion, an element emerging from the fact of limited resources). In Norway, social assistance caseworkers must 'carefully calculate' the appropriate levels of benefit to motivate people to move into the labour market.

In many of our study settings, anti-poverty measures have been structured in such a way that programme logic has been subordinated to macroeconomic logic. The predominance of labour market policies in Norway, described above, is also observable in South Korea, where a self-sufficiency principle has been accorded huge importance. In Uganda and India too, human capacity building anti-poverty programmes emphasise 'productivity'. These examples indicate how the agency of people in poverty has been undervalued when the 'social' is subordinated to the economic.

In the arena of anti-poverty policy shaping/structuring and shaming potential, Norway and the UK present huge similarities, as movement into work has been the predominant focus. Despite their striking welfare regime differences (Esping-Andersen, 1990)[1] – not to mention their vastly different frames of reference – the similar potential to shame via the work-oriented distinction between 'worthy' and 'unworthy' shows how the welfare state, judged from the point view of subjective experiences, may, in part, collapse marked macro differences.

Still, the framing of policy has a great bearing on the structures that follow. In Norway, the structure of its new higher tier of social assistance (the Qualification Programme) mirrors the strategy of building human capacity to meet the larger goal of integrating people into the workforce. A focus on building capacity is reflected in the fact that some may receive 'more', both in terms of benefit level and services. On the other hand, successive governments in the UK have tightened the contractual relationship between benefit recipients and the state, with an increasing preoccupation with the work-oriented duties/obligations of recipients, successively weakening the state's obligations from 'security' to grudging 'support' and punitive sanctions. This increasing conditionality has reduced the citizenship ethos for all recipients.

In Uganda and India an interesting comparison may be made between the promise of 'inclusive growth' that shapes some of the measures studied in these two settings and the ways in which programmatic structure may heighten the shaming of programme participants. Ugandan NAADS, which targets the 'economically active poor' to increase their level of output production, is comparable with the Indian employment guarantee policy (NREGA) that targets 'able-bodied men and women' who are ready to do gruelling and stigmatised manual labour. Similarly, the UPE policy of Uganda, whose implicit – if not publicly stated – intention has been to provide education to children from low-income rural families, is comparable with India's PDS, which subsidies food grain for people living in poverty. The very structure of these programmes reflects the mantra that 'poor people's services are always poor services' (Titmuss, 1968). It is this characteristic that generates the stigma that is attached to those participating.

The most astonishing element of shaming at the policy moment of *shaping* is the absence of voice present within some segments of the population. Some of the most vulnerable groups have been left out of sight of the state, and thus from the policy design itself. In China, it has been migrant workers moving from rural to urban areas. In India, the poorest of those living in poverty have been treated as non-entities and have been neglected by the state. Within this setting, anti-poverty policies have largely benefited those who are less vulnerable. In Pakistan the Islamic ethic driving much of social policy-making has disregarded the single mother who has borne children out of wedlock. Here, too, religious sentiments to appease the Sharia community have shaped the Zakat programme, and have resulted in measures that have excluded religious minorities.

Common across the seven settings has been an attempt to make citizens 'productive'. The measures studied in welfare settings in the global North have been specifically structured around an 'activation' aim, and those in the global South have moved away from poverty reduction to a focus on investment in productive citizens (Surender and Walker, 2012). Reflecting a contemporary neoliberal agenda, conditional cash transfers, with some success stories in Latin America, are now being advocated as a policy model for the entire global South (Dornan and Porter, 2012). Chapter Ten, the concluding chapter, shows how the conditionalities that are attached have the potential to create new spaces for shaming.

Delivering policy

Across the seven settings, claimants described how the requirement to articulate their 'need' in order to gain access to benefits heightened their sense of shame. In China, articulation takes place during the community vetting process to identify 'deserving' claimants. In India, applicants must compete for their 'eligibility to be poor' (to receive a place on the BPL list). In Norway, social assistance claimants must 'appear needy' in order to receive sufficient benefits. In Pakistan, applicants must actively work to appeal to state officials. In Uganda, applicants must prove that they are 'economically active'. In South Korea and in the UK, applicants must continuously take care to be identified as the 'real needy' rather than as 'fraudsters'. The process of shaping oneself to 'fit' into the state's categories of 'deserving' welfare recipient was dehumanising to our low-income respondents. Their stories reflected the reality on the ground that 'poverty, disability, and discrimination … are not facts but interpretations and combating them is the expression of a value based on interpretation rather than a theory based on fact' (O'Brien and Penna, 1998, p 196). In contrast, anti-poverty policy becomes empowering when the frailty of human existence is acknowledged and citizenship status is accorded to collectively help each other to negotiate this condition.

The articulation of need at the point of delivery has been institutionalised through two types of policy structures. Both involve the use of discretion when determining eligibility. The first is the discretion that is exercised at the moment of policy *shaping*, when the ideal target group or institution is determined (see Table 9.2). For instance, in China and India the poverty lines that have been created are arbitrary. In India, people have been moved on and off the 'below poverty level' (BPL) list, depending on how and at what level this line has been fixed. In China, there has been huge variation between municipalities as to where the poverty line has been set, largely depending on the local fiscal situation. Such shifts have generated a sense in the claimants that their 'welfare rights' have been at the mercy of the state. Another example of discretion at the point of setting targets is Uganda, where the earlier target group for UPE was needy families, and yet, in a populist rent-seeking move, schools suddenly became the targets and were thus stigmatised.

A second type of discretion occurs at the individual level, wherein welfare officers and public officials distinguish one claimant from another. This has been observed in all of the settings. In countries such as Korea, Pakistan, China and India, the ratio of welfare officer to claimant has been very high. This has resulted in a system interface that is of poor quality with little sensitivity to the claimant. In this, it must be acknowledged that fiscal constraints do create poor institutions and ill-trained human resources, which then stigmatise poor people. Even in highly resourced settings such as Norway, however, welfare caseworkers exercise discretion, selecting one candidate over another for the Qualification Programme, often according to local fiscal constraints and welfare office priorities. With limited staff resources and top-down pressures to deliver transitions into work, 'creaming' results and good risks (those with higher employability) are preferred over bad risks. The rejection of applications has been hugely shameful in a context where employability has been held very high.

The history of social policy has shown that welfare administration cannot purely depend on law-based allocation (Adler and Bradley, 1975; Titmuss, 1987; Evans, 2010). Discretion is an important element in service provision (Molander et al, 2012). As described in the next chapter, the absence of professional judgement within the context of the global South has been a limitation at the point of delivery. Yet personal normative stances have tended to dominate over professional discretion (Terum and Nergård, 1999). Respondents in South Korea, Norway and Pakistan report that when professionals have been unable to exercise discretion or have been hard-pressed with time to make sound decisions, they tend to make choices based on the stereotyped biases attached to 'deserving' categories or culturally valued groups. This has the impact of stigmatising those belonging to negatively stereotyped categories. It is clear that the best practices for providing welfare services without shaming, yet enabling local discretion, are still to emerge.

Our data suggest that discretion at the individual level is particularly shaming in settings where corruption is rampant. In India, Pakistan and Uganda, local officials exercise discretion in tandem with the rent-seeking practice of petty corruption. Applicants who have been able to afford to pay a bribe are perceived as 'smart' as they have managed to access the welfare system. At a structural level, corruption has led to poor services. In India, food grain meant for people in poverty has been diverted to private markets, leading to stigmatised and poor quality grain access for those most in need. Rather than placing the focus, however, on the inefficiency and injustice that corruption breeds at the point of delivery, the answer in the settings studied in the global South has been to follow the model set by advanced welfare states. Thus, has there been a concerted effort to establish surveillance systems to identify 'fraudster' claimants. The stigma attached to being identified as such is evidenced in the moral policing that occurs in Pakistan, where a person making a false claim is branded as having committed a 'great sin'. In South Korea, welfare officers view claimants primarily with distrust and suspicion and verification mechanisms are hugely stigmatising. In China and Korea claimants are asked to produce reports from potential employers as to why they have not been hired. With such scrutiny, even rightful claimants are conscious of a harsh public gaze (see Table 9.3).

Table 9.3: Anti-poverty policy delivery and its effect on shaming across seven settings

Setting	Policy evidence	Shaming potential
China	*Dibao*: although introduced as a 'right' compared to earlier charity programmes, at the stage of access, the community vetting process to determine deservingness is personally intrusive and the application of local standards while making decisions counterproductive	While the move to introduce a 'rights-based' programme is progressive, applicants must face a committee of their peers/neighbours in a rigorous vetting process
India	Programmes are targeted at those placed on the BPL list, and political fixing of the list creates competition to get on; corruption leads to poor quality food grain via PDS; morally damaged participation in NREGA; bias against the most poor in BPL designation	Lessened shame for the poorest people managing to get onto the 'BPL' list, as they gain access by competing successfully against well-off people who gain easier access through corruption. However, welfare programmes are generally stigmatised as they offer 'poor' services
Norway	Applying the principle of discretion, welfare caseworkers decide how 'needy' social assistance claimants are and who is fit for the Qualification Programme	Those remaining on social assistance are further marginalised in the presence of new possibilities and services; those in the Qualification Programme may experience an offer of 'more'
Pakistan	Identity-based targeting of Zakat and BISP creates both stigma as well as clientelism	Those excluded from measures have no way to escape poverty and may experience heightened frustration and anger
South Korea	High administrative workload coupled with high levels of discretion provided to officials of NBLSS results in insensitive treatment of claimants	Suspicion and expectation by officials that claimants live a 'needy' life belittles their welfare rights
Uganda	UPE schools experience 'access shock', leading to poor quality services and resulting in stigma; inability to raise voices against bias in award of services and benefits towards those who are better off in the NAADS and PFA programmes	Heightened sense of shame and anger experienced by the poorest people since resources meant for them are diverted to better-off people and groups
United Kingdom	Increased conditionality placed on pre-existing programmes; activation programmes turning more in the direction of workfare; move from a pre-1996 focus on security to an increasingly punitive system, with reduced access to benefits and stringent conditions placed, often under the guise of pro-user rhetoric ('customer', 'client', 'personalisation')	In a situation of high levels of unemployment poor workless people and the working poor are increasingly portrayed as abusing the system and in need of corrective measures. Mixed reports on customer satisfaction, ranging from finding advisers supportive and helpful, to feeling belittled by encounters with job centres

Conclusion and implications

This chapter has summarised the mechanisms that emerged from our data linking the potential for shame to the framing, structuring and delivery of anti-poverty policies. What conclusions can be drawn from this summary of widely different contexts? On the one hand, one might resist drawing any conclusion, much in the same way as there has been resistance towards the delineation of an internationally acceptable definition of poverty (see Townsend's challenge against this practice in Spicker, 2007). In this volume we take a different approach. Experiences across the seven case countries offer policy lessons that are translatable across culturally differentiated contexts.

One of the ambitious tasks this book has attempted is to examine the interlinkages of policy processes (framing–structuring–delivery), and how these may have an impact at the individual level (via the shame that individuals living in poverty may experience). This has been with the aim of transcending the disconnect that exists between the worlds of policy researcher and policy-maker (Birnbaum, 2000). Needless to say, different frames lead to different policy tools. Further, two states adopting similar policy tools, but differing on the frames, might generate wholly different impacts concerning the variable of shame. A good example among the case countries is the differential impact of 'activation' policies in Norway, the UK and South Korea. Norway's policy frame is more narrowly concerned with minimising long-term dependency on social assistance via human capital formation – with this has come a consideration of its impact on individuals receiving the benefit. The UK's activation policies have their roots in explicitly delineating citizens into 'deserving' and 'undeserving', following a long established tradition of the social contract. South Korea's policy frame has been overwhelmingly aimed at achieving economic growth by self-sufficiency and by encouraging hard-working individuals. Comparatively, one could see, the policy tool of 'activation' per se is not shaming. Rather, it is the larger policy frame and its delivery that determines the shaming mechanism. In Korea, the 'social' has been completely neglected, creating hugely shaming situations in which welfare officers perceive claimants with suspicion. The UK's increased conditionality within its 'activation' policy has become instrumental for shaming. In Norway one group (social assistance recipients) experience shame compared to others (those in the Qualification Programme). These diverse shaming experiences reveal how policy tools are hugely embedded with the political frames and designs that give shape to such tools.

Policy tools are not neutral. Challenging this neutrality was a key contribution when the Marxian and Liberal traditions of the welfare state came under criticism beginning in the 1970s (O'Brien and Penna, 1998; Pierson, 1998). Policy neutrality is based on rationalist assumptions about the relationship between citizens and the state. Sen (1977) wittingly described the strategy of aiming to achieve social justice through the application of strict ideas concerning the economic man to be attempts by 'rational fools'. The meticulous artefacts of surveillance and monitoring for the efficient implementation of social policies are against the very aims of welfare itself. Attempts by policy-makers to create optimal and efficient policies have all too often resulted in the destruction of a space within which such policies might be effective. Policies addressing the satisficing (satisfying and sufficient) requirements of the target population have not been found to undermine macroeconomic concerns, in particular, those matching welfare state objectives (Akerlof and Yellen, 1987).

In contrast, policies established in many of the settings studied in this volume have reacted predominantly to changing macroeconomic conditions, without considering the necessary requirements for citizens to live in dignity. South Korea and China, for instance, have witnessed very similar trajectories in their move away from a Confucian ethic. In Korea, families resent having to shame their families when taking up the state's offer. In China, the community vetting procedure involved with claiming *dibao* resembles a communitarian spirit that is not coherent with other aspects of the policy, thus leading to shame.

Structural transitions in welfare fiscal approaches are visible in India and Uganda, where poverty reduction has taken a back seat to an emphasis on 'productivity'. Such policy transitions often neglect the germinating social forces, which act as strong undercurrents for policy acceptance. Thus, however well designed the policies may be, they result in unintended consequences. In other words: 'Designed or planned social order ignores essential features of any real, functioning social order' (Scott, 1998, p 6). One fails to notice that behind such wishful policies it may be the 'unreason' of the state machinery that disciplines the citizens to behave according to dominant economic, social and political orders (Foucault, 1977, 1982). Citizens in such settings, however, perceptively recognise such 'unreason', and respond with shame-proof behaviour, such as resorting to corruption in the face of the state's illegitimacy or competing to get onto a BPL list, as in India.

One of the significant comparative contributions in this book has been to focus on the policy neglect of certain sections of the population. Our evidence has shown that, as a result of this neglect, these segments experience stigma and shame as non-entities in their own states. Very often this social displacement is, in fact, a political act. To reclaim this social space, citizens have resorted to identity politics as a mechanism to assert their social needs (Fraser, 1989). On the other hand, a political (non-normative) engagement with social rights (Dean, 2007) will bring recognition and autonomy as a part of dignity-based policy-making (Fraser and Honneth, 2003). As we have shown in this chapter, it is the value-informed policy frames that displace citizens from the gaze of the welfare state. A move towards dignity-based policies must be rooted in changing the foundational discourses shaping the policy-making process, as much as in the design of policies themselves.

Note
[1] The influential classification of the UK as a liberal welfare state and Norway as a social democratic welfare state.

References
Adler, M. and Bradley, A.W. (1975) *Justice, discretion and poverty*, London: Professional Books.

Akerlof, G.A and Yellen, J.L. (1985) 'Can small deviations from rationality make significant differences to economic equilibria?', *American Economic Review*, vol 75, no 4, pp 708-20.

Birnbaum, R. (2000) 'Policy scholars are from Venus; policy makers are from Mars', *The Review of Higher Education*, vol 23, no 2, pp 119-32.

Bradshaw, J.R. and Terum, L.I. (1997) 'How Nordic is the Nordic model? Social assistance in a comparative perspective', *Scandinavian Journal of Social Welfare*, vol 6, no 4, pp 247-56.

Campbell, J.L. (1998) 'Institutional analysis and the role of ideas in political economy', *Theory and Society*, vol 27, no 3, pp 381-92.

Chase, E. and Bantebya Kyomuhendo, G. (eds) (2014) *The shame of poverty: Global experiences*, Oxford: Oxford University Press.

Dean, H. (2007) 'Social policy and human rights: Re-thinking the engagement', *Social Policy and Society*, vol 7, no 1, pp 1-12.

Dornan, P. and Porter, C. (2012) 'The implications of conditionality in social assistance programmes', in R. Surender and R. Walker (eds) *Social policy in a developing world*, Cheltenham: Edgar Elgar, Chapter 8.

Esping-Andersen, G. (1990) *The three worlds of welfare capitalism*, Cambridge: Polity Press.

Evans, T. (2010) *Professional discretion in welfare services*, London: Ashgate.

Foucault, M. (1977) *Discipline and punish*, Harmondsworth: Penguin.

Foucault, M. (1982) *Madness and civilization: A history of insanity in the age of reason*, London: Tavistock.

Fraser, N. (1989) *Unruly practices: Power, discourse and gender in contemporary social theory*, Cambridge: Polity Press.

Fraser, N. and Honneth, A. (2003) *Redistribution or recognition? A political-philosophical exchange*, London: Verso.

Lister, R. (2004) *Poverty*, Cambridge: Polity Press.

Lødemel, I. (1997) *The welfare paradox: Income maintenance and personal social services in Norway and Britain – 1946-1966*, Oslo: Scandinavian University Press.

Molander, A., Grimen, H. and Eriksen, E.O. (2012) 'Professional discretion and accountability in the welfare state', *Journal of Applied Philosophy*, vol 29, no 3, pp 214-30.

O'Brien, M. and Penna, S. (1998) *Theorising welfare*, London: Sage Publications.

Pierson, C. (1998) *Beyond the welfare state?*, Bristol: The Policy Press.

Pinker, R. (1971) *Social theory and social policy*, London: Heinemann Educational Books.

Ragin, C. (1997) 'Turning the tables: How case-oriented research challenges variable-oriented research', *Comparative Social Research*, vol 16, no 4, pp 27-42.

Scott, J.C. (1998) *Seeing like a state*, New Haven, CT: Yale University Press.

Sen, A. (1977) 'Rational fools: A critique of the behavioural foundation of economic theory', *Philosophy and Public Affairs*, vol 6, no 2.

Spicker, P. (2007) 'Definitions of poverty', in P. Spicker, S.-A. Leguizamon and D. Gordon (eds) *Poverty: An international glossary*, London: International Studies in Poverty Research, pp 229-43.

Stake, R. (2005) 'Qualitative case studies', in N.K. Denzin and Y.S. Lincoln (eds) *The Sage handbook of qualitative research* (3rd edn), London: Sage Publications, pp 435-454.

Surender, R. and Walker, R. (2012) *Social policy in a developing world*, Cheltenham: Edward Elgar.

Terum, L.I. and Nergård, T.B. (1999) 'Medisinsk skjønn og rettstryggleik', *Tidsskrift for Den norske lægeforening*, vol 119, no 15, pp 2192-6.

Titmuss, R. (1968) *Commitment to welfare*, New York: Pantheon Books.

Titmuss, R. (1987) 'Welfare "rights" law and discretion', in *The philosophy of welfare: Selected writings of Richard M. Titmuss*, London: Allen & Unwin, pp 201-15.

Walker, R. (2012) 'Social security: Risks, needs and protection', in R. Surender and R. Walker (eds) *Social policy in a developing world*, Cheltenham: Edward Elgar, Chapter 7.

Walker, R. (2014) *The shame of poverty: Global perspectives*, Oxford: Oxford University Press.

Weigand, C. and Grosh, M. (2008) *Levels and patterns of safety net spending in developing and transition countries*, Social Protection Discussion Paper no 0817, Washington, DC: The World Bank.

TEN

Towards global principles for dignity-based anti-poverty policies

Erika K. Gubrium and Ivar Lødemel

The context in which policy-making and delivery occurs is important when analysing the impact of policy. A brief example illustrates this point. One of the low-income respondents in rural Uganda invited us to her homestead. Her home was a hut made of dried mud with no windows. She hoped to be able to mend the thatch roof before the next rainy season. The empty dirt floor was just big enough for the floor mats that were rolled out at bedtime. Her family of five spent most of the time outside in front of the hut, where they prepared meals, washed and did homework for as long as daylight allowed. We were not invited to the homes of the Norwegian respondents, but we can imagine a contrasting scenario from stories told to us and the wealth of statistics that support it. A low-income respondent with a family of three is likely to live in a four-room apartment, built to high Norwegian building standards, with a fully equipped kitchen and bathroom. The children will likely have their own bedroom. When they are driven to school in a 15-year-old car the children wear clothes that only the inquisitive eyes of their peers can distinguish from that of other children. The respondent is unemployed and has not established entitlement to unemployment insurance, yet the local authority is obliged by law to pay her means-tested social assistance sufficient to maintain the resources and activities described.

The poverty experiences that have been relayed in the empirical chapters and the analysis presented in Chapter Nine demonstrate vastly different worlds with varying normative expectations concerning those on the receiving and delivering end of policy. Despite these differences, however, the low-income respondents in Uganda and Norway expressed strikingly similar feelings and experience of shame as they contrasted their own socioeconomic positions with that of their peers. Our analysis of the policy–shame nexus across the seven settings took account of both the surprising similarities and the enormous contextual differences.

Rather than effectiveness in the sense of providing a minimum income guarantee or the necessary food items, the definition of the impact of policy in this volume boils down to the psychosocial impact that policies have had on individual recipients. We focused in particular on the potential of policy to heighten shame or to build dignity. Related to this focus, three primary themes emerged from the empirical stories told: first, the 'social matters'; second, the mismatch between national strategies and realities on the ground; and third, the potential for shaming in the programmes that are predicated on conditionality. The themes took shape in the three policy moments explored across the seven settings, and have an impact on policy framing, influencing *what* is delivered. Framing also shapes the norms and assumptions concerning measure receipt, having a great impact on those at the receiving end. They are found within policy shaping and structuring, determining *how* measures are delivered. And most notably, they have an impact on delivery, determining where and how policy *functions*.

This concluding chapter consists of three sections, each devoted to issues introduced in Chapter One. First, we demonstrate how the emergent themes are strongly supported by the interplay of the poverty–shame nexus and policy across the settings investigated. Second, we discuss the promise offered by International Labour Organization (ILO) Recommendation 202 (2012), whose signatory countries have agreed to provide a nationally defined minimum of income for its people in the form of a 'social protection floor'. Among its 185 signatory nations, the Recommendation was signed by the seven in discussion here. Its focus on the social aspects of vulnerability offers a means for addressing the issues of dignity and shame. Pointing further to the future, the third section presents the possible application of relevant principles within the Recommendation. While the similarities in experiences are striking, so also are the differences in the economic, political and policy context of the nations covered in this volume. Our evidence therefore warns against any effort to make 'one-size-fits-all' policy recommendations. Instead, we develop a rubric consisting of general recommendations that may later be used in the development of new, and the reform of existing, policies in these very different settings.

Emerging themes

The stories told in each of the seven settings describe particular policy-related issues that may heighten the shame that individuals living in poverty experience. However, three themes emerged that resoundingly shaped the interplay between policy and the poverty–shame nexus across these vastly different settings.

The social matters

The empirically rich volume by Chase and Bantebya Kyomuhendo (2014) demonstrates that poverty is not just about lacking economic accumulation and material resources; it is also characterised by vastly reduced abilities to withstand social risks and to live life according to prevailing social norms. At the same time, the empirical chapters in this volume demonstrate that the social context and consequences of policy-making have not often been accounted for, a flaw that has been intensified by poor insight and planning in many of the settings. What's good for business has superseded what's good for society as a whole. Welfare strategies have been predicated on rational choice assumptions concerning individual 'economic man' throughout the policy cycle.

There is growing scholarly awareness that poverty has social and psychosocial aspects (Townsend, 1979; Sen, 1983; Marlier et al, 2007; Alkire and Foster, 2011; Taylor, 2011; Walker et al, 2013). Yet the overwhelming anti-poverty policy emphasis to date across the global North and South has been on the individual and the economic (Dean, 2003; Holmes and Jones, 2009; Voipio, 2012; Wright, 2012; Walker, 2013). This lack of recognition has further heightened the shame experienced by the policy recipients with whom we spoke. The empirical chapters illustrate policy-making and implementation processes in which attention is placed on 'troubled' individuals, yet their particular motivations, needs and realities are not often considered. The chapters substantiate that the vast social divisions that mark many of the settings are not solved through a purely economic approach. Rather, the visibility of such distinctions may be heightened and the lives of the most vulnerable not improved.

As shown in Chapter Three, India's public works programme (National Rural Employment Guarantee Act, NREGA) demonstrates these negative impacts. Notably, the programme has provided women belonging to lower castes with the opportunity to escape heavily exploitative situations of forced labour in the agricultural sector. In this sense, it can be said to have provided a limited amount of dignity to a particularly vulnerable population. Yet, rather than addressing the issue of prevailing caste-driven hierarchies within the labour market, the programme instead assumes a stigmatised workfare function by compelling participants to engage in stigmatising forms of work. The type of work assigned, the pay offered and the workers themselves have become a national 'joke', reinforcing morally laden understandings concerning the 'deservingness' and rights of the lower castes.

In Uganda, the introduction of universal education has merged children across a highly differentiated socioeconomic hierarchy into the same schools. As Chapter Eight suggests, the inclusion of low-income children has been publicly linked to degraded school quality. This understanding and the visible material disparity between themselves and their peers has led to a heightened sense of embarrassment and shame for the low-income students and their families taking part in the Ugandan study. In the Indian and Ugandan contexts, poverty 'relief' efforts have not only failed to effectively grapple with and relieve social exclusion, they have also reinforced it.

Lack of attention to deep social divisions is also reflected in the failure to develop an appropriate mechanism for ensuring that those who are *most* vulnerable benefit from anti-poverty approaches. A standard social policy assumption is that the more selective the policy, the more potentially redistributive it is. While this may hold true from a narrow economic perspective, Chapters Five and Seven, set in Norway and the UK respectively, support the contention that selectivity often results in a heightened sense of moral superiority on the one side, and of stigma and social exclusion on the other (see Titmuss, 1968; Eales, 1989). Selectivity has similar effects in our study settings from the global South. The process of selecting eligible claimants is frequently predicated on a claimant's possession of social or economic capital, or according to their moral 'deservingness', doing little to reduce inequality. Weak targeting of anti-poverty policies across the settings that possess deep socioeconomic disparities results in outcomes wherein the lowest income quintile quite often do not have access to much-needed programmes and benefits. In the chapters presenting Uganda, India, China and Pakistan, selectivity has been skewed toward individuals who possessed a modicum of resources and who were seen as more 'deserving'. Given the low level of coverage in these settings, those who are most vulnerable have the degrading task of being forced to compete at a contest in which they have little chance of coming out ahead. Chapter Five demonstrates that those who are most marginalised in Norway and who have very real barriers to work, and yet are still within the main target group of the Qualification Programme, have similarly been excluded from the possibilities connected to participation in its new human capital-based work approach.

Finally, our evidence demonstrates a (resounding) lack of consideration by national policy-makers to the fact that, like everyone else, low-income people are concerned with status and have hopes and expectations for themselves. In this sense, it is reasonable to expect that stigmatised and poor services result in low take-up. Thus, it is ineffective to reduce them to mere economic actors. Chapter Eight reports on the emptying out of low-quality universal public education schools in Uganda, as better-off students in urban areas have moved to private schools and children from low-income families feel 'forced' to attend. In Norway and in the UK it has long been recognised that there is a discrepancy between the number of people eligible for social assistance and those claiming benefits (Eardley et al, 1996). Chapter Two similarly demonstrates reluctance by former state employees in urban areas of China to enter into a demeaning eligibility process that typically only yields minimal financial support, at best. Chapter Three illustrates a similar problem in India, where the stigma attached to its public works programme (NREGA) has followed the 'less eligibility' strategy typically associated with the British workhouse (Dornan and Porter, 2012), ensuring that only those most in need of such work were willing to participate.

A mismatch between strategy and reality

This volume is informed by data that speak both to the world of policy recipients and to the language and structures particular to the policy development cycle. The data provide a rare opportunity to contrast policy rhetoric and the personal impact of policy practice. They support earlier contentions that there was a general mismatch between assumptions and strategies at the level of national policy-making and the more local interpretation and implementation of policy on the ground (Hargrove, 1975; Mazmanian and Sabatier, 1983; Hogwood and Gunn, 1984; Pressman and Wildavsky, 1984). They also provide evidence to substantiate earlier claims concerning the complex world of policy implementation (Lipsky, 1980; Barrett and Fudge, 1981; Hjern and Hull, 2007), and do so in two ways. Chapter Nine has established that the reality that we see in delivery is determined not only by the structure of policies, but also, crucially, by the framing discourses that surround the process of policy-making itself. Below, we consider a second means by which mismatch occurs, illustrating a broad failure by policy-makers to recognise the different contexts and realities circumscribing the creation and application of anti-poverty measures, even where local differences are taken into account.

Earlier scholarship complicating the idea of a discrete policy cycle focused largely on complexities situated in the global North. Yet perhaps most notable in our research was evidence supporting the contention of a general failure by national policy-makers in the global South to account for the reality of broad corruption (see Tanzi and Davoodi, 1997; The World Bank, 2004; Hall, 2012). This feature is compounded by the ways in which deep social hierarchies and strongly engrained public assumptions concerning the limited rights and roles of individuals living in poverty may pervade the intended purpose of the policy. The presence of corruption in conjunction with infrastructural weakness further heightens the impact. The effects of corruption and clientelism are compounded at the point of framing when there are few individuals with any expertise involved in policy-making and at the point of delivery when there are few qualified professionals in charge of implementation (Voipio, 2011).

India has moved to the use of central 'expert' policy Planning Commissions (often comprised of economists), who apply a technical approach towards social policy. At the national level, the matter of distinguishing who is 'below poverty level' (BPL) and eligible for a range of benefits is considered an objective exercise. In reality, as Chapter Three reports, the award of this status is far from objective and involves the interference of local bureaucrats who tend to follow the highest bidder. The heavy competition that surrounds the gaining of access to benefits means that their attainment may be a matter of pride *for those who can*. Given the reality of a weak infrastructure and low levels of coverage, the majority of those who are most in need, however, are those who gain the least. Furthermore, for those who have attained the status, corruption results in shame at the point of policy delivery. While the Public Distribution System (PDS) programme is aimed at providing affordable food to India's poor, the low-income respondents in the India study who have gained the right to subsidised grain have only had access to below standard products, while better quality grain has been siphoned off to those who can pay the highest premium.

Pakistan's largest social welfare scheme, the Benazir Income Support Programme (BISP), is intended to empower low-income women through the delivery of cash transfers. However, Chapter Six shows how, similar to the award of BPL status in India, the award of programme benefits is perverted by the corruptive intervention of local bureaucrats in the decision-making process. Low-income respondents suggested that clientelist discretion at the local level has meant that their geographical location, political affiliation and level of social clout determine the likelihood of access to this scheme. For the women who were potential recipients, corruptive discretion at the point of determining their eligibility necessitated the coercion of men outside the family (bureaucrats 'on the make'). Low-income female respondents described the emotional impact of feeling forced to make contact with these men, a highly stigmatised activity given overtly religious norms concerning female propriety. This dilemma forced potential recipients to be more dependent on the men in their lives and reinforced for them their lack of real power.

In Chapter Eight the Ugandan National Agricultural Advisory Services (NAADS) and the Prosperity for All (PFA) programme likewise reflects the difference between lofty intention and delivery realities. At the national level, both aim to increase the self-sustainability and empowerment of poor subsistence farmers. However, cronyism and corruption by bureaucrats at all levels means that those with the fewest social or financial resources literally cannot afford to partake in the services and benefits offered.

In part, the mismatch may also derive from a key difference that exists between anti-poverty measures and other welfare policy measures. Unlike, for example, social insurance, anti-poverty measures are always more local. In the welfare states of the North and South that are based on the Bismarckian model, the overriding goal has been social cohesion more than poverty relief (Walker, 2014). This goal has shaped the strategies applied. The presence of clear categories and entitlements tied to, for example, work-generated pensions, are easy to calculate using technical strategies that can be done from a removed central/national office. The people being served by anti-poverty measures, however, fit into unclear and diffuse categories whose needs are not best served using a one-size-fits-all technical approach.

Norway's work approach is aimed at a narrow target group. As Chapter Five reports, however, today the broad majority of individuals claiming social assistance face a diffuse set of social, structural and financial obstacles. The evidence presented suggests that while the work approach may be useful for some, it is not the answer for most claimants. The discrepancy between a government that resoundingly supports the idea of full employment and the everyday realities of claimants who are unable to either find or engage in work is a powerful means for generating shame. The mismatch is reflected in critiques from service providers themselves that the approach is not, on the whole, useful (Røysum, 2012).

The UK story presented in Chapter Seven provides one of the strongest illustrations of the damaging effects of the mismatch between policy and target group. In this case, the vast gap between national policy-making rhetoric and the everyday realities of claimants has resulted in a blurred political distinction between who may be considered 'deserving' and who may not. The gap was broadened after the separation of policy-making ministers from benefit-providing agencies taking place in the late 1990s. It is today reflected in the state's increasingly alienating language concerning benefit claimants, crystallised in the upcoming Universal Credit scheme, as all claimants have become suspect in the eyes of the state and the media, as any demand for recognition by those who are struggling to make ends meet is actively reviled.

A mismatch also exists between strategy and macroeconomic climate. As Chapter Four describes, South Korea's National Basic Living Security Scheme (NBLSS) represents a historic shift from charity- to rights-based social assistance. At the level of structure and delivery, its supply-side work approach provides minimal benefits. Its productivist strategy of promoting self-sufficiency is better matched to an economic climate that no longer exists. The approach gained strength during a period of intense economic growth, and sought to address the issue of those few who found themselves outside the labour market. In contrast, the most vulnerable in today's Korea are made up of widely disparate groups: young college graduates either incapable of finding work or precariously employed, the very old and single-headed households – in other words, those who cannot find work or who are unable to work. A similar point can be made concerning the shift towards workfare in the UK, created in the 'boom years' and yet only fully realised at a time of austerity post-2007. In both cases, a supply-side only approach is not appropriate.

Heightened shaming potential in conditional programmes

Social assistance (and other safety net programmes) is always more conditional than other forms of social protection. This follows mainly from its last resort function. In order to determine eligibility, the claimant must prove that other sources of maintenance are not available. This typically includes earnings from income and savings, but may also include family resources, and that of extended family. Over the past two decades, we have, however, witnessed a global trend where new requirements have been added in order to secure entitlement. Conditionality – defined here as the granting of cash transfers or services on the condition that the recipient carries out activities or meets certain behavioural requirements – has been increasingly applied in social assistance programmes in the global North (Lødemel and Trickey, 2001; Griggs and Bennett, 2010). It is a relatively new strategy, however, to anti-poverty efforts in the global South (Dornan and Porter, 2012).

The intensified conditionality that has taken place in the global North (in the form of work activation) has been placed on pre-existing programmes. In such cases we have witnessed a change in the social contract as new requirements have been added to a previously established set of entitlements. In its modern form, policies first developed in the US gained popularity in Europe in the 1990s and soon became the standard throughout the European Union (EU). Over the past two decades, therefore, rights have been curtailed and duties intensified (Lødemel and Trickey, 2001; Lødemel and Moreira, 2014). It is also associated with last resort 'residualist' tendencies: it is stigmatising, associated with low take-up and with limited anti-poverty effectiveness (Spicker, 1984; Behrendt, 2002; van Oorschot, 2002; Halvorsen and Stjernø, 2008; Matsaganis et al, 2010). It has been suggested that new compulsion, when placed on pre-existing programmes, has the potential to undermine the quality of the welfare offer, as the provider may choose whether or not to give high-quality offerings to recruits (Grimes, 1997). Furthermore, when compelled to do something that they perceive as meaningless, people's sense of self (worth) is undermined (Lødemel and Trickey, 2001). If claimants are already vulnerable, this may then undermine the efficacy of the measure offered.

This version of conditionality was represented by the increased stringency that took place within Norway's social assistance in the 1990s (Lødemel, 2001). Today, it is seen in the curtailed social assistance programmes in the UK, where, as is reported in Chapter Seven, the language of 'tough love' has been used to rationalise cuts to benefits and to place more stringent requirements to work or search for employment. Claimants have felt a markedly negative impact. Low-income respondents in the UK describe a sense of humiliation and unfair recrimination resulting from an increasing application of 'workhouse' test strategies designed to curtail their access to much needed benefits and services.

In the global South, the trend is similar, but the policy implications differ. In the absence of pre-existing entitlement-based social assistance, new conditional programmes have been introduced as the first instance of nationwide safety nets. In this situation we do not witness a similar change in the social contract. For the individual participant/recipient, the implication, however, is similar, as described below.

The more recently established social (including conditional) cash transfer schemes in the global South have been said to represent the realisation of T.H. Marshall's (1965/1981) vision of an offer of 'more'. These have taken the form of newly introduced human capital-oriented programmes that have been said to create new possibilities and, potentially, increased rights for anti-poverty measure participants (Leisering, 2008, 2009). Conditional cash transfer schemes make payments to poor households on the condition that those households invest in the human capital of their children in specific ways. Optimistic prognoses (especially those offered by The World Bank) have touted their use in the alleviation of poverty (Rawlings and Rubio, 2005; Fiszbein and Schady, 2009), whereas others highlight negative aspects such as reduced school attendance and increased labour demand on children associated with public works programmes (Dornan and Porter, 2012), the spread of clientelism and patronage (Hall, 2012), and the creation of new avenues through which corruption can take place (Alcázar, 2010).

Despite potentially negative aspects, the sort of 'new' conditionality taking place in the global South may, at the very least, be less likely to offer 'less', as it is attached to the provision of new benefits and does not, on the face of it, constrain pre-existing rights (see, for example, Lødemel and Dahl, 2000). Given this, the promise that has been attached to new conditionality in the global South has led to its description as opening a possibility for policy learning across the global divide (see Øverbye, 2012; Rawlings, 2004). In fact, South-originating approaches have been adopted or considered in the North in the form of minimum income guarantees, conditional cash transfers and microfinance schemes. For example, the Norwegian Qualification Programme resembles the approach of 'more' offered in the South, and New York City adopted a conditional cash transfer programme that was directly inspired by a similar programme in Mexico (Peck and Theodore, 2010). The focus that such approaches place on human capital should be especially appealing given the recent adoption of the ILO Recommendation 202 on social protection floors.

Yet the empirical evidence provided in this volume paints a picture that is not altogether encouraging. Our analysis demonstrates that, across the global North and South, the introduction of new conditionality – whether tied to old or new programmes – has introduced new arenas of shaming for low-income respondents. Conditionality has been used as a way to reduce spending on those deemed not to be in need. Furthermore, the shame that is attached to these programmes has been reflected North to South in reduced levels of take-up (Walker et al, 2013), and thus the effectiveness of this strategy is called into question.

The paternalism of conditionality is reflected in its therapeutic function, as policy-makers at the national level have determined what people 'need', and have applied rational choice assumptions when interfering with the income and lives of those who are to be 'helped' (Dornan and Porter, 2012). Solutions designed to avoid abuse or to motivate have had a negative impact on both those who are eligible and non-eligible. Relatively new social assistance schemes, in contrast to those in Norway and the UK, China's *dibao* system and South Korea's NBLSS have nonetheless been described as 'residual' welfare, with reference to their strict eligibility rules (often tied to a supply-side work-for-benefits approach) and limited coverage (Gao et al, 2011). In Chapters Two and Four, Chinese and South Korean respondents describe the heavy emotional toll endured in the process of attempting to gain eligibility. As activation must occur locally (Lødemel and Trickey, 2001; Künzel, 2012), a move towards increased conditionality has also added to the pressure to move to the personal. In China, this has taken the form of claimants facing a committee of neighbourhood peers in eligibility determinations. In South Korea, it has meant the need to contact close and distant relatives for financial support before being declared worthy of state aid. In both settings, claimants have had to both prove and explain why they have not been able to support themselves through regular employment. This intrusion has both heightened the shame they have felt and emphasised the idea that they are suspect until proven 'deserving'. Moreover, in South Korea, the stigma associated with claiming benefits has resulted in low take-up, thus casting doubts on the effectiveness of this strategy in alleviating poverty.

Indeed, the impact of conditionality on claimants has been especially marked in the study sites in the global South, where resources have often been limited and corruption typically rampant. Within this context, intensified requirements for face-to-face meetings with bureaucrats have been particularly troubling to low-income respondents. Chapter Six reports that the requirement in Pakistan to engage in personal interactions with rent-seeking bureaucrats has been shaming for claimants, especially for women seeking benefits via BISP. Pakistan's Zakat scheme is result of the adoption of a personal version of charity, with individual decision-making, to the national and public level. The combination of state interference and high levels of individual discretion does not translate well, and has resulted in increased shaming for potential benefactors and recipients.

Chapter Eight demonstrates how conditionality at the point of delivery in Uganda has undermined the aim of sustainable poverty reduction through the NAADS and PFA programme. Conditionality has introduced new expectations and a new means for dehumanisation through discrimination. The worthiness of claimants has been predicated on their possession of social and financial resources. Economically vulnerable respondents bemoaned the fact that this characteristic was the very reason that NAADS committees and the Savings and Credit Cooperative Organizations (SACCOs) attached to the programme had deemed them least eligible. The punitive financial and not-so-hidden social sanctions emerging from interactions with committees and SACCOs had heightened their sense of hopelessness and vulnerability, making their overall situation worse.

The evidence provided above suggests that it is the discretionary aspect of conditionality that results in heightened shame for low-income claimants. Yet shame may emerge from the basic presumptions of conditionality concerning the agency of low-income people and their reduction to mere economic actors. This includes the assumption that they lack individual motivation to participate in society, work or raise their children properly and that they must therefore be steered into 'correct' behaviour. India's public works programme (NREGA), for example, has introduced a new programme that offers benefits (pay) in exchange for work, without discretion. Yet as Chapter Three reports, it is by dint of the work itself being so undesirable and stigmatised and the pay so low that selectivity can be said to be high. It is the residual nature of their work and remuneration that programme participants have found so shameful. More broadly speaking, many of the study's low-income respondents had long been struggling to find paid work, to send their children to school and to live up to society's norms. Rather than seeing conditions as incentives, most have found that the attachment of pre-defined conditions to the offer of benefits has undermined any sense of real autonomy or agency.

Norway's Qualification Programme is, in part, an exception to this rule. It offers a new human capital-based approach to social assistance and is a move away from a workfare ideal (Gubrium et al, forthcoming, 2014). Users often accept new conditional programmes as fair when the activities and programmes are perceived as more meaningful (see, for example, Gubrium, 2013), when they add 'more' to pre-existing rights, or when they offer a new right to additional opportunities. Conditionality is perceived as a curtailment of rights ('less') when this is not the case (Lødemel and Trickey, 2001). Chapter Five reports that many of the low-income respondents engaged in the programme did not describe a sense of heightened shame from its newly imposed conditions, but rather described it as an offer of better future prospects. Similar to the low-income respondents across the seven settings, most had long wanted to work. In fact, rather than emphasising the positive aspects of the higher benefit they had received in connection with programme participation, most emphasised as positive the requirement that they engage in work-oriented activity. To them, this offered the possibility to move toward a 'normal' life. Notably, however, was the negative impact of the programme on those claimants who were not deemed eligible for the programme, as well as on those who did not gain work through the programme. These respondents described a reinforced understanding that they had, once again, not been able to meet society's broader expectations. What had been a new opportunity for some had, for those unable to meet or make use of the new conditions, been a further means of marginalisation and stigmatisation.

Policy-making and dignity

The three themes emerging from the analysis demonstrate the importance of recognising and integrating the voices and needs of anti-poverty policy recipients in the policy-making process. The data presented strongly substantiate the claim that policy-makers who fail to prioritise the dignity of the policy recipients are prone to introduce policies ranging from the ineffectual to the entirely counterproductive. Yet global development and aid organisations working in the global South have overwhelmingly focused their attention on attaining beneficial material outcomes from anti-poverty policies and programmes (Walker, 2013). These strategies have focused primarily on getting people to engage in prescribed actions in order to surpass a certain economic threshold, often taking the form of *quid pro quo* arrangements. Our evidence demonstrates, on the other hand, that a dignity-based approach is beneficial for recipients/participants. And, if we are convinced that the strategy of human capital development and resulting self-sufficiency is, indeed, an aim, this approach is also more effective for the provider.

It has been proposed that for social protection schemes to be transformative, they must move beyond the material in conceptualising the ideas of risk and vulnerability, and they must address the structural issues of social inequity and exclusion (Devereux and Sabates-Wheeler, 2007; Holmes and Jones, 2009). Social exclusion and inclusion have been a key part of the discourse of anti-poverty policy-making in the global North (Ferrera et al, 2002; Atkinson et al, 2004; Walker, 2014). With the rise of social cash transfer strategies in the global South, the conversation has now turned to the social and structural. Increasing focus has been placed on the capacity that people may or may not have to engage in the 'healthy' activities that have been prescribed by policy-makers. This newer conversation has taken into consideration the everyday lives of anti-poverty measure recipients. Increasing the capacity of low-income people means addressing both social and economic risks that they face. One promising strategy for doing so is through the establishment of a social protection floor (Voipio, 2012), and the recent passage of ILO Recommendation 202 (2012) provides a means for moving this strategy forward.

The Recommendation is the culmination of decades of efforts to provide minimum social security standards (Walker et al, 2012). The principles outlined within speak to an array of considerations involved in the development of rights-based social protection measures. It is committed to two primary goals: reducing poverty through the guaranteed provision of a social protection floor and the reduction of inequalities through strategies enabling pro-poor growth via empowerment and democratic participation. These goals are to be carried out according to a human rights framework based on dignity and respect at all levels of policy development and provision (Lister, 2008; Voipio, 2012; Walker, 2014). The human rights side is predicated on the secure guarantee of a global socioeconomic 'floor' of income security measures. In contrast to charity or needs-based approaches that overwhelmingly focus on individual duties, the Recommendation moves to a system of rights and entitlements, with an emphasis on the state's obligations and accountability (ILO, 2012). Participatory and accountability mechanisms ensure that the voices of social protection recipients are actively taken into account. They aim to build individual agency and empowerment by mitigating the personal and social impact of poverty as much as the material (Walker et al, 2012).

Notably, preliminary findings from the more broadly focused cross-national comparative study were used in the call for inclusion of the Recommendation's 6th principle: 'respect for the rights and dignity of people covered by the social security guarantees'. This principle speaks directly to the psychosocial impact of both poverty and policy-related approaches. Moreover, as the data demonstrates, it speaks to the effectiveness of anti-poverty policies. The evidence provided in this volume provides support to the contention that a consideration of recipient dignity is crucial to the longer-term success of any anti-poverty effort. The ILO Recommendation suggests a framework for assessing how closely integrated social protection assistance has been between those providing and those receiving social protection assistance. It is especially aimed at redressing failed policy-making efforts in the global South. Yet our evidence suggests that there is also work to be done in the anti-poverty policy arena in settings in the North (see Walker et al, 2012). Our evidence demonstrates that, in both the South and North, social inclusion strategies that merely aim to encourage civic participation without addressing the origins of socioeconomic disparities may only heighten the impact of these differences.

Given the recent global economic downturn, organisations such as The World Bank and the United Nations (UN), long having had a dominant position in anti-poverty efforts taking place in the global South, are now shifting their financial heft towards the establishment of social protection floors in the North and South (see The World Bank, 2009; ILO, 2012). In the global South as well as in those nations most affected by the crisis in the North, their clout and history of investment make a real push for this strategy and its associated tenets more likely. Yet at the same time, the global economic situation also means that, while the 'social protection floor' movement is promising, it will be implemented in a rather harsh climate. We have witnessed calls for welfare tightening usually associated with austerity in most places (including, quite recently, in relatively unaffected Norway). These calls are linked to close-to-universal global support for stronger conditionality in welfare provisions. It is within this climate that our evidence provides the most compelling message: that treating the recipients of anti-poverty measures with respect and promoting their dignity makes policy *more* effective.

Attuned to the aim of respecting the dignity of anti-poverty measure recipients, we now conclude with the shared implications that arise from our focus on instances of shaming across three policy moments, as well as from the three themes that emerged from the analysis. We have not conducted a formal implementation study, yet we have talked with the people affected by social policy. Based on the perspectives of the individuals receiving social protection, we offer some lessons learned concerning anti-poverty policy and its consideration of dignity.

Relevant lessons

The experiences relayed by the low-income respondents suggest that poverty is not an identity, but a relation. Most had high expectations for themselves. Most wanted to work and live a life according to the sociocultural norms of their particular setting. Yet they told us that the state policies they had encountered emphasised that they were different, and therefore subject to different rules and regulations than members of 'normal' society. Ironically, the predominantly economically focused anti-poverty programmes and policies that were supposed to alleviate and relieve poverty had instead largely heightened the pressure, shame and stigma they experienced. In some cases, this was because the policies offered less than promised. In most cases, however, it was because the policy strategy and instruments were distorted at the point of delivery.

Our evidence underscores the fact that policy learning is not a simple matter. The strong message that emerged is that any assessment of policy success needs to take into account the whole policy process. The structure of policy measures is important, yet also at issue is why particular policies have been used, the framing factors that may enable or constrain successful implementation, as well as how appropriate it is to apply a chosen approach within a particular setting (Dolowitz and Marsh, 1996; Benson and Jordan, 2011). This includes a focus on the aims and causes of particular policy choices. Our analysis has attended to these aspects of policy-making. Furthermore, we have merged these broader contextual considerations with a focus on the experiences and perceptions of policy recipients, something previously missing from the world of comparative social policy. Using our assessment of the anti-poverty policies in the seven settings, we now provide a brief overview of relevant lessons learned.

The low-income people we spoke with described a strong interplay between security and dignity. They suggested that when policy-making was framed as a conditionally based provision, as subject to bureaucratic discretion both in a positive sense (with a charitable function) and a negative one (with a punitive function to weed out the 'undeserving'), it was inherently demeaning. They described as degrading those policies that were framed according to essentialist notions concerning how and why they were living in poverty, as well as concerning what was necessary to individually motivate them to leave their situations. This is in contrast to rights-based strategies recognising the importance of recipient dignity and psychosocial 'wellbeing' in order to achieve longer lasting positive results (Sage, 2013). The stories told in the seven settings support the contention that policy developments are experienced by recipients as empowering when they enhance their citizen-based rights and limit the conditional and discretionary power of institutions, bureaucrats and providers (Standing, 2008).

Respondents also described a gap between policy-making, policy implementation and recipient realities. Service must be personal enough to recognise the everyday needs and constraints of users. Yet the more personal and relational the service, the greater the potential for stigma (Pinker, 1971). One potential strategy for building awareness of the different contexts and realities of policy target groups would be to generate communication networks between those living in poverty and decision-makers. The democratic participation of policy recipients in the development and implementation process offers one means to provide voice and collective strength to these individuals. This can be encouraged during initial policy development (via focus groups), and implementation (building agency through the inclusion of carefully selected, trained and remunerated target group members in system administration). It also offers a means for generating grassroots-driven systems of accountability (Molander et al, 2012) and redress (Alcázar, 2010), helping to relieve the more arbitrary and shaming aspects of discretion and conditionality.

Furthermore, evaluations of policy implementation and delivery might do well to focus on process as well as outcome, with a primary aim at determining how the *most* vulnerable fare. Such a focus might involve the use of pilot studies in which shame and social exclusion are among the key considerations. It might be further augmented through the development and financial support of social networks and forums for recipient dignity building. For example, in India, groups of lower caste women in Kerala have been involved in the implementation and monitoring of its public works programme. This has resulted in increased awareness of rights, a stronger collective voice for the most vulnerable and more sensitivity to the needs of target groups during implementation (Vijayanand and Jithendren, 2008, as cited in Singh, 2012). Employing a similar strategy, anti-poverty efforts might engage in South-to-South learning and enhance the collective strength of most vulnerable groups elsewhere.

Our analysis in Chapter Nine demonstrates that, while the themes that have emerged can be parlayed into general recommendations, the application of recommendations must acknowledge particular welfare settings and cultural understandings of shame and dignity. A rubric for crafting dignity- and rights-based anti-poverty policy would support the effective application of the ILO's new social protection floor recommendation. Yet while we are able to provide more general lessons learned from our data, it is still too soon to move beyond this to the world of concrete suggestions for the improvement of practice.

Our evidence suggests that shaming takes place throughout the policy cycle, yet it is especially relevant at the point of policy delivery. The evidence presented in this volume speaks especially to the experiences of policy recipients. Yet the mechanisms of delivery and the voices of the professionals delivering the measures are an equally important story to be explored (Voipio, 2011). With this aim in mind, the national teams whose research has filled this volume have begun to embark on a new study, one that takes further the considerations and lessons that have been shared here, examining anti-poverty policy processes at the point of delivery. The research will incorporate the voices of policy recipients and providers. It will also focus on the interactions that take place during the delivery process. In this way, we may begin to move toward a rubric for anti-poverty policy-making that respects the dignity of policy recipients.

References

Alcázar, L. (2010) *The uses and abuses of social programmes: The case of conditional cash transfers*, U4 Brief No 3, July, Norway: U4 Anti-Corruption Resource Centre.

Alkire, S. and Foster, J. (2011) 'Counting and multidimensional poverty measurement', *Journal of Public Economics*, vol 95, no 7-8, pp 476-87.

Atkinson, A.B., Marlier, E. and Nolan, B. (2004) 'Indicators and targets for social inclusion in the European Union', *Journal of Common Market Studies*, vol 42, no 1, pp 47-75.

Barrett, S. and Fudge, C. (1981) *Policy and action: Essays on the implementation of public policy*, London: Methuen.

Behrendt, C. (2002) *At the margins of the welfare state. Social assistance and the alleviation of poverty in Germany, Sweden and the United Kingdom*, Aldershot: Ashgate.

Benson, D. and Jordan, A. (2011) 'What have we learned from policy transfer research? Dolowitz and Marsh revisited', *Political Studies Review*, vol 9, pp 366-78.

Chase, E. and Bantebya Kyomuhendo, G. (eds) (2014) *The shame of poverty: Global experiences*, Oxford: Oxford University Press.

Dean, H. (2003) 'The third way and social welfare: The myth of post-emotionalism', *Social Policy & Administration*, vol 37, no 7, pp 695-708.

Devereux, S. and Sabates-Wheeler, R. (2007) 'Social protection for transformation', *IDS Bulletin*, vol 38, no 3, pp 23-8.

Dolowitz, D.P. and Marsh, D. (1996) 'Who learns what from whom? A review of the policy transfer literature', *Political Studies*, vol 44, no 2, pp 343-57.

Dornan, P. and Porter, C. (2012) 'The implications of conditionality in social assistance programmes', in R. Surender and R. Walker (eds) *Social policy in a developing world*, Cheltenham: Edgar Elgar, Chapter 8.

Eales, M. (1989) 'Shame among unemployed men', *Social Science & Medicine*, vol 28, no 8, pp 783-9.

Eardley, T., Bradshaw, J., Ditch, J., Gough, I. and Whiteford, P. (1996) *Social assistance in OECD countries*, Synthesis Report No 46, OECD Department of Social Security, Paris: OECD.

Ferrera, M., Matsaganis, M. and Sacchi, S. (2002) 'Open coordination against poverty: the new EU "social inclusion" process', *Journal of European Social Policy*, vol 12, no 3, pp 227-39.

Fiszbein, A. and Schady, N. (2009) *Conditional cash transfers: Reducing present and future poverty*, World Bank Policy Research Report, Washington, DC: The World Bank.

Gao, Q., Yoo, J., Yang, S.-M. and Zhai, F. (2011) 'Welfare residualism: A comparative study of the Basic Livelihood Security systems in China and South Korea', *International Journal of Social Welfare*, vol 20, pp 113-24.

Griggs, J. and Bennett, F. (2010) *Rights and responsibilities in the social security system*, Occasional Paper 6, London: Social Security Advisory Committee (www.ssac.org.uk/pdf/occasional/Rights_ Responsibilities_Social _Security.pdf).

Grimes, A. (1997) 'Would workfare work? An alternative approach for the UK', in A. Deacon (ed) *From welfare to work: Lessons from America*, London: Institute of Economic Affairs, pp 97-107.

Gubrium, E.K. (2013) 'Participant meaning-making along the work trajectory of a labour activation programme', in J.F. Gubrium and M. Järvinen (eds) *Turning troubles into problems: Clientization in human services*, London: Routledge, pp 137-154.

Gubrium, E.K., Harsløf, I. and Lødemel, I. (forthcoming, 2014) 'Norwegian activation reform on a wave of wider welfare state change: A critical assessment', in I. Lødemel and A. Moreira (eds) *'Workfare revisited.' The political economy of activation reforms*, New York: Oxford University Press.

Hall, A. (2012) 'The last shall be the first: Political dimensions of conditional cash transfers in Brazil', *Journal of Policy Practice, vol 11, pp 25-41.*

Halvorsen, K. and Stjernø, S. (2008) *Work, oil and welfare: The welfare state in Norway*, Oslo: Universitetsforlaget.

Hargrove, E.C. (1975) *The missing link: The study of the implementation of social policy*, Paper 797-1, Washington, DC: The Urban Institute.

Hjerne, B. and Hull, C. (2007) 'Going interorganisational: Weber meets Durkheim', *Scandinavian Political Studies*, vol 7, no 3, pp 197-212.

Hogwood, B.W. and Gunn, L.A. (1984) *Policy analysis for the real world*, New York: Oxford University Press.

Holmes, R. and Jones, N. (2009) *Putting the social back into social protection: A framework for understanding the linkages between economic and social risks for poverty reduction*, Background Note, August, London: Overseas Development Institute.

ILO (International Labour Organization) (2012) *Recommendation concerning national floors of social protection adopted by the Conference at its one hundred and first session*, Recommendation 202, 14 June, Geneva: ILO.

Künzel, S. (2012) 'The local dimension of active inclusion policy', *Journal of European Social Policy*, vol 22, no 1, pp 3-16.

Leisering, L. (2008) 'Social assistance in the global South – A survey and analysis', *ZIAS*, vol 1-2, no 22, pp 74-103.

Leisering, L. (2009) 'Extending social security to the excluded: Are social cash transfers to the poor an appropriate way of fighting poverty in developing countries?', *Global Social Policy*, vol 9, no 2, pp 246-71.

Lipsky, M. (1980) *Street-level bureaucracy: Dilemmas of the individual in public services*, New York: Russell Sage Foundation.

Lister, R. (2008) 'A human rights conceptualisation of poverty', Paper presented at the International Conference on 'Exclusion, a challenge to democracy. How relevant is Joseph Wresinski's thinking?', Paris: Paris Institute of Political Studies, 19 December.

Lødemel, I. (2001) 'Discussion: Workfare in the welfare state', in I. Lødemel and H. Trickey (eds) *'An offer you can't refuse: Workfare in international perspective*, Bristol: Policy Press, pp 295-343.

Lødemel, I. and Dahl, E. (2000) 'Public works programs in Korea: A comparison to active labour market policies and workfare in Europe and the US', Paper presented at the International Conference on 'Economic crisis and labour market reform: The case of Korea, Korea Labour Institute and World Bank', Seoul, May.

Lødemel, I. and Moreira, A. (eds) (2014) *'Workfare revisited.' The political economy of activation reforms*, New York: Oxford University Press.

Lødemel, I. and Trickey, H. (2001) *'An offer you can't refuse': Workfare in international perspective*, Bristol: Policy Press.

Marlier, E., Atkinson, A.B., Cantillon, B. and Nolan, B. (2007) *The EU and social inclusion: Facing the challenges*, Bristol: Policy Press.

Marshall, T.H. (1965/1981) *The right to welfare*, London: Heinemann Educational Books.

Matsaganis, M., Levy, H. and Flevotomou, M. (2010) *Non take up of social benefits in Greece and Spain*, Working Paper No EM7/10, Colchester: EUROMOD.

Mazmanian, D.A. and Sabatier, P.A. (1983) *Implementation and public policy*, Glenview, IL: Scott Foresman.

Molander, A., Grimen, H. and Eriksen, E.O. (2012) 'Professional discretion and accountability in the welfare state', *Journal of Applied Philosophy*, vol 29, no 3, pp 214-30.

Øverbye, E. (2012) 'Land i Sør - laboratorier for ny sosialpolitikk', *Velferd*, vol 101, no 6.

Peck, J. and Theodore, N. (2010) 'Recombinant workfare, across the Americas: Transnationalizing "fast" social policy', *Geoforum*, vol 41, pp 195-208.

Pinker, R. (1971) *Social theory and social policy*, London: Heinemann Educational Books.

Pressman, J.L. and Wildavsky, A. (1984) *Implementation: How great expectations in Washington are dashed in Oakland*, Berkeley, CA: University of California Press.

Rawlings, L.G. (2004) *A new approach to social assistance: Latin America's experience with conditional cash transfer programs*, Social Protection Discussion Paper 0416, Washington, DC: The World Bank.

Rawlings, L.B. and Rubio, G.M. (2005) 'Evaluating the impact of conditional cash transfer programs', *World Bank Research Observer*, vol 20, no 1, pp 29-55.

Røysum, A. (2012) 'The reform of the welfare services in Norway: One office – one way of thinking?', *European Journal of Social Work* (iFirst version), pp 1-16.

Sage, D. (2013) 'Activation, health and wellbeing: Neglected dimensions?', *International Journal of Sociology and Social Policy*, vol 33, no 1/2, pp 4-20.

Sen, A. (1983) 'Poor, relatively speaking', *Oxford Economic Papers*, vol 35, pp 153-69.

Singh, A.K. (2012) 'Caste – the actual cost of empowerment? Dalit women and NREGA', Master's thesis, Oslo: Oslo and Akershus University College.

Spicker, P. (1984) *Stigma and social welfare*, London: Croom Helm.

Standing, G. (2008) 'How cash transfers promote the case for basic income', *Basic Income Studies*, vol 3, no 1, pp 2-30.

Tanzi, V. and Davoodi, H. (1997) *Corruption, public investment, and growth*, IMF Working Paper 97/139, Washington, DC: International Monetary Fund.

Taylor, D. (2011) 'Wellbeing and welfare: A psychosocial analysis of being well and doing well enough', *Journal of Social Policy*, vol 40, no 4, pp 777-94.

Titmuss, R.M. (1968) *Commitment to welfare*, London: George Allen & Unwin Ltd.

Townsend, P. (1979) *Poverty in the United Kingdom*, Harmondsworth: Penguin.

van Oorschot, W. (2002) 'Targeting welfare: on the functions and dysfunctions of meanstesting in social policy', in P. Townsend and D. Gordon (eds) *World poverty: New policies to defeat an old enemy*, Bristol: Policy Press, pp 171-193.

Vijayanand, S.M. and Jithendran, V.N. (2008) *Implementation of NREGA – Experience of Kerala*, Kerala: Government of Kerala.

Voipio, T. (2011) 'Social Protection for All – An agenda for pro-child growth and child rights', Social and Economic Policy, UNICEF Policy and Practice, January (www.unicef.org/socialpolicy/files/Jan2011_ChildPovertyInsisghts_ENG(4).pdf).

Voipio, T. (2012) 'Empowerment through social protection – Social Protection Floor Initiative (SPF-I)', UN-DESA Expert Group Meeting, 10-12 September (www.un.org/esa/socdev/egms/docs/2012/ppt/Timo-Voipio.pdf).

Walker, R. (2013) 'Towards the analysis of social policy in a developing world', in R. Surender and R. Walker (eds) *Social policy in a developing world*, Cheltenham: Edward Elgar, pp 258-284.

Walker, R. (2014) *The shame of poverty: Global perspectives*, Oxford: Oxford University Press.

Walker, R., Chase, E. and Lødemel, I. (2012) 'The indignity of the Welfare Reform Act 2012: Why the ILO matters for UK antipoverty programmes', *Poverty*, vol 143, pp 9-12.

Walker, R., Bantebya Kyomuheno, G., Chase, E., Choudhry, S., Gubrium, E.K., Jo, N.-Y., Lødemel, I., Mathew, L., Mwiine, A., Pellissery, S. and Yan, M. (2013) 'Poverty in global perspective: Is shame a common denominator?', *Journal of Social Policy*, vol 42, no 2, pp 215-233.

World Bank, The (2004) *World development report 2004: Making services work for poor people*, Washington, DC: The World Bank.

World Bank, The (2009) *World Bank Group operational response to the crisis*, Washington, DC: The World Bank.

Wright, S. (2012) 'Welfare-to-work, agency and personal responsibility', *Journal of Social Policy*, vol 41, no 2, pp 309-28.

Index

Note: Page numbers in *italic* type refer to tables.

A

absolute poverty
  in China 18, 30
  in India 37
  in Pakistan 114
  in South Korea 62, 64
  in Uganda 160
access shock 164, 165
activation policies *see* work approach
agency and autonomy x, 6, 190, 210
  in India 48
  recommendations 212, 215
  in South Korea 74, 77, 79
  in UK 152
  see also self-sufficiency
agriculture *see* rural economy
Andersen, K. 92
ATD Fourth World xi

B

Bantebya Kyomuhendo, G. 1–2, 179
'basic needs' approach 26
behavioural effects of shame 7, 166,
  173
'below the poverty level' (BPL) 43–4,
  50, 204
Benazir Income Support Programme
  (BISP) 116
  delivery 122, 124–6, 204–5
  recommendations 128–9
  structure 118, 120, 121–2
benefit levels
  in China 28
  in Norway 89
Benefits Agency (UK) 139
Bhutto, Z.A. 113
BISP *see* Benazir Income Support
  Programme
Bjorkman, J. 42
Blair, T. 140, 141
blame

conceptualising in UK policy
  135–9
crystallising in UK policy 139–47
and policy in South Korea 71
and provision in Pakistan 126–8
see also responsibilities/duties
BPL ('below the poverty level') 43–4,
  50, 204
bribery see corruption
bureaucracy *see* civil service;
  procedural formalities

C

Cameron, D. 149
capabilities approach 6, 126
  see also employability; work
  capability
cash transfer schemes 115–16, 191,
  207–8
caste system 38, 44, 55, 201–2
charity see international aid; Zakat
  programme
Chase, E. 1–2, 179
cheating see welfare fraud
child poverty, in UK 140–1, 144–5
Child Poverty Act (2010) (UK)
  140–1
China 10, 181
  historical context 17–18, 196
  policy delivery in 26–9, 31–2, 191,
  192, 193, *194*, 209
  policy framing in 19–23, 186, *187*,
  188
  policy implications and
  recommendations 29–32
  policy structuring in 23–6, 188,
  189, 191
civil service
  in Pakistan 111, 127–8, 130
  in UK 133
community vetting, in China 26–7,
  28, 29, 31

community-based programmes, in
Pakistan 129
conditional cash transfers (CCTs)
115–16, 191, 207–8
conditionality
in Norway 96–8
in Pakistan 115–16
and shaming 206–11, 214
in UK 137–8, 141
consumption, in South Korea 63, 64
corruption 193, 204
in India 50–1, 53, 55, 204
in Pakistan 115, 119, 121, 123,
204–5
in Uganda 158, 169, 175, 205
cross-national concepts of shame 7–8
cultural context, and policy framing
185

D

danwei 19–20, 24
delivery *see* policy delivery
Deng Xiaoping 20
Department for Work and Pensions
(DWP) (UK) 145
dependency *see* welfare dependency
deservingness
articulation of need 191–2
concept in China 27, 28, 31
concept in Norway 92, 93, 94–5,
100
concept in South Korea 70, 73
concept in UK 134, 136, 206
and programmes in Uganda 173,
174
and selectivity 202
see also eligibility
dibao system (China) 22, 24–6
benefit level 28
criteria and eligibility 26–7
implications and recommendations
29–32
recipient perceptions 27, 28–9
dignity
and interactionism 5
link with security 214
and NREGA programme in India
47, 48, 52
policy lessons 213–16
and policy-making xi, 3, 211–13
and Qualification Programme in
Norway 99, 100, 101, 103

and Universal Credit in UK 150
discourse
impact on anti-poverty policy
185–6
see also media; perceptions; political
rhetoric
discretion
and shame 214
types of 192–3
see also local discretion; poverty lines;
targeted provision
discrimination 38, 127
documentation
and shame 77, 80
see also procedural formalities
Duncan Smith, I. 149–50
duties *see* responsibilities/duties

E

economic context
policy mismatch with 206
policy as response to 196
social protection in 213
economic crisis, in South Korea
64–5, 70
economic growth and development
modernisation in UK 139–41
in Pakistan 113, 114
prioritised over social 66–9, 71, 81,
113, 114, 190, 201–2
in South Korea 61, 62, 63, 66–9,
71, 81
transition in China 17, 18, 19, 20–1,
31
in Uganda 159, 162, 170–2
economy
agriculture-based in Uganda 157
see also rural economy; urban
economy
education
and class in Uganda 160, 165
and conditionality in Pakistan
115–16
UPE in Uganda 159, 163–7, 172–3
eligibility
articulation of need 191–2
in China 26–7, 30
effects of selectivity 202
in India 43–4, 49–51, 204
in Norway 92, 94–6
in Pakistan 119–26

in South Korea 69, 72, 73, 74, 77, 80

in Uganda 163–4

see also conditionality; deservingness; exclusion from provision; local discretion; targeted provision; universal provision

employability 95

see also work capability

employment

impact of Chinese economic reform on 20–3

NREGA programme in India 47–9, 52–3, 201–2, 210

rural and urban in India 37–8

UK approach to welfare and *see* United Kingdom

under planned economy in China 19–20

women's participation 39, 116

see also work approach

Employment and Support Allowance 143

exclusion from provision 191, 202

in China 25

in Pakistan 119–20

in South Korea 73–4

in Uganda 169, 171, 173

expenditure on welfare

in China 23

comparisons 188

in Pakistan 118, 121

in South Korea 69

in Uganda 162, 164

in UK 139

F

family, as safety net in South Korea 64, 68, 74, 75–6

family obligation support clause 75–6

farming *see* rural economy

federally administered tribal areas (FATAs) (Pakistan) 117

Field, F. 141

food security, PDS in India 45–7, 51–2

food subsidies 127

foreign aid 64, 72, 119

Fowler reforms (UK) 135–7

framing *see* policy framing

fraud *see* welfare fraud

Frembgen, J. 117

funding of welfare

in Pakistan 118–19

see also expenditure on welfare

G

Gandhi, M. 43

gender

and shame in India 39

women welfare recipients in Pakistan 116, 121, 124–6

geography

and poverty in Uganda 160

and stigma in India 38

Goetz, J. 8

H

Hanssen, B.H. 92

HIPC (Heavily Indebted Poor Countries) list 161

honour

concept in India 39, 41

and tribal custom in Pakistan 117

see also Zakat programme

households

and poverty surveys 125–6

and welfare eligibility 74

see also family

human capital approach

conditional cash transfers (CCTs) 208

in Norway 91, 190, 210–11

in Uganda's UPE 163

Hussain, A. 114

I

identity

collective in Pakistan 112

and diversity in India 42

and interactionism 5

and internalised shame 88

see also social stratification

illiteracy 122

immigrants 88

implementation *see* policy delivery

income inequality

in China 18, 21, 26, 30

low in Norway 89

stable in South Korea 62

in Uganda 160–1, 162
Income Support (UK) 136
India 10, 181–2
  diversity and complexity in 37, 42, 53–4
  economic prioritised over social policy 201–2
  history of policies 40–1
  NREGA 47–9, 52–3, 201–2, 210
  PDS 45–7, 51–2, 204
  policy delivery in 42–3, 49–53, 191, 192, 193, *194*
  policy framing in 41–4, 186, *187*
  policy implications and recommendations 53–5
  policy structuring in 45–9, 188, *189*, 190–1, 210
  poverty level in 37, 43–4, 50, 204
  poverty, stratification and shame in 38–40, 44
  recipient participation 215
  strategy-reality mismatch 204
individualism
  in Norway 88, 91, 101
  policy focus on 201
  in South Korea 64, 68
  and UK welfare discourse 148–9
  see also agency and autonomy; responsibilities/duties; self-sufficiency
industrialisation, in South Korea 62, 63, 66–9
inequality
  in China 18, 21, 26, 30
  low in Norway 89
  neglected in policy-making 201–2
  in Pakistan 112–17, 126–7
  stable in South Korea 62
  in Uganda 160–1, 162, 165–6, 169, 172–3
  underlying policy-making 204
  see also social stratification
interactionism 5
international aid 64, 72, 119
International Labour Organization (ILO) xi, 3, 200, 212–13
internships *see* Qualification Programme
'iron rice bowl' 19
izzat *39*

J

Jinnah, M.A. 112
Jobcentre Plus (UK) 145
Jobseekers Allowance (UK) 137–9, 142, 143

K

Keltner, D. 8
Kim Dae-Joong 70
Kim Young-Sam 69

L

land ownership
  in Pakistan 112
  in South Korea 62
Li Peng 22
Lister, R. 5
Livelihood Protection Law (South Korea) 64, 69, 72
loans (Uganda) 171, 174
local discretion 192, 204–5, 209–10, 214
  in China 26–7, 28, 29, 31
  in India 49–50
  in Norway 94–6
  in Pakistan 117, 120–1, 123
  in South Korea 78, 79–80
  in UK 150
  see also corruption
Lødemel, I. 87
lunch fees, in Ugandan schools 166

M

'making work pay' (UK) 143–4
market economy
  in China 17, 19, 20–1
  in India 41
Marshall, T.H. 98
Mathur, K. 42
MDGs (Millennium Development Goals) 3
means-testing
  in Norway 94
  in Pakistan 125
  in South Korea 73, 75
media
  in India 43, 49, 55
  in Norway 88
  in UK 138, 148, 149

middle class, in Uganda 160–1, 162, 165
migrants, and welfare provision in China 25
Millennium Development Goals (MDGs) 3
modernisation *see* economic growth and development
motivation 210
  in Norway 93, 96, 101, 102, 103
  see also sanctions
Museveni, Y. 161–2, 166
Musharraf, P. 115
Mustahqeen *122–3*

N

National Agricultural Advisory Services (NAADS) (Uganda) 159, 167–70, 173, 175, 205, 209–10
National Basic Living Security Scheme (NBLSS) (South Korea) 65, 70, 206
  delivery 77–81
  structure 71–7
National Development Plan (NDP) (Uganda) 159, 161–3, 170–2, 173–4
National Insurance Service (Norway) 91, 93
National Rural Employment Guarantee Act (NREGA) (India) 47–9, 52–3, 201–2, 210
national settings 9–11, 180–4, 199
  see also economic context
nationalisation in Pakistan 113–14
NBLSS *see* National Basic Living Security Scheme
NDP *see* National Development Plan
need
  articulation of 191–2
  'basic needs' approach 26
Nehru, J. 43
'New Deal' programmes (UK) 142
New Labour policy (UK) 139–47
newspapers 43, 49, 88, 138
Noh Tae-Woo 69
Norway 10–11, 182–3
  compared with Uganda 199
  policy delivery in 92–100, 191, 192, 193, *194*
  policy frames and tools 195
  policy framing in 87–9, 186, *187*

policy implications and recommendations 100–3
  policy shaping in 89–92
  policy structuring in 92–100, *189*, 190, 207, 210–11
  strategy-reality mismatch 205
  welfare state in 85–7
NREGA (National Rural Employment Guarantee Act) (India) 47–9, 52–3, 201–2, 210

O

officials
  interaction with recipients 79–80, 94, 146
  see also local discretion

P

Pakistan 11, 183
  background 111
  BISP 116, 118, 120, 121–2, 124–6, 128–9, 204–5
  historical context and framing 112–17, 186, *187*
  policy delivery in 122–8, 191–2, 193, *194*
  policy implications and recommendations 128–30
  policy structuring in 118–22, 188, *189*, 191, 209
  strategy-reality mismatch 204–5
  Zakat 114–15, 118, 119, 120–1, 122–4, 128, 129
Park Jung-Hee 66–7
participation of recipients in policy 212, 215
Pathways to Work (UK) 143
PDS *see* Public Distribution System
PEAP *see* Poverty Eradication Action Plan
perceptions
  relating to poverty
    in China 20, 21, 22, 28
    in India 43, 49, 52–3, 54
    in Norway 88
    in South Korea 61, 63, 65–6, 71
    in UK 146–7, 148, 151
  relating to social assistance
    in Norway 99–100

in UK 136, 140, 148–50
see also policy recipients
Pinker, R. 1
Plan for Modernisation of Agriculture
    (PMA) (Uganda) 159, 167–70,
    173, 175, 205, 209–10
planned economy in China 17,
    19–20, 23
Planning Commission (India) 43–4,
    204
policy
  comparisons 12, 179–80
  and conditionality *see* conditionality
  diversity of 4
  economic prioritised over social
    66–9, 71, 81, 113, 114, 190, 201–2
  foundational discourses 195–7
  global initiatives 3–4, 200, 212–13
  link with shame x–xi, 4, 5–6, 179,
    195
  and national contexts 9–11, 180–4,
    199
  research on 4, 5–6
  social psychological impact 5–6
  see also shame and shaming
  strategy-reality mismatch 186,
    203–6, 214–15
  translatability of 180–1, 195
policy delivery
  in China 26–9, 31–2, 191, 192, 193,
    194, 209
  comparisons of 191–4
  delivery-strategy mismatch 203–6
  further research on 215–16
  in India 42–3, 49–53, 191, 192, 193,
    194
  in Norway 92–100, 191, 192, 193,
    194
  in Pakistan 122–8, 191–2, 193, *194*
  in South Korea 77–81, 192, 193,
    194
  in Uganda 165–7, 168–70, 171–2,
    192, 193, *194*
  in UK 138–9, 145–6, 192, *194*
policy framing
  in China 19–23, 186, *187*, 188
  comparisons of 185–8
  impact of 195
  in India 41–4, 186, *187*
  in Norway 87–9, 186, *187*
  in Pakistan 112–17, 186, *187*
  in South Korea 65–71, 81, *187*, 195

in Uganda 160–3, 186, *187*
in UK 134–7, 139–41, 147–50, 152,
    187, 195
policy implications and
    recommendations 12–13, 213–16
  in China 29–32
  in India 53–5
  in Norway 100–3
  in Pakistan 128–30
  in South Korea 81–2
  in Uganda 172–5
  in UK 151–2
policy recipients
  agency of *see* agency and autonomy
  common experiences of 199–200,
    213–14
  experiences in China 27, 28–9,
    31–2
  experiences in India 45, 48, 49, 50,
    51–3, 54
  experiences in Norway 90–1, 94,
    95–7, 98, 99, 100, 102, 103
  experiences in Pakistan 126–7
  experiences in South Korea 74,
    75–6, 77–81
  experiences in Uganda 165–7,
    168–70, 171–2
  experiences in UK 145–6, 152
  marginalisation in Uganda 162–3
  receipt perceived as not shameful
    29, 45, 50, 54, 126, 143–4
  research on experiences of 2
  voice and participation 44, 175,
    185, 191, 212, 215
  see also exclusion from provision
policy shaping and structuring
  in China 23–6, 188, *189*, 191
  comparisons of 188–91
  in India 45–9, 188, *189*, 190–1
  in Pakistan 118–22, 188, *189*, 191
  shaping in Norway 89–92
  in South Korea 71–7, *189*, 190
  structuring in Norway 92–100,
    189, 190
  in Uganda 163–5, 167–8, 170–1,
    188, *189*, 190–1
  in UK 138–9, 142–5, 150, *189*, 190
policy-makers
  disconnect between people and 186
  see also civil service; politicians
policy-making
  and dignity xi, 3, 211–13

welfare and anti-poverty 205
political context
  and policy framing 185
  in South Korea 62
  in UK 133
political influence, and rural elite
  46–7, 112
political reform in Uganda 161–2
political rhetoric 186, 188
  in China 22
  in India 40–1, 42, 45, 46
  in Uganda 161, 164, 170–1, 172
  in UK 136, 137–8, 139, 140, 141,
  144, 146–7, 149–50
politicians
  corruption and welfare delivery in
  India 50–1, 53
  and welfare structure in Pakistan
  120, 121–2, 129
Poor Law ideology
  in Norway 87, 93, 102
  in UK 134–5
positive shame 7, 8
poverty
  differing concepts of 5
  discourse of *see* perceptions; political
  rhetoric
  importance of social component
  201–3
  link with shame x–xi, 1–2
  research on 1–2
  shame and stratification in India
  38–40, 44
  in South Korea 62–5
  see also absolute poverty; child
  poverty; relative poverty; rural
  poverty; urban poverty
Poverty Action Fund (Uganda) 161
Poverty Eradication Action Plan
  (PEAP) (Uganda) 159, 161, 162,
  163–70
poverty lines 192
  BPL in India 43–4, 50, 204
  setting in China 26, 30
  in Uganda 158
poverty surveys, in Pakistan 125
poverty trap 30, 74, 135
privatisation, in China 18, 19
procedural formalities 77, 80, 122,
  146
production
  policy focus on 191

see also work approach
Prosperity for All (PFA) (*Bonna
  Bagaggawale*) (Uganda) 159, 162,
  170–2, 174, 205, 209–10
Public Distribution System (PDS)
  (India) 45–7, 51–2, 204
Public Employment Service
  (Norway) 91, 93
public opinion *see* perceptions
public pressure
  and policy in India 55
  and policy in South Korea 68–9, 70
Pukhtunwali *117*

Q

Qualification Programme (2007)
  (Norway) 92, 210–11
  implications and recommendations
  100, 101, 102, 103
  structure and delivery 93, 95, 97–9
queues 52, 127

R

Ramesh, J. 43
  recipients *see* policy recipients
Recommendation 202 (ILO) xi, 3,
  200, 212–13
relative deprivation 165
relative poverty
  in China 18, 21, 30
  in Norway 88–9
  in Uganda 160
religion, Zakat provision in Pakistan
  114–15, 118, 119, 120–1, 122–4,
  128, 129
renewal of eligibility 77, 80
reservation system in India 38–9
residual welfare schemes 180–1, 183,
  209, 210
  in China 22
  in Norway 87, 93, 100
  in South Korea 63, 64, 78, 81
resources *see* expenditure on welfare;
  funding of welfare
responsibilities/duties
  and Norwegian policy 88, 92, 96,
  101
  and UK policy 136, 137, 141, 147,
  152, 183–4
  see also blame; social contract
rights

dibao in China 25, 29, 32
and dignity 48
and Norwegian policy 90, 92–3, 96, 97, 101
in South Korea 70, 71, 72, 77
and UK policy 137, 141, 147, 152, 184
see also social contract
rights-based policy 212, 214
rural economy
in India 37–8
influence of rich farmers 46–7
in Uganda 157
see also NREGA; rural support programmes
rural elite, political influence of 46–7, 112
rural poverty
in China 17–18, 25
in India 38
in Uganda 157
rural schools, in Uganda 164, 165
rural support programmes
in Pakistan 129
PMA/NAADS in Uganda 159, 167–70, 173, 175, 205, 209–10
see also NREGA
rural-urban system in China 17–18, 25

S

SACCOs (Savings and Credit Cooperative Organizations) (Uganda) 171, 210
sanctions, against recipients 137, 142, 146
scheduled tribes and castes in India 38
selectivity
impact of 202
see also eligibility; targeted provision
self-sufficiency
in South Korea 68, 73–4
see also agency and autonomy
Sen, A. x, 6, 126, 196
shame and shaming
cross-national concepts 7–8
dimensions in India 38–40, 54
impact of conditionality 206–11, 214
impact of discretion *see* local discretion

and interactionism 5
link with anti-poverty policies x–xi, 4, 5–6, 179, 195
link with poverty x–xi, 1–2
modern incarnation in Norway 88
and neglect by State in Pakistan 116–17
not felt for welfare receipt 29, 45, 50, 54, 126, 143–4
and policy delivery 191–4
in China 27, 28–9, 31–2
in India 48, 49, 51–3, 54
in Norway 87, 93, 94, 95–7, 98, 99, 100–1, 102
in Pakistan 122–9
in South Korea 71, 77–81
in Uganda 165–7, 168–70, 171–3, 174
in UK 146, 152
and policy framing 186–8
and policy structuring 188–91
in India 45, 50
in Norway 87, 93, 94, 95–7, 98, 99, 100–1, 102
in Pakistan 119, 121
in South Korea 72–7
in UK 137, 150
and Poor Law ideology 93, 134–5
recipient experiences
in China 27, 28–9, 31–2
in India 45, 48, 49, 50, 51–3, 54
in Norway 94, 95–6, 98, 99, 100
in Pakistan 126–7
in South Korea 74, 75–6, 77–81
in Uganda 165–7, 168–70, 171–2
in UK 146, 152
research on 1–2, 4, 5–6
shaping *see* policy shaping and structuring
shopkeepers, corrupt 51
Smart Cards 128–9
Social Action Programme (Pakistan) 115
Social Care Act (1964) (Norway) 90, 95, 96, 101
social change and continuity 63–4, 186–7
social citizenship, in Norway 98–100
social class, in Uganda 160–1, 162, 165
social component of poverty 201–3

economic growth prioritised over 66–9, 71, 81, 113, 114, 190, 201–2
social context and consequences of policy 201–3
social contract 41–2, 142–3, 190, 207
social control
and honour in India 41
and illiteracy in Pakistan 122
Social Fund (UK) 150
social mobility, in Norway 88
social policy
background in UK 133–5
neglect of subjective experience in 1
social protection floor 212, 213
Social Services Act (1991) (Norway) 96
social stability, in China 20, 22
social status
and economic reform in China 23, 31
and perceptions of poverty in India 39, 43
in South Korea 63
social stratification
in India 38–40, 44, 55, 201–2
neglected in policy-making 201–2
underlying policy-making 204
see also inequality; social class
socialism, in Pakistan 113
South Korea 10, 182
historical context 61, 62–5, 196
NBLSS *see* National Basic Living Security Scheme
policy delivery in 77–81, 192, 193, *194*
policy frames and tools 195
policy framing in 65–71, 81, *187*
policy implications and recommendations 81–2
policy structuring in 71–7, *189*, 190, 209
poverty in 62–5
strategy-reality mismatch 206
Standing, G. 48
State
relationship with people in India 41–2
see also policy-makers
state-owned enterprises (SOEs) 18, 20
stigma

and conditionality 207
geographical in India 38
and policy structuring
in Norway 87
in South Korea 72–7
of welfare receipt 203, 209
in China 27, 28–9, 30, 32
in Pakistan 123, 205
in UK 143–4, 146, 152
see also shame and shaming
structure *see* policy shaping and structuring
Sure Start (UK) 144
Sustenance (*Guzara*) allowance 122

T

targeted provision 180–2, 184, 202
of BISP in Pakistan 121, 123
and diverse claimants 205
of PDS in India 46, 52
of Qualification Programme in Norway 97–8
of Sure Start in UK 144
in Uganda 162, 163, 173, 174
taxation, in Pakistan 113–14
'thicker society', in India 37
tribal custom in Pakistan 117

U

Uganda 11, 184
compared with Norway 199
economic prioritised over social policy 202
NDP framework 159, 161–3, 170–2
PEAP framework 159, 161, 162, 163–70
policy delivery in 165–7, 168–70, 171–2, 192, 193, *194*
policy framing in 160–3, 186, *187*
policy implications and recommendations 172–5
policy structuring in 163–5, 167–8, 170–1, 188, *189*, 190–1, 209–10
socioeconomic context 157–8, 161
strategy-reality mismatch 205
summary 184
unemployment
in South Korea 64, 70
and urban poverty in China 21–2
and welfare policy in UK 137–8

unemployment trap 135
United Kingdom (UK) 11, 183–4
  Fowler reforms 135–7
  Jobseekers Allowance 137–9, 142, 143
  New Labour policy 139–47
  policy delivery in 138–9, 145–6, 192, *194*
  policy frames and tools 195
  policy framing in 134–7, 139–41, 147–50, 152, 186–8, *187*, 195
  policy implications and recommendations 151–2
  policy structuring in 138–9, 142–5, 150, *189*, 190, 207
  social policy context 133–5
  strategy-reality mismatch 205–6
  Universal Credit 147–50
United Nations (UN) 3, 213
Universal Credit 147–50
universal primary education (UPE) (Uganda) 159, 163–7, 172–3
universal provision
  in China 25, 26
  in Norway 85–6
  in South Korea 70
  UPE in Uganda 159, 163–7, 172–3
UPE *see* universal primary education
urban economy, in India 37
urban elite, in Pakistan 112–13
urban poverty
  in China 21–3
  dibao system as response to 24–5
urban-rural system in China 17–18, 25
Utility Stores 127

V

voice of people in poverty 44, 175, 185, 191, 212, 215

W

wages, under NREGA programme 48, 53
Walker, R. 1–2
welfare dependency
  concerns in China 26, 28, 30–1
  concerns in South Korea 70, 73
  concerns in UK 134, 140, 147–8
  and Norwegian policy 96
  see also unemployment trap

welfare fraud 193
  concerns in China 26, 27, 30–1
  concerns in UK 139, 149
welfare officers *see* officials
welfare provision
coverage *see* targeted provision; universal provision
  delivery of *see* policy delivery
  exclusion from *see* exclusion from provision
  framing *see* policy framing
  quality of 51–2, 203, 204, 207
  structuring *see* policy shaping and structuring
welfare recipients *see* policy recipients
Welfare Reform Act (2012) (UK) 147
welfare state, Norwegian 85–7
'welfare to work' (UK) 142–3
women
  and honour in India 39
  as policy recipients in Pakistan 116, 121, 124–6
work approach 195, 207
  in Norway 85, 86, 89–90, 91–2, 95–8, 100, 101, 102, 205
  in South Korea 66–8, 70–1, 73–4, 78–9, 80
  and welfare structuring 190
  see also United Kingdom; workfare approach
work capability
  in South Korea 70–1, 73
  see also employability
work ethic, in South Korea 66–8
Work Programme (UK) 147
work-focused interviews (WFIs) (UK) 143
workfare approach
  of NBLSS in South Korea 73, 78–9, 80
  in Norway 90
  of NREGA programme in India 48
  UK New Labour approach 142
  see also work approach
Working Families' Tax Credit (WFTC) 143
World Bank 213
worthiness *see* deservingness

Z

Zakat programme (Pakistan) 114–15
  delivery 122–4
  recommendations 128, 129
  structuring 118, 119, 120–1
Zia ul Haq, M. 114, 118